Leadership: Theory and Practice

Leadership: Theory and Practice

Ben Kinkaid

CLANRYE INTERNATIONAL
www.clanryeinternational.com

Clanrye International,
750 Third Avenue, 9th Floor,
New York, NY 10017, USA

ISBN: 978-1-64726-079-8

Cataloging-in-Publication Data

Leadership : theory and practice / Ben Kinkaid.
p. cm.
Includes bibliographical references and index.
ISBN 978-1-64726-079-8
1. Leadership. 2. Management. 3. Industrial management. I. Kinkaid, Ben.
HD57.7 .L43 2021
658.409 2--dc23

For information on all Clanrye International publications
visit our website at www.clanryeinternational.com

CLANRYE INTERNATIONAL

Contents

Preface VII

Chapter 1 **Understanding Leadership** 1
- a. Leadership Skills 7
- b. Leadership Development 8
- c. Leadership Training 13
- d. Strategic Leadership 15
- e. Leadership Pipeline 36
- f. E-Leadership 38

Chapter 2 **Types of Leadership Styles** 40
- a. Emotional Leadership Styles 42
- b. Executive Leadership 43
- c. Transactional or Managerial Leadership 44
- d. Opinion Leadership 47
- e. Innovation Leadership 48
- f. Autocratic Leadership 50
- g. Bureaucratic Leadership 53
- h. Laissez-Faire Leadership 58
- i. Charismatic Leadership 67
- j. Task-Oriented Leadership 69
- k. Relationship-Oriented Leadership 70
- l. Participative Leadership 71
- m. Ethical Leadership 74
- n. Authentic Leadership 76
- o. Self-leadership 77

Chapter 3 **Leadership: Philosophies, Models and Theories** 80
- a. Development of Leadership Philosophy 80
- b. Authentic Leadership 87
- c. Servant Leadership 88
- d. Contingency Theory of Leadership 91
- e. Fiedler's Contingency Theory 94
- f. Situational Theories of Leadership 96
- g. Vroom-Yetton-Jago Decision Model 100
- h. Social Identity Theory of Leadership 104

i. Path-Goal Leadership Theory 111
j. Evolutionary Leadership Theory 114
k. Trait Theory of Leadership 126
l. Great Man of Leadership Theory 128
m. Transformational Leadership Theories 130
n. Tannenbaum and Schmidt Continuum 133
o. Leadership Models 135
p. Hersey-Blanchard Model 144

Chapter 4 **Leadership Qualities, Traits and Ethics** **147**
a. Self-Motivation for Leaders 149
b. Leadership Traits 152
c. Leadership Vision 169
d. Role of Optimism in Leadership 172
e. Traits of a Charismatic Leadership 173
f. Traits of an Ethical Leader 174
g. Leadership Values and Workplace Ethics 176
h. Compassion in Leadership 178

Chapter 5 **Leadership Practices and Challenges** **181**
a. Team Building 181
b. Role of Leader in Strengthening the Bond 194
c. Challenges of Leadership 195
d. Motivation and Inspiration 204
e. Leader and Conflict Management 206
f. Leadership and Conflict Resolution 208

Chapter 6 **Gender and Leadership** **210**
a. Women in Leadership 220

Permissions

Index

Preface

The practical skill that involves the ability of a person or organization to guide other people, teams, or organizations is termed as leadership. The method of providing direction, implementing plans and motivating people is termed as a leadership style. It depends upon the personal experiences, philosophy and personality of the leader. A few of the common leadership styles are autocratic, participative, paternalism, free-rein, task-oriented and relationship-oriented. There are several qualities common in most leaders such as assertiveness, authenticity, character strengths, emotional intelligence, etc. One of the primary practices which are associated with leadership is team building. This involves assembling a group of individuals and turning them into a team where each member is committed to each other as well as to a common purpose. This textbook provides comprehensive insights into the area of leadership. Some of the diverse topics covered herein address the varied branches that fall under this category. This book will provide comprehensive knowledge to the readers.

A foreword of all chapters of the book is provided below:

Chapter 1 - The process through which an executive can guide, influence and direct the work and behavior of others in order to achieve a specific set of goals is known as leadership. There are several skills which are associated with leadership such as the capability to inspire, delegate work and communicate in an effective manner. This is an introductory chapter which will introduce briefly all these significant aspects of leadership.; **Chapter 2** - A leader can choose from a large number of behavioral patterns in order to inspire and influence the followers. Some of these styles are transactional or managerial leadership, opinion leadership, innovation leadership, autocratic leadership and executive leadership. All the diverse principles related to the different styles of leadership have been carefully analyzed in this chapter.; **Chapter 3** - The leadership philosophy is an important factor which has a profound impact on the success or failure of any person as a leader. Some of the different philosophies and theories related to leadership are authentic leadership, servant leadership, path-goal leadership theory and evolutionary leadership theory. This chapter discusses in detail these theories and methodologies related to leadership.; **Chapter 4** - Some of the qualities which are important in a leader are motivation, vision, thoroughness, continuous improvement and creativity. Compassion is another value which is highly regarded in a leader. This chapter discusses in detail these qualities, traits and ethics which are desired in a leader.; **Chapter 5** - There are various practices and challenges which are associated with the role of a leader. Primary among these is the ability of team building. The leader also plays an integral role in strengthening the bonds between team members. The chapter closely examines these key concepts of leadership practices and challenges to provide an extensive understanding of the subject.; **Chapter 6** - Gender in leadership has been a topic of study for the past few decades, after women have increasingly began to take on leadership positions in different industries. The topics elaborated in this chapter will help in gaining a better perspective about the role which gender plays in leadership as well as the different approaches which men and women undertake in order to lead their teams.

At the end, I would like to thank all the people associated with this book devoting their precious time and providing their valuable contributions to this book. I would also like to express my gratitude to my fellow colleagues who encouraged me throughout the process.

Ben Kinkaid

1

Understanding Leadership

The process through which an executive can guide, influence and direct the work and behavior of others in order to achieve a specific set of goals is known as leadership. There are several skills which are associated with leadership such as the capability to inspire, delegate work and communicate in an effective manner. This is an introductory chapter which will introduce briefly all these significant aspects of leadership.

Leadership is a process by which an executive can direct, guide and influence the behavior and work of others towards accomplishment of specific goals in a given situation. Leadership is the ability of a manager to induce the subordinates to work with confidence and zeal.

Leadership is the potential to influence behaviour of others. It is also defined as the capacity to influence a group towards the realization of a goal. Leaders are required to develop future visions, and to motivate the organizational members to want to achieve the visions.

According to Keith Davis, "Leadership is the ability to persuade others to seek defined objectives enthusiastically. It is the human factor which binds a group together and motivates it towards goals."

Characteristics of Leadership

1. It is a inter-personal process in which a manager is into influencing and guiding workers towards attainment of goals.
2. It denotes a few qualities to be present in a person which includes intelligence, maturity and personality.
3. It is a group process. It involves two or more people interacting with each other.
4. A leader is involved in shaping and moulding the behaviour of the group towards accomplishment of organizational goals.

Leadership is situation bound. There is no best style of leadership. It all depends upon tackling with the situations.

Role of a Leader

Following are the main roles of a leader in an organization:

1. Required at all levels- Leadership is a function which is important at all levels of management. In the top level, it is important for getting co-operation in formulation of plans and policies. In the middle and lower level, it is required for interpretation and execution of plans and programmes framed by the top management. Leadership can be exercised through guidance and counseling of the subordinates at the time of execution of plans.

2. Representative of the organization- A leader, i.e., a manager is said to be the representative of the enterprise. He has to represent the concern at seminars, conferences, general meetings, etc. His role is to communicate the rationale of the enterprise to outside public. He is also representative of the own department which he leads.

3. Integrates and reconciles the personal goals with organizational goals- A leader through leadership traits helps in reconciling/integrating the personal goals of the employees with the organizational goals. He is trying to co-ordinate the efforts of people towards a common purpose and thereby achieves objectives. This can be done only if he can influence and get willing co-operation and urge to accomplish the objectives.

4. He solicits support- A leader is a manager and besides that he is a person who entertains and invites support and co-operation of subordinates. This he can do by his personality, intelligence, maturity and experience which can provide him positive result. In this regard, a leader has to invite suggestions and if possible implement them into plans and programmes of enterprise. This way, he can solicit full support of employees which results in willingness to work and thereby effectiveness in running of a concern.

5. As a friend, philosopher and guide- A leader must possess the three dimensional traits in him. He can be a friend by sharing the feelings, opinions and desires with the employees. He can be a philosopher by utilizing his intelligence and experience and thereby guiding the employees as and when time requires. He can be a guide by supervising and communicating the employees the plans and policies of top management and secure their co-operation to achieve the goals of a concern. At times he can also play the role of a counselor by counseling and a problem-solving approach. He can listen to the problems of the employees and try to solve them.

Leadership and Management - Relationship and Differences

Leadership and management are the terms that are often considered synonymous. It is essential to understand that leadership is an essential part of effective management. As a crucial component of management, remarkable leadership behaviour stresses upon building an environment in which each and every employee develops and excels. Leadership is defined as the potential to influence and drive the group efforts towards the accomplishment of goals. This influence may originate from formal sources, such as that provided by acquisition of managerial position in an organization.

A manager must have traits of a leader, i.e., he must possess leadership qualities. Leaders develop and begin strategies that build and sustain competitive advantage. Organizations require robust leadership and robust management for optimal organizational efficiency.

Differences between Leadership and Management

Leadership differs from management in a sense that:

1. While managers lay down the structure and delegates authority and responsibility, leaders provides direction by developing the organizational vision and communicating it to the employees and inspiring them to achieve it.

2. While management includes focus on planning, organizing, staffing, directing and controlling; leadership is mainly a part of directing function of management. Leaders focus on listening, building relationships, teamwork, inspiring, motivating and persuading the followers.

3. While a leader gets his authority from his followers, a manager gets his authority by virtue of his position in the organization.

4. While managers follow the organization's policies and procedure, the leaders follow their own instinct.

5. Management is more of science as the managers are exact, planned, standard, logical and more of mind. Leadership, on the other hand, is an art. In an organization, if the managers are required, then leaders are a must/essential.

6. While management deals with the technical dimension in an organization or the job content; leadership deals with the people aspect in an organization.

7. While management measures/evaluates people by their name, past records, present performance; leadership sees and evaluates individuals as having potential for things that can't be measured, i.e., it deals with future and the performance of people if their potential is fully extracted.

8. If management is reactive, leadership is proactive.

9. Management is based more on written communication, while leadership is based more on verbal communication.

The organizations which are over managed and under-led do not perform upto the benchmark. Leadership accompanied by management sets a new direction and makes efficient use of resources to achieve it. Both leadership and management are essential for individual as well as organizational success.

Authority vs. Leadership

The authority exercised is a kind of legitimate power and people follow figures exercising it, because their positions demand so irrespective of the person holding the position. Leaders in organizations and elsewhere may have formal authorities but they mostly rely on the informal authority that they exercise on people to influence them. Leaders are trusted for their judgment and respected for their expertise, integrity etc and hence followed and not because they hold a certain position. For e.g. M. K. Gandhi for most part did not hold any official position to lead the Indian freedom struggle.

It is also important to understand that a formal authority and power emerging from it, might not always be able to influence people in the desired manner as; in times of crisis and difficulties people view it as coercion. On the other hand leadership tends to create followers out of free will and choice without forcing them to accept anything thrown their way. Authority rarely provides a scope for feedback, constructive criticism or opinions of the people on whom it is exercised however leaders provide ample platform to their followers to voice their thoughts and feedback.

When dealing with adults, the sole use of authority to direct and discipline them hardly works, leadership provides a better approach of sharing and involving thus building rapports with followers and creating long term relationships. Authority can hardly make people change their attitudes and behaviors with lasting effects and results however a leader inspires followers through self modeled ways and hence leadership displays greater effectiveness in addressing attitudes and behaviors of people.

Exercising authority sometimes limits the approaches to arrive at solutions for issues and problems while leadership encourages people to look beyond the obvious and think innovatively and sometimes emerge with radical solutions.

Apart from it, the biggest difference between the two as cited by Stephen R Covey is the moral authority held by leaders over the followers which is absent in the case of power from authority. Within the organizational setup when leaders also have moral authority on their subordinates by establishing a synchrony in their words and actions; the rest of the structure and processes of the organization also get aligned to it, thus creating a robust and transparent culture.

Authoritative way of working also encourages individuals to work in silos while in the organizations of today; the leaders need to have a complete picture and coordinate with other functions and departments as and when required. It is indeed difficult for mangers and leaders to move out of their circle of authority and coordinate and interact with external people. However the need of the hour and the more effective approach to leadership and management is when leaders come out of their comfort zone and move from exercising authority on a small group to leading the entire organization.

Individuals, who do not rely on authority but lead people, are the ones who enjoy the privilege of their ideologies and thoughts practiced by later generations long after they are gone. Even with individuals who held positions of responsibilities, the ones who actually led their people are the ones remembered and followed.

Emotional Intelligence for Leaders

An organization is made up of people and when people are involved, emotions automatically come into play, and a workplace is no different. It would be unwise to assume that a workplace is all objective, no-emotion only performance kind of a packed room where hormones have no scope to creep in however the fact is that emotions alone are the biggest motivator or de-motivator of an employee. The emotions alone, govern the performance and efficiency of a worker and had it not been the case, we would have never talked about the importance of work-life balance and for the present context, the need of emotionally intelligent leaders.

The current times are very dynamic not just economically but also socially where the social fabric is rapidly evolving due to globalization and other influences. The average age of the workforce is reducing and the leaders now look forward to managing people belonging to different cultures and backgrounds. In such a situation, it is important for a leader to be highly sensitized to the emotional aspects of his/her transactions with people. Emotional Intelligence is basically the ability to recognize and understand one's own feelings and emotions as well as those of others and use that information to manage emotions and relationships. The 4 important aspects of EI as proposed by Daniel Goleman are:

- Self Awareness
- Self Management
- Social Awareness
- Relationship Management or Social Skills

A leader tends to have a huge influence on the thoughts and motivation of people. He/she has the capacity to enthuse optimism and confidence in the followers and lead them to constructive endeavors which is called resonance and on the other hand they can negatively influence them to destruct, e.g of such leaders being Hitler and d Osama Bin Laden which is opposite to resonance called desonance.

Leaders are closely observed in terms of their body language, facial expressions etc. So, it is important for a leader to consider the non-verbal form of expressions as well, which may positively or negatively influence followers. Therefore, if a leader is talking about ethics in business with a slightly unconvinced and bemused look on his face, the followers make a note of it and the message is not received by them. A leader has to act as a role model too, supporting his statements, ideologies and values with appropriate actions.

As a leader one also has to be aware of one's own capabilities and weaknesses, it is difficult to accept guidance from a leader who is not self aware. As managers, leaders have to empathize as well with the situations, emotions, aspirations and motivations of the subordinates. A decreasing performance of a team member might be because of a number of reasons, a disruptive worker might be facing motivation issues and a subordinate who uses abusive language with others might be lacking confidence in his own abilities. A leader needs to discern facts and try and reach to deeper levels and understand things beyond obvious.

Apart from the above reasons, Emotional Intelligence is also important because the followers or subordinate expect it from their leaders. A subordinate working closely with the manager would expect the manager to understand his situation and priorities. And not surprisingly, whether manger does so or not, affects his level of commitment and performance at work. A leader has to suitably know and understand when he/she needs to be directive and when he needs to delegate. He/she needs to be aware, when the team members are acting as one unit and when there are differences.

It is sometimes awkward to address emotional aspects of transactions between people but leaders need to understand the importance and relevance of it as it has a huge impact on the performance outcomes. While conducting reviews and development dialogues, the feedback has to be delivered in a manner which is acceptable. The leader needs to be sensitive to the insecurities and apprehensions of the subordinates which sometimes might be expressed and sometimes kept undisclosed. At the senior level it is all the more important as the senior executives find it hard to clearly outline their anxieties and differences and the leader has to anticipate some of them.

So, to be able to attract and retain talented subordinates and keep them motivated, a leader needs to brush up on his people skills and emotional intelligence, as all of them are not born with the charisma to hold people. Fortunately, emotional intelligence with practice and carefully directed efforts can be increased.

Organizational Leadership

Organizations need strong leadership for optimum effectiveness. Leadership, as we know, is a trait which is both inbuilt and can be acquired also. Organizational leadership deals with both human psychology as well as expert tactics. Organizational leadership emphasizes on developing leadership skills and abilities that are relevant across the organizations. It means the potential of the individuals to face the hard times in the industry and still grow during those times. It clearly identifies and distinguishes the leaders from the managers. The leader should have potential to control the group of individuals.

An ideal organizational leader should not dominate over others. He should guide the individuals under him, give them a sense of direction to achieve organizational goals successfully and should act responsibly. He should be optimistic for sure. He should be empathetic and should understand the need of the group members. An organizational leader should not only lead others individually but also manage the actions of the group.

Individuals who are highly ambitious, have high energy level, an urge to lead, self-confidence, intelligence, have thorough knowledge of job, are honest and flexible are more likely to succeed as organizational leaders. Individuals who learn the organizational leadership develop abilities and skills of teamwork, effective communication, conflict resolution, and group problem solving techniques. Organizational leaders clearly communicate organizational mission, vision and policies; build employees morale, ensure efficient business operations; help employees grow professionally and contribute positively towards organizations mission.

Tips for Effective Organizational Leadership

1. A leader must lead himself, only then he can lead others. He must be committed on personal and professional front, and must be responsible. He must be a role model for others and set an example for them.

2. A leader must boost up the morale of the employees. He should motivate them well so that they are committed to the organization. He should be well acquainted with them, have concern for them and encourage them to take initiatives. This will result in more efficient and effective employees and ensure organizational success.

3. A leader must work as a team. He should always support his team and respect them. He should not hurt any employee. A true leader should not be too bossy and should not consider him as the supreme authority. He should realize that he is part of the organization as a whole.

Organizational leadership involves all the processes and possible results that lead to development and achievement of organizational goals. It includes employees' involvement, genuineness, effective listening and strategic communication.

Leadership Skills

Leadership skills are the strengths and abilities individuals demonstrate that help the oversee processes, guide initiatives and steer their employees toward the achievement of goals.

Leadership skills are an essential component in positioning executives to make thoughtful decisions about their organization's mission and goals, and properly allocate resources to achieve those directives. Valuable leadership skills include the ability to delegate, inspire and communicate effectively. Other leadership traits include honesty, confidence, commitment and creativity.

Good leaders share a series of leadership skills that make them the best people to head teams. They know how to ask for advice, have a high degree of emotional intelligence, act with fairness and empathy, take risks. These are just some of the leadership skills every leader needs to success.

Surround yourself with People Smarter than you are

Good leaders achieve success when they're surrounded by teams of people who are experts in their areas, and even who are smarter than the manager that hired them. Good leaders let their team work and innovate. In exchange, teams with a good leader make it so this leader feels comfortable and prepared for the challenge of creating good work.

Be Transparent

A team that feels like something is being hidden from it is mistrustful. The group has to know what's going so that everyone rows in the same direction. If you hide information, you'll lose the trust of your team, because they'll believe that you aren't taking them into account and turn their backs on you. If you tell them what's happening, you head off possible fears and at the same time inject a healthy dose of motivation.

Show Empathy

When someone brings up a problem or concern, a good leader tries to understand the problem and the point of view of the person. Showing empathy is proof that the leader has listened. Your response must address the concerns the other person has brought up, even it's not always the response this person was hoping for.

Be Altruistic

Your taking an interest in the well-being of others will make the teams work better and give back better results. Making room for emotions helps you get to know your people, and them you, it connects you on a personal level. It's not a question of being "best buddies" but rather of making the relationship more human. Asking "how are you?" in the morning, or taking an interest from time to time in family members or hobbies, helps close the gap between "bosses" and "employees".

Be Responsible

Leadership is also a responsibility. Effective leaders are aware of their responsibility for the team they head, and that's their biggest concern. If you ever lose your empathy with or dedication to the people you're leading, you're not being a good leader.

Involve them in your Vision

Be as transparent as you can with your team. The more they know, the more they'll share the same dream and the harder they'll work to reach the goal as a team. Share your passion.

Have a Clear Vision and Communicate it to the Team

Have a clear and convincing vision of the future of your project and communicate it to your team. This will motivate and center the group. Act as if the vision were a reality and share it with the others so that they can also visualize this idea and do everything necessary to achieve it.

Develop the Management Skills of your Team

A solid leader is one of the pillars of success of any company. People, however, aren't born with leadership skills. In other words, a leader isn't born, a leader is made. The people in an organization must be trained and have the tools, resources and development necessary to assume leadership.

Earn their Respect

Leaders with character have no need to pull rank to get results: they get them by generating trust and respect, that's why they're more effective. They don't need to impose rules or micro-manage to get their teams to complete their tasks.

Be Optimistic and Show Curiosity

Optimistic leaders inspire and motivate teams. If you show curiosity, you'll learn and collaborate with the team. This closeness avoids unnecessary conflicts that can grow out of lack of understanding and indifference. Curiosity will allow you to get closer to people and rise to the challenge of leadership in new times.

Some of these qualities have traditionally been seen as weaknesses, but the truth is that these aptitudes can become powerful tools for business people and future leaders who are willing to develop leadership skills.

Leadership Development

Leadership development refers to activities that improve the skills, abilities and confidence of leaders. Programmes vary massively in complexity, cost and style of teaching. Coaching and mentoring are two forms of development often used to guide and develop leaders.

According to Baldwin and Ford, the success of leadership development is influenced heavily by the quality of the programme, level of support and acceptance from superiors, and the characteristics/learning style of the person being developed.

Some commentators differentiate between leadership development and leader development, the former being used when referring to development programmes focusing on collective leadership in an organisation and the latter on individuals.

Leadership development is a common process in succession planning, which aims to produce high-calibre leaders to take over senior positions when they become vacant. High-performers are typically identified for these leadership development programmes, which may be longer-term and broader than programmes focusing on tighter end-goals.

Elements to Include in Leadership Development Programs

While all leaders have common leadership challenges, there are aspects of leadership unique to each leader level. Making the transitions from leading self as an individual contributor to leading others to leading other leaders all require enhanced capabilities.

That's where leadership development programs come in. To deepen talent bench strength, you'll need two things:

- General development programs applicable to all.
- Targeted employee leadership training specifically designed for the needs of each audience's next-place and in-place roles.

Developing leaders at all levels means approaching each leader level with respect to their current skills and the desired capabilities to ensure there are no gaps in development. Incorporating these key elements of leadership development programs for each level of leader can ensure development in targeted skills.

Developing Emerging Leaders

Emerging or high-potential leaders are just starting out on their leadership journey. Often, the first steps are to identify the emerging leaders, increase self-awareness, build relational skills, and focus on evidence-based leadership skills to prepare for the shift from managing self to managing others in the future. These early-level leaders are becoming acquainted to the organizational leadership style and common language as they grow and form their leadership plan.

Emerging leader development programs can include elements such as the following:

- Self-assessment to identify current areas of improvement.
- Leading a key functional project to practice increased responsibility and accountability.
- Group coaching to allow emerging leaders to grow together, connect across organizational functions, consider future scenarios and roles, or develop a management mindset.
- Mentoring and coaching relationships to expose high-potential leaders to other parts of the business.

Developing Middle Management

Seasoned leaders typically have different needs than emerging or senior-level leaders and developing middle managers has to take into special consideration their prior experience. These supervisor, manager, or director-level leaders need learning designed around deepening current skills, engaging and influencing others to amplify results, operating strategically, leading other leaders, and establishing teams.

Middle management development programs can include elements such as the following:

- Exposure to higher-level or senior leaders outside of the organization to deepen outsight.
- Professional or industry association involvement to gain deeper knowledge and connections in the industry.
- Action learning to practice solving a high-level, complex, real-world business issue with a diverse, cross-functional group.
- Individual mentoring and coaching relationships with higher-level or senior leaders to gain understanding of the business as a whole.
- Acting as a coach or mentor for emerging, high-potential leaders to develop or strengthen coaching and relational skills.
- Cross-functional, cross-level, or international business assignments to diversify experience within the organization across business units or functions.
- Leading a major organizational initiative or full-time strategic project assignment to practice building high-performing teams and leading other leaders.
- Volunteer leadership or board role in an industry or professional association to build experience influencing others.
- 360-degree assessments to identify areas of improvement and how they show up to others.

Developing Senior Leaders

As leaders rise to enterprise-wide executive roles, the complexity of what success looks like increases as well. C-suite leaders are expected to strategically manage the business as a whole and/or specific business units, no longer just manage groups of leaders. These leaders are expected to act as forward-looking visionaries, driving action through others.

Senior leadership development programs can include elements such as the following:

- Individual coaching to discuss complex business issues and development goals.
- Executive team coaching to increase team cohesion and ability to identify a shared vision.
- 360-degree assessments to identify areas of improvement and how they show up to others as leaders.
- Executive education programs and advanced degrees to build business acumen and critical industry-specific skills.

Bersin by Deloitte found that on average the investment in development per level of leader varies from $8,204 for executives to $2,551 for first-level leaders. These numbers reflect the increasing complexity of skills required as leaders move throughout our organizations.

Above all, the most critical part of development programs is, of course, reinforcement. Part of the impact that technology has on leadership development includes the personalization of leadership plans and development programs, allowing employees to choose from on-demand resources and activities geared toward leaders' learning style, pace, interests, and goals.

Each level of leader will prefer different types of reinforcement, but technological options may help bridge the gap between the leader's day-to-day actions and the skills and development gained in sessions. In-the-moment reinforcement allows for consistent, regular reminders about why achieving the desired skill or behavior change is important to them, how they can master the new knowledge or skills, and what to apply and when to apply it.

Leadership Development Plan

Leadership is a continually evolving skill. By learning more about yourself, your strengths and weaknesses, you can determine your developmental needs and gain a bright idea about the areas in which you need to improve. For encouraging both personal and professional growth of an individual, tailored leadership plans can be developed. Customized plans help in guiding you, where you want to be within a particular span of time by improving self-awareness and behavior modification. Good leaders know how to change their behaviors and for changing their behavior, they develop their self-awareness, which further contributes to behavior modification. In this way, leadership is a self-perpetuating cycle. Behavioral changes range in scope from becoming a better listener, to creating an organization-wide change or an attitude to diversity.

Leadership development plan is a comprehensive plan which helps in establishing your career on a strategic path of leadership. In a nutshell, it is your vision statement which aims at determining where you want to be within next 3-5 years by analyzing the current situation and the strategic strengths.

As a leader, you try to react more appropriately and respond to different situations effectively. By improving your self-awareness as a leader, you can enhance your ability to manage your learning by creating a Leadership development plan. An effective leadership plan should be documented and have easy accessibility. As discussed, it should be customizable and have the scope for adapting it to the requirements of the changing circumstances.

The fundamental questions which you should be asking yourself before embarking on a Leadership Development Plan are:

- Before developing a Leadership Plan, find out how ready you are to commit yourself towards this kind of an endeavor.
- Assess what skills or competencies you already have as a leader.
- Decide whether or not you will be able to implement and follow your plans for a sustained amount of time preferably for 8 to 24 months for best results.

- Determine, whether you have the patience and perseverance to stick to the process even when you encountered obstacles.

Leadership development is an ongoing process. It is essential for every individual no matter how knowledgeable they are or equipped with the required competencies and skills as a leader, leadership development is a continuous process and helps in addressing the professional challenges.

Steps of Developing a Leadership Plan

Before writing the plan, you should gather the necessary information from self-assessment to collate and analyze your data. Using this analysis, you can articulate the vision and set objectives for Leadership development.

Collating Data and Analysis of the Self Assessment Data

By analyzing the data which you have organized, decide which goals you wish to target for improvement over next few years. Five elements can be considered:

Situation: You can analyze your existing situation around the following pointers:

- Question yourself on whether or not the work environment promotes a positive ambiance for growth and high morale?
- Is it hindering your productivity or helping you by anyway?
- Identifying the possible measures of rectification which can be implemented for improving the existing situation.

Exemplification:

- This stage involves assessment of your current behaviors.
- Determination of the possible guidelines or action plans for modifying or improving those behaviors which you want to change.

Assessment:

- Decide about the possible ways by which you can assess your existing competencies and the potential techniques which you can deploy throughout the plan during the self-assessment process.

Know-How:

- You can think about the areas in which you have already gathered strong expertise and the areas in which you need to improve or require some more experience.
- Decide whether you need to spend some more time working with individual departments for overcoming your weaknesses and developing your know-how in specific areas?

Education:

- Decide upon those areas in which you need further training or education.

- Decide if you just require a practical or ethical knowledge which you can acquire from your peers, instead of going ahead with formal training which may sometimes sound too idealistic.

Articulating your Vision for Success and set Objectives for Realizing the Vision

Next step is to think about your overall vision for the year ahead and the next 3-5 years. Establish a personal vision and a plan for where you want to be within next 3-5 years. Write some solid objectives you want to achieve for realizing the vision. Goals should be SMART- Specific, Measurable, Achievable, Realistic and Time-Bound.

- Specific Objectives: Clearly and accurately highlight what kind of objectives you wish to fulfill over a specified period, how and why you want to attain those objectives.
- Measurable Objectives: A Measurability criterion is very crucial, as it helps in the assessment of the areas of success and failure in the realization of your objectives.
- Achievable Objectives: Objectives which a leader wishes to attain should be feasible and possible; otherwise it may lead to a loss in the motivation level.
- Realistic Objectives: The pre-defined objectives are supposed to be realistic in the sense that a leader should have the necessary resources and competencies for realizing those objectives.
- Time-Bound: Establish the objectives around a specific time frame or set deadlines, as this would create a sense of urgency and improve the motivation level.

Writing the Plan

The process of writing the plan involves setting developmental objectives into several competency areas. It can be broken down into three sections:

- Your future goals.
- The current and future responsibilities.
- Timelines in which you want to achieve things.

From your analysis, fill in your vision and smart objectives; List your current responsibilities and what you feel future ones might be. Outline your timelines for achieving goals and pinpoint areas you want to work on for leadership character development.

Leadership Training

The success of leadership training always depends on how it is done. Great leaders move us and inspire us to do our best work. That said, it is important that you have effective leaders in your workplace to empower and influence your people to achieve business and team goals.

The Benefits of Leadership Training

Six of the big benefits *that leadership train*ing can offer your organization:

Increase Productivity

The right, consistent leadership can increase the productivity of your people. At its primal level, leadership is about understanding your people emotionally. In his book The New Leaders, Daniel Goleman states that emotional intelligence is critical to the success of a leader. Emotional intelligence involves being smart about emotions and using empathy effectively to empower and engage employees. Leadership training that encompasses emotional intelligence can hone these emotional skills in your people managers and leaders.

Retain your People

75% of people voluntarily leaving jobs don't quit their jobs, they quit their bosses! That's right, employees leave ineffective leaders. By investing in leadership training, you can retain your people and reduce costly recruitment expenses.

Nurture Future Leaders

You need to be strategic about developing and nurturing future leaders. Without strategy, leadership roles are often given to the most forward candidates with dominant personalities. Quality leadership is a combination of the right qualities and the right training. Identify those who have what it takes and provide them with targeted leadership training. Nurturing future leaders supports succession planning and offers career pathways to employees, further increasing retention.

Increase Employee Engagement

We all like to know how we are progressing in our roles, receiving praise when it is well-earned and constructive feedback as necessary. In fact, 43% of highly engaged employees receive feedback at least once a week compared to only 18% of those with low engagement. Giving feedback is a skill of successful leaders. Through leadership training, you can teach effective ways to give feedback to motivate and increase the skill level of your people.

Implement an Effective Leadership Style

Leadership training can assist in implementing the most appropriate leadership style for your organization and the work you do. There are several leadership styles, all with their own advantages and disadvantages. Leadership training can also help individual leaders develop their own personal leadership style that their team members will best respond to.

Make Better Decisions

Last, but absolutely not least: Leadership training can result in better decision-making. How? Because leaders functioning at a high level of emotional intelligence have the perspective to make informed, intelligent business decisions. For that reason alone, you can consider your leadership training investment returned.

Strategic Leadership

In order to understand what the strategic framework looks like in action, you need to dissect it. This essentially means looking at the definition of strategy and how it can be linked to leadership. Furthermore, you need to examine the purpose of strategic leadership, as it can help realize the requirements and objectives of using this style.

Strategy

Strategy is definitely a word the business world can't get enough of. It is regularly flashed around, but what exactly does it mean to define things as strategic?

Strategy is about drawing up a set of steps and processes, which can help in achieving a pre-determined objective. To have a strategy, you need to first formulate an understanding of the situation and the objectives at hand. Once you've formulated an action plan, you must implement it, following the guidelines you've established.

If you consider strategy as a selection of decisions or choices, which are aimed at achieving a specific goal in order to succeed, you can notice the link it has to leadership. In essence, leadership is about the ability to take actions that guide a group, such as an organization, towards set objectives.

Therefore, strategy adds another layer to leadership and is just another framework to use when leaders are considering the actions and processes they want to use in order to communicate, motivate and direct the group they are supposed to lead. Just like the authoritarian leadership or the charismatic leadership, the strategic leadership provides the leader with the framework for guiding the troops.

There are a number of different ways to define strategic leadership. According to the definition, strategic leadership is *"the process of using well considered tactics to communicate a vision for an organisation or one of its parts"*. Furthermore, the framework uses a specific set of actions in order to achieve its objectives. The tactics referred to in the definition combine different management methods, motivation of subordinates, and persuasion techniques.

Aim of Strategic Leadership

It's essential to understand that strategic leadership isn't just a tool for organizing a group or managing the operational aspect of a company. The purpose of the strategy involves changing or creating an organizational structure, which is better equipped for achieving the organization's goals. Therefore, the aim of strategic leadership always includes an aspect of transformation. It is about creating a vision that helps to move the organization from point A to point B.

The requirement for change can stem from a variety of places and it doesn't need to necessarily be about saving a failing organization, for instance. While strategic leadership is helpful in boosting company performance and could help solve the structural issues within an organization, the transformation can be driven by a positive need to reinvent rather than just finding ways to survive.

Nonetheless, improvements in productivity are often at the heart of strategic leadership. In a typical strategic leadership framework, these changes are supported by subordinate development rather than cuts in the operational structure.

The style believes in empowerment through enhanced understanding, which is mainly driven by its focus on both short- and long-term objectives. Strategic leadership is never about a quick fix, as it requires the organization to look to the future whenever it is implementing a change or making a decision. Therefore, things, such as firing employees, can be seen as counterproductive in terms of future growth and succession planning, for example.

Overall, the aim of strategic leadership is to prepare the organization for whatever future might bring. The style calls for predictive behavior and analytical decision-making. Actions should not be taken simply by focusing on the current, but each decision needs to implement an understanding of different future events and possibilities. The vision for the organization should focus on the future and the strategic leadership model needs to prepare the organization for whatever the future might have in store for it.

The Core Elements of Strategic Leadership

The above provides the basis for understanding strategic leadership, as it helps to forge the basis components of what the style is about. In order to go deeper into the workings of the framework, you need to examine the different components of it.

we'll first explore the essential components of the leadership style, before outlining the key steps a strategic leader needs to take for the framework to work efficiently and effectively.

The Essential Components of Strategic Leadership

As we've mentioned before, strategic leadership is often considered similar to any operational leadership, i.e. the creation of an action plan. But the differences are there, with the most obvious issue being how operational leadership is just about directing resources to a certain part of the business to achieve a specific goal. On the other hand, strategic leadership is more about the transformation of the business, rather than achieving a specific goal. It's about an overall vision and leadership, rather than a specific way of obtaining a desired outcome.

Richard L. Hughes and Katherine Colarelli Beatty, faculty members of Center for Creative Leadership (CCL), explored the core elements of the strategic leadership framework and found there to be three major elements that set the style apart from other leadership frameworks.

Firstly, the strategic leadership framework is broad in scope. In order for the style to work efficiently, the leader's role is to understand the business is both interdependent and interconnected. Unlike in the operational leadership style, the focus is not on examining the impact of a single action to the immediate surroundings, but rather discovering how a decision in one sector will influence the whole of the organization. Therefore, strategic leadership is constantly evaluating the broad impact of actions and decisions, even when they don't seem directly connected to different parts. The strategic leadership framework requires awareness of the whole organization, instead of just certain aspects of it.

The second defining element of the framework is its future-focused application. Strategic leadership is aimed at finding a balance between the long-term focus of styles, such as transformational leadership, and the short-term focused style of transactional leadership. The aim is to integrate the short-term decisions, which are a necessary part of any organization and its decision-making, with the far-reaching outlook. The leadership needs a long-term focus and vision to be part of the decision making process when it comes to implementing short-term solutions. In essence, the strategic leader must look at the impact an action might have on the short- and long-term.

Thirdly, the leadership framework is change oriented. There is a strong transformational element to strategic leadership. The framework sets out to have a deep impact on the organization's vision and values, as well as its structure and systems. The style sets out to create more clarity and operational strength throughout it, with the leader having the biggest role in achieving this. the strategic leader must possess specific qualities and abilities in order to have a deep impact on the operational culture.

The above elements provide the cornerstone for strategic leadership. Perhaps more importantly, they also set it apart from some of the other leadership styles. Although many styles utilize the above points to some extent, they aren't always working simultaneously.

The Key Steps of Strategic Leadership

When it comes to the implementation of strategic leadership, the structure that requires is rather direct. It starts with the understanding of the organization. The first step to starting a company-wide transformation begins with the realization of why the company exists. Every organization has a mission; a goal it works towards.

Before a leader can start fixing the processes or help subordinates be more productive, he or she needs to be aware of the purpose of the organization. For example, a company such as Soylent, which produces food supplements, has a purpose that is about ensuring people can stay healthy and get their nutrients whenever and wherever they are. In order for the strategy to work, and frankly for the company to survive in today's market, it has to answer the question 'Why?'

Related to the understanding of the company's purpose is the realization of facts about its customers. The second step is therefore about figuring out who the customers are and what they want from the company. It might seem rather obvious, but the strategic leader has to understand the customer base as much as possible. The most important questions to answer are:

- What are the different types of customers the organization has?
- Why are the customers choosing the organization?
- What can the organization do better to increase the value the customers receive?

As the above questions are answered, the strategic leader is more able to devise an operational vision for the organization that will help the company achieve its objectives, both in the short- and long-term.

Once the above concepts are understood and analyzed, the leadership framework can move on to the third step of creating a vision for the organization, matching the demands of the customers and the company. The leader's role essentially is to align the purpose of the company with the customer needs, creating a strategy that helps the organization to fulfill it's goals and to provide customers the value they are looking for. The vision will be the framework for further action and it should guide the decision-making at all times.

The final step is, therefore, a process of crafting a strategy of steps that help realize the vision. The idea is for the leadership model to transform the company from its current state to the defined and desired state. It's important to note that this doesn't necessarily mean strategic leadership only works for organizations that are in trouble. An organization can wish to move from place A to place B without it being driven by financial trouble, for instance. The transformational element of strategic leadership is simply about enhancing the company's operations and perhaps changing the direction completely.

Hughes and Colarelli Beatty suggested that strategic leadership is essentially about answering three important questions: What? Who? How? You can see these questions clearly if you look at the steps above, as well as the three key elements of the framework.

The 'What' question for strategic leadership is about identifying the aspects the organization can improve and focus on in order to achieve better results. It closely deals with understanding the purpose of the organization and the needs of the customer. According to Hughes and Colarelli Beatty, the strategic leadership framework needs to focus on establishing strategy as a learning process. This is comprised of the following five points:

- Identify your current position.
- Recognize your purpose and the position you want to achieve.
- Realize the steps required to get there.
- Put the strategy in action.
- Assess and re-evaluate your progress.

The 'Who' in strategic leadership is about identifying the people that are crucial for the implementation of the above plan. Although the strategic leader is key in the process, the framework doesn't exclude the input and involvement of the subordinates, such as some other leadership styles might do. The strategic leadership should include both bottom-up decision-making, as well as the traditional top-down leadership. Hughes and Colarelli Beatty emphasize that strategic leadership is not a framework solely created by individuals, such as the leader, but a collaborative activity.

Finally, the framework deals with the 'How', which is about the processes used for achieving the 'what' by the 'who'. According to the book, the strategic leadership framework is driven by:

- Strategic thinking, which means having a vision for the organization and seeing innovative ways to overcome challenges.
- Strategic acting, which is an effort to implement the above discoveries.
- Strategic influencing, which deals with creating the right conditions for the organization to operate.

The Qualities of Strategic Leader

When it comes to being a leader, it often takes specific personality traits and skills to pull off a certain leadership style. Strategic leaders are no different and the qualities of these leaders have been extensively studied as well. Below are some of the core traits strategic leaders should have and the abilities they need in order to lead strategically.

The Characteristics of a Strategic Leader

The strategic leadership model requires plenty from its leader. Since the leader has to be involved with every aspect of the organization, the needed characteristics emphasize the leader's people skills and organizational abilities. The below five are the key characteristics a strategic leader should focus on developing in order to succeed.

Inquisitive

Strategic leaders need to be able to look at complex situations and come up with the best solutions for moving forward. Therefore, the leader must be curious about the options and be able to question things. If you don't feel inquisitive, you won't be able to find strategic solutions to questions, as you'll just rely on things you've previously learned.

Inquisitive personality can provide leaders a number of benefits. It can help in building relationship with other people because you are curious about their worldview and opinions. But it also makes learning new things easier. If you are able to find an angle that interests you, learning about almost anything is much easier and more fun.

When you learn new things, you naturally become better at leading since your understanding of the world is better. You can make connections and get a fresh insight by looking at things from new perspectives, rather than just staying inside your comfort zone.

Improving your inquisitive nature isn't difficult to do. You simply need to start asking more questions, commit yourself to trying out new things and in immersing yourself with whatever you are doing. But it also requires you to admit that you don't have all the answers and that you occasionally will be wrong about things.

Resourceful

The above trait relates to the second characteristic strategic leaders possess which is all about resourcefulness. By becoming more curious about the world and the industry you work in, you'll also enhance your ability to provide more things to the table. You become resourceful, as you have different skills, knowledge and understanding in your luggage.

There are two types of resourcefulness you need to use. The first is about the internal resources you have at your grasp, directly related to your ability to be innovative. The second type is about the external things you need, but which you can't control. These require you to interact with others and to find different ways to answer your problem. To improve your resourcefulness in terms of both these types, Shen suggests you need to be able to:

- Endure discomfort: This is about handling rejection, uncertainty and even the odd case of failure without it being the end of you or your goals.
- Communicate clearly: You need to develop the skills to convince people of your vision.
- Persevere through the storms: Being a leader or building a business are not easy things to do, but resourceful people have the grit to get through these with tenacity and determination.

Finally, Shen believes it takes three steps to become a truly resourceful person: improving your knowledge, taking action, and repeating the two steps until you reach your destination.

Influential

The above two characteristics are not enough to convince other people of your leadership qualities or guarantee they trust your vision. You need to be able to use your influence to get people on board. Influential people can succeed in achieving objectives because they make it easy for others to trust and listen to them. If you can't get others to buy into your plan, you won't be able to achieve it.

The ability to influence is especially important for strategic leaders because they are often implementing strategies others might not find as easy to follow. Changing a system around in a business, for example, can be difficult. The better you are at ensuring others trust you vision, the easier it will be to move towards the goals.

Seven easy ways you can improve your influence over others:

- Becoming a better listener.
- Learning to read body language and making decisions based on that.
- Acknowledging the accomplishments of other people.
- Seeking advice and assistance, even if you don't necessarily always need it.
- Improving your ability to remember personal details of your subordinates.
- Letting other people know you trust their abilities.
- Finding common ground with the people you meet.

Compassionate

You might have noticed how all of the above characteristics emphasize the leader's ability to listen to others and to understand their perspective. Therefore, for the strategic leader to achieve his or her objectives, compassion becomes a key trait to use. If you are able to show compassion to other people, especially to your subordinates, you are able to gain their trust and respect. This can help in achieving the objectives and getting the followers on board with your vision.

In addition, compassion towards others also helps you to understand more about the different ways of looking at things and it could teach you a lot about creative thinking. By asking questions and looking at the view of the subordinate, you can perhaps find new and better ways of dealing with certain issues.

Tiny Buddha has plenty of materials on the website for embracing compassion. But in one of the posts, Kavetha Sundaramoorthy, sets out six simple ways you could show more compassion:

- Focusing more on listening to other people.
- Understanding the emotion behind people's actions.
- Creating a support system around you.
- Seeing people as a whole person, not just focusing on the negative or positive aspects of them.
- Placing yourself in the other person's shoes and focusing on the emotional experiences they might be going through.
- Forgiving failure whenever it happens, whether you make the mistake or when someone else fails.

Communicative

Finally, a strategic leader must possess brilliant communication skills. Since you need to be able to manage and inspire the workforce, you must be able to get your message across in a clear manner. Furthermore, strategic leaders are often hands on with the job, which means communicating directly with customers and other stakeholders. If you can converse easily, you can get other people more invested in your chosen strategy.

While most characteristics on the list are qualities anyone can improve and train, communication skills are perhaps the easiest trait to master – you don't need to be a natural in communication, as you can implement easy strategies in order to improve your skills. The key to a good communication comes from:

- Learning to listen – Don't listen passively and wait for your turn to speak, but engage in the listening process. Pay attention to what the person is saying and even repeat the key points in your head.
- Use the BRIEF method – When you are communicating with a person, you should use the BRIEF method to keep your message concise and clear. The acronym stands for background, reason, information, end, and follow-up.
- Pay attention to your body language – Sometimes our body language can tell a bigger story than the words we use. If you are turned away from the person you are talking to, you look elsewhere when he or she speaks, or you play with your thumbs constantly, you will implicate boredom to the person.

The Core Abilities you need to Lead Strategically

On top of the above traits, strategic leaders also need three core abilities, which lay out the foundation for the action plan in the strategic leadership framework. These three abilities include:

- The ability to interpret: A strategic leader must be able to interpret complex situations in order to draw the right conclusions for making decisions. The leader must be able to review the situation at hand and understand the intricate details surrounding the issues. This includes things such as interpreting the current subordinate mood and productivity, the direction of the company and the industry, and customer needs.
- The ability to anticipate: As well as being able to read the current situation and what the different elements around the business or project mean, the leader must be forward-looking. Strategic leadership requires the ability to anticipate the future and the different outcomes, as well as the situations that could influence and change these predictions. The actions the leader takes now must be aware of the different roads ahead for the business.
- The ability to decide: But the leader cannot be inactive or spend too much time simply thinking about the different possibilities. The future and its many outcomes cannot stop the strategic leader from making decisions, because inaction can damage the business. Therefore, a strategic leader is able to interpret and predict and then come to a conclusion which tells the direction the company will move towards. Although strategic leadership is not about barking orders to subordinates, the leader's role is still to point out the direction and coach the team towards it.

Advantages and Disadvantages of Strategic Leadership

When it comes to analyzing any leadership framework, you can't just examine the strengths of the theory and the possible benefits of it. You must also focus on understanding the possible drawbacks of the style.

Not only can a balanced view of the advantages and disadvantages of the leadership theory help you realize whether it is the right style for you as a leader or for the organization, but also to ensure you implement the framework correctly and minimize the risk of the disadvantages.

So, what are the strengths and weaknesses of strategic leadership?

Advantages of Strategic Leadership

The implementation of strategic leadership has the obvious benefit of strategy. Any framework, which utilizes carefully constructed ideas of how to move forward, will benefit over a system of reactive actions. If you create a plan focusing on the long-term vision, as well as the short-term actions that support the vision, you create a stronger structure for operating.

The framework essentially provides more clarity in the decision-making process because it sets out the benchmarks of which actions and choices are measured against. The leader and the subordinates have a roadmap ahead of them, which guides them in all of their actions. Furthermore, since strategic leadership emphasizes the whole organization, rather than a narrow focus on specific sections, the entire organization will be moving towards the same goal.

Choices within the team or the organization are not done by narrow-minded understanding of what is best for the specific moment, but with the clarity of realizing the impact the decision has on other parts of the organization and the long-term goals of the company. Therefore, it removes or at least limits the possibility of the organization not following the same guidelines or working in hindrance to other parts of it. The internal conflict is limited, as the decision-making process always requires consideration of other parts of the business.

Overall, strategic leadership adds more clarity to operations as well. Having a clearly defined vision will make it easier for subordinates to understand why things are done the way they are. The objectives are clear, making it easier to implement procedures that move the organization towards them. Strategic leadership doesn't just focus on the operational structure and the decision-making processes of the organization, but also the corporate culture and values.

Therefore, it adds clarity since each of these aspects are clearly outlined, ensuring there are boundaries to guide the overall direction of the business. This can have a strong impact in ensuring the success and positive transformation within the organization and its operations.

In addition, the strategic leadership's action plan creates a set of objectives and tasks, which are clearly defined. This creates a situation where each of these goals and processes can be measured. By measuring performance and achievement, the organization can create a stronger understanding of what it is doing right and the areas it needs to develop and improve further. Furthermore, as studies have shown, the ability to measure performance can improve productivity much faster than if you don't examine the elements while working towards an objective.

Finally, strategic leadership has the advantage of providing an organizational perspective. What this means is that by examining the different components and trying to predict the future, the leadership framework has a wider understanding of the organizational components. Not only does the framework help understand how specific sectors within the company impact each other, it also provides a deeper insight into how the organization relates to the wider industry.

This organizational perspective can help the company better prepare against competition and the future changes within the market, ensuring it is equipped to answer when changes take place in the sector.

Disadvantages of Strategic Leadership

Despite its numerous advantages, strategic leadership does have elements that can cause problems to an organization and its followers. Most of the drawbacks could be limited with proper implementation, but it's nonetheless crucial to understand the limitations of the framework.

First problem comes from the style's reliance on predicting the future. When it comes to drafting the policies and guidelines, the framework tries to assess what the future might bring and therefore to understand its impact on the operations. After the predictions, the strategic framework implements the decisions it sees fit with this information in mind.

The problem is that predicting the future is not only hard, but it's impossible. It naturally helps to consider the different elements and to look into the possibilities of 'what might be'. But relying on guesswork will never guarantee the choices you make are the correct ones.

The issue can manifest in two different ways. First, the organization might take a gloomy approach to the future and try reading into different worst-case scenarios. But if you try limiting problems too much, you can end up stalling the company's growth and productivity. Risk-taking is not always a bad idea. On the other hand, you could predict the future with rose-tinted glasses and end up hurting the organization by avoiding proper risk-management.

Finding a balance between the two is not necessarily as easy as it might sound either. Finally, the future can always throw unforeseen elements in the company's path. Even by carefully analyzing history and the current market conditions, it's impossible to predict what the industry would look like in ten or even five years time because of the technological advancements, for instance.

Although strategic leadership framework tries to find a balance between the short- and long-term objectives, even the limited focus on long-term goals can hinder the short-term profitability and productivity of a company. As the choices the company makes will always consider the long-term impact of them, the creation of profit and improvements in productivity might take a second-place in the decision-making process. In certain companies, this could be a potential problem in dealing with investors and other stakeholders. Furthermore, if an organization is in an immediate trouble financially, for example, the strategic leadership style can be too slow to react to the issues.

Overall, the strategic leadership style can be rather inflexible. In order to counter the rigidness, the framework has to emphasize innovation in its action plan. If it doesn't, creativity can stifle. This is down to the fact that strategy often creates established routines, which can lead to the organization becoming slow in reacting to change. In addition, the formal processes can generate an environment where new opportunities are not properly explored, but are simply rejected based on the set vision and strategy. In addition to inflexibility, the strategic leadership framework is a rather complex one to implement.

In general, the proper implementation of it can be difficult and lead to many of the above problems. The complexity stems from the need to consider both short- and long-term objectives, as well as the ability to analyze the current and future trends within the organization and outside of it. Therefore, the style is rather difficult to implement, and it can take a long-time for it to provide the results the leader and the organization are after.

Famous Strategic Leaders

The world has witnessed plenty of leaders and some have been excellent, while others have failed to convince the public of their leadership qualities. Different leaders have also used various leadership styles and studying these leaders' examples is a good way to learn about the specific frameworks.

In terms of strategic leaders, there are examples in the world of business, sport, politics and even entertainment, such as the film industry. Below are three examples of strategic leaders.

Hillary Rodham Clinton

Politics requires plenty of strategic abilities because of the dynamic nature of the industry. A political leader needs to have a vision and a plan for achieving the objectives in order to succeed. While there are many examples of political leaders who've used strategic leadership, Hillary Rodham Clinton is one such example. The former Secretary of State and the First Lady of the US has applied visionary thinking with actual strategies of getting things done.

One of the clearest examples of her strategic abilities came during her husband's first presidency. Mrs Clinton was in charge of transforming the country's healthcare system, even at a great personal cost. The issue had been brewing in the US for a long time, but no one had the vision and strength to implement change within the sector. Although Mrs Clinton failed to implement the kind of healthcare plan she and her husband wanted to, the process did start a conversation in the country and eventually helped President Barack Obama pass his healthcare reforms.

Further more, Mrs Clinton applied the steps of a strategic leader during the process. She studied the healthcare system in the country closely and the problems it faced, she set up systems to get the citizens involved with the process, she outlined a detailed program for achieving the objectives the committee set out, and worked together with both American political parties in order to implement those changes.

Steven Spielberg

A rather different example of a strategic leader comes from the world of entertainment. The award-winning director Steven Spielberg has showcased how the leadership framework can be used when contributing to the world of cinema as well.

Not only has his movies applied visionary and strategic tactics that enthral the audience – consider, for example, his decision to not show the shark until the final stages of Jaws – but also in how he approaches his projects as a whole. Spielberg is not afraid to tackle the big social issues that are being debated and his style of creating movies is therefore challenging and forward-looking.

Ed Burns, an actor who worked with Spielberg in the movie Saving Private Ryan, gave interesting insights into how the director operates in his book Independent Ed. Business Insider reported on how Burns writes about Spielberg's unique way of leading actors to discover their own way, instead of fully directing them towards the right direction. The director simply explains the vision and then leaves the actors to making the right decisions based on this vision. To Spielberg, it's not about telling others what to do, but helping them understand the direction together.

Interestingly, Spielberg has also directed a film of another strategic leader, US President Abraham Lincoln. The award-winning film clearly showcases an understanding of the strategic leadership framework and in the below interview, Spielberg discusses the movie and Lincoln's leadership in an interesting way.

Howard Hughes

Howard Hughes might be among the most eccentric leaders the business world has ever seen, but the mysterious and elusive billionaire showcased certain strategic leadership qualities during his time. Although the businessman will be best remembered for spending his final years in secret and in fear of germs, he was able to completely transform the world of aviation and entertainment before his compulsive problems took hold.

Hughes was born into a wealthy family, but he had to quickly take responsibility of the business empire when his mother died when he was just 16 and his father soon followed her. Hughes understood himself as a leader and an entrepreneur, but not as a crafter. He hired an administrator to help with the daily grind. The account named Noah Dietrich ran most of the operations, but Hughes outlined the vision for the business and indulged himself with other projects on the side.

His love affair with airplanes led him to start building his own aircrafts. Hughes had a clear vision: he wanted to create the fastest aircraft in the world. Eventually, he managed to do that and simultaneously transformed the aviation industry as we know it with the introduction of better aerodynamics.

The eccentric billionaire also continued to make movies that he knew the public would like. One of his films, The Outlaw, was banned at the time, but this publicity only helped make it a popular hit after it was eventually released. He was able to implement his ideas in a manner that responded to the consumer needs of the time.

Hughes' quote regarding airplane design highlights how passionate he was and how responsibly he took the implementation of his vision.

Principles of Strategic Leadership

Most companies have leaders with the strong operational skills needed to maintain the status quo. But they face a critical deficit: They lack people in positions of power with the know-how, experience, and confidence required to tackle what management scientists call "wicked problems." Such problems can't be solved by a single command, they have causes that seem incomprehensible and solutions that seem uncertain, and they often require companies to transform the way they do business. Every enterprise faces these kinds of challenges today.

Given the small percentage of senior leadership equipped to manage large-scale transformation, companies are often forced to bring in leaders from outside. But as we've observed in countless organizations over the years, significant change in a company is more likely to succeed if it is led from within. Perhaps most alarming, the leadership gap is typically hidden from view. No one recognizes that the company's top executives aren't acting strategically, or people do realize it, but no one is willing to call attention to the problem. The gap thus comes to light only when a company faces a major challenge to its traditional way of doing business. It's in the do-or-die moments, when companies need a strategic leader most, that they discover the current leadership isn't up to the task.

Fortunately, companies can build the capacity for strategic leadership. It starts with recognizing that your organization undoubtedly already has emerging strategic leaders within it whose skills are being overlooked or even stifled. The problem can be traced back to how organizations traditionally promote and develop their leaders. In many companies, the individuals who make their way to the top of the hierarchy do so by demonstrating superlative performance, persistent ambition, and the ability to solve the problems of the moment. These are valuable traits, but they are not the skills of a strategic leader.

The following 10 principles can help unlock the potential strategic leadership in your enterprise. These principles represent a combination of organizational systems and individual capabilities - the hardware and software of transformation. You may have already adopted some of these tenets, and think that's enough. But only when you implement all of them together, as a single system, will they enable you to attract, develop, and retain the strategic leaders who've eluded you thus far.

Systems and Structures

The first three principles of strategic leadership involve nontraditional but highly effective approaches to decision making, transparency, and innovation.

Distribute Responsibility

Strategic leaders gain their skill through practice, and practice requires a fair amount of autonomy. Top leaders should push power downward, across the organization, empowering people at all levels to make decisions. Distribution of responsibility gives potential strategic leaders the opportunity to see what happens when they take risks. It also increases the collective intelligence, adaptability, and resilience of the organization over time, by harnessing the wisdom of those outside the traditional decision-making hierarchy.

In an oil refinery on the U.S. West Coast, a machine malfunction in a treatment plant was going to cause a three-week shutdown. Ordinarily, no one would have questioned the decision to close, but the company had recently instituted a policy of distributed responsibility. One plant operator spoke up with a possible solution. She had known for years that there was a better way to manage the refinery's technology, but she hadn't said anything because she had felt no ownership. The engineers disputed her idea at first, but the operator stood her ground. The foreman was convinced, and in the end, the refinery did not lose a single hour of production.

When individuals like the plant operator are given responsibility and authority, they gain more confidence and skill. And when opportunities to make a difference are common throughout an organization, a "can-do" proficiency becomes part of its identity. At Buurtzorg, a Dutch neighborhood nursing organization, most decisions are made by autonomous, leaderless teams of up to a dozen nurses. A small central management team supports and coaches the frontline nurses; there is no other middle management. The company achieves the highest client satisfaction levels of all community nursing delivery in the Netherlands, at only 70 percent of the usual cost. Patients stay in care half as long, heal faster, and become more autonomous themselves. And the nurses gain skills not just for leading their part of the enterprise, but in community leadership as well.

Be Honest and open about Information

The management structure traditionally adopted by large organizations evolved from the military, and was specifically designed to limit the flow of information. In this model, information truly equals power. The trouble is, when information is released to specific individuals only on a need-to-know basis, people have to make decisions in the dark. They do not know what factors are significant to the strategy of the enterprise; they have to guess. And it can be hard to guess right when you are not encouraged to understand the bigger picture or to question information that comes your way. Moreover, when people lack information, it undermines their confidence in challenging a leader or proposing an idea that differs from that of their leader.

Some competitive secrets (for example, about products under development) may need to remain hidden, but employees need a broad base of information if they are to become strategic leaders. That is one of the principles behind "open-book management," the systematic sharing of information about the nature of the enterprise. Among the companies that use this practice are Southwest

Airlines, Harley-Davidson, and Whole Foods Market, which have all enjoyed sustained growth after adopting explicit practices of transparency.

Transparency fosters conversation about the meaning of information and the improvement of everyday practices. If productivity figures suddenly go down, for example, that could be an opportunity to implement change. Coming to a better understanding of the problem might be a team effort; it requires people to talk openly and honestly about the data. If information is concealed, temptation grows to manipulate the data to make it look better. The opportunity for strategic leadership is lost. Worse still, people are implicitly told that there is more value in expediency than in leading the enterprise to a higher level of performance. Strategic leaders know that the real power in information comes not from hoarding it, but from using it to find and create new opportunities for growth.

Create Multiple Paths for Raising and Testing Ideas

Developing and presenting ideas is a key skill for strategic leaders. Even more important is the ability to connect their ideas to the way the enterprise creates value. By setting up ways for people to bring their innovative thinking to the surface, you can help them learn to make the most of their own creativity.

This approach clearly differs from that of traditional cultures, in which the common channel for new ideas is limited to an individual's direct manager. The manager may not appreciate the value in the idea, may block it from going forward and stifle the innovator's enthusiasm. Of course, it can also be counterproductive to allow people to raise ideas indiscriminately without paying much attention to their development. So many ideas, in so many repetitive forms, might then come to the surface that it would be nearly impossible to sort through them. The best opportunities could be lost in the clutter.

Instead, create a variety of channels for innovative thinking. Some might be cross-functional forums, in which people can present ideas to a group of like-minded peers and test them against one another's reasoning. There could also be apprenticeships, in which promising thinkers, early in their careers, sign on for mentorship with leaders who are well equipped to help them build their skills. Some organizations might set up in-house courses or sponsor attendance at university programs. Reverse mentoring — in which younger staff members share their knowledge of new technology as part of a collaboration with a more established staff member — can also be effective.

Google has made use of a number of channels to promote innovation. A few examples: Employees can directly email any of the leaders across the organization; the company established "Google cafés" to spark conversation by encouraging interaction among employees and across teams; and executives hold weekly all-hands meetings (known as TGIFs) to give employees at every level in-person access to senior leaders. People at Google learn to make the most of these opportunities — they know the conversations will be tough, but that genuinely worthwhile innovative thinking will be recognized and rewarded.

People, Policies and Practices

The next four principles involve unconventional ways of thinking about assessment, hiring, and training.

Make it Safe to Fail

A company's espoused statement of values may encourage employees to "fail fast" and learn from their errors. That works well until there is an actual failure, leading to a genuine loss. The most dreaded phone call in the corporate world soon follows; it's the one that begins: "Who authorized this decision?" Big failures are simply unacceptable within most organizations. Those who fail often suffer in terms of promotion and reward, if not worse.

You must enshrine acceptance of failure — and willingness to admit failure early — in the practices and processes of the company, including the appraisal and promotion processes. For example, return-on-investment calculations need to assess results in a way that reflects the agreed-upon objectives, which may have been deliberately designed to include risk. Strategic leaders cannot learn only from efforts that succeed; they need to recognize the types of failures that turn into successes. They also need to learn how to manage the tensions associated with uncertainty, and how to recover from failure to try new ventures again.

Honda is one enterprise that has taken this approach to heart. Like several other industrial companies, the automaker has had a dramatic, visible failure in recent years. The installation of faulty equipment from its favored airbag supplier, Takata, has led Honda to recall about 8.5 million vehicles to date. Although the accountable executives were fired, the company's leaders also explicitly stated that the airbag failure, in itself, was not the problem that led to dismissal. The problem was the lack of attention to the failure at an early stage, when it could have been much more easily corrected. As one Honda executive told Jeffrey Rothfeder, author of *Driving Honda: Inside the World's Most Innovative Car Company* (and an *s+b* contributing editor), "We forgot that failure is never an acceptable outcome; instead, it is the means to acceptable outcomes."

Some organizations have begun to embrace failure as an important part of their employees' development. The Bill & Melinda Gates Foundation and the U.K.-based innovation charity Nesta have held "failure fests," at which employees discuss decisions that went wrong and derive lessons from them. In addition to establishing such forums, you can provide managers with opportunities to oversee smaller change initiatives, some of which may not work out, to develop the skills they'll need to lead larger-scale transformations.

Provide Access to other Strategists

Give potential strategic leaders the opportunity to meet and work with their peers across the organization. Otherwise, they remain hidden from one another, and may feel isolated or alone. Once they know that there are others in the company with a similar predisposition, they can be more open, and adept in raising the strategic value of what they do.

The first step is to find them. Strategic leaders may not be fully aware themselves that they are distinctive. But others on their team, and their bosses, tend to recognize their unique talents. They may use phrases like "she just gets it," "he always knows the right question to ask," or "she never lets us get away with thinking and operating in silos" to describe them. A good way to learn about candidates is to ask, "Who are the people who really seem to understand what the organization needs — and how to help it get there?" These may be people who aren't traditionally popular; their predisposition to question, challenge, and disrupt the status quo can unsettle people, particularly people at the same level.

Of course, you don't want to create the impression that some people deserve special treatment. Instead, cultivate the idea that many managers, perhaps even most, have the potential to become strategic leaders. Then bring the first group together. Invite them to learn from one another, and to explore ways of fostering a more strategic environment in the rest of the enterprise.

Develop Opportunities for Experience-based Learning

The vast majority of professional leadership development is informative as opposed to experiential. Classroom-based training is, after all, typically easier and less expensive to implement; it's evidence of short-term thinking, rather than long-term investment in the leadership pipeline. Although traditional leadership training can develop good managerial skills, strategists need experience to live up to their potential.

One vehicle for creating leadership experiences is the cross-functional "practice field," as organizational learning theorist Peter Senge calls it. Bring together a team of potential strategic leaders with a collective assignment: to create a fully developed solution to a problem or to design a new critical capability and the way to generate it. Give them a small budget and a preliminary deadline. Have them draw plans and financial estimates of their solutions. Then run the estimates through an in-depth analysis. This project might include a simulation exercise, constructed with the kind of systems simulation software that has been used to model and participate in wargames since the 1980s. You can also let reality be their practice field. Have them create the new capability or initiative on a small scale, and put it into effect. Then track the results assiduously. Assign mentors with experience to help them make the most of their effort — without sidetracking it.

Whether you set up the project in reality or as a simulation, the next step should be the same. Schedule a series of intensive discussions about the results. Explore why these results appeared, what the team might have done differently, and how things could be different in the future if the group changed some of the variables. The goal is to cultivate a better understanding than would be possible without this type of reflection, and to use that understanding as the basis for future efforts.

Hire for Transformation

Hiring decisions should be based on careful considerations of capabilities and experiences, and should aim for diversity to overcome the natural tendency of managers to select people much like themselves.

Test how applicants react to specific, real-life situations; do substantive research into how they performed in previous organizations; and conduct interviews that delve deeper than usual into their psyche and abilities, to test their empathy, their skill in reframing problems, and their agility in considering big-picture questions as well as analytical data. In all these cases, you're looking for their ability to see the forest and the trees: their ability to manage the minutiae of specific skills and practices, while also being visionary about strategic goals. The better they are at keeping near and far points of view simultaneously available, the better their potential to be strategic leaders.

For those hired, the on-boarding processes should send explicit signals that they can experiment, take on more responsibility, and do more to help transform the organization than they could in their previous career. They need to feel that the culture is open to change and to diverse views.

Focus on the Self

The final three principles are aimed at the potential strategic leaders themselves. Following these tactics can help them prepare for their personal evolution.

Bring your whole Self to Work

Strategic leaders understand that to tackle the most demanding situations and problems, they need to draw on everything they have learned in their lives. They want to tap into their full set of capabilities, interests, experiences, and passions to come up with innovative solutions. And they don't want to waste their time in situations (or with organizations) that don't align with their values.

Significantly, they encourage the people who report to them to do the same. In so doing, strategic leaders create a lower-stress environment, because no one is pretending to be someone else; people take responsibility for who they truly are. This creates an honest and authentic environment in which people can share their motivations and capabilities, as well as the enablers and constraints in their life.

Find Time to Reflect

Strategic leaders are skilled in what organizational theorists Chris Argyris and Donald Schön call "double-loop learning." Single-loop learning involves thinking in depth about a situation and the problems inherent in it. Double-loop learning involves studying your own thinking about the situation — the biases and assumptions you have, and the "undiscussables" that are too difficult to raise.

Your goal in reflection is to raise your game in double-loop learning. Question the way in which you question things. Solve the problems inherent in the way you problem-solve. Start with single-loop learning, and then move to double-loop learning by taking the time to think: Why did you make that decision? What are the implications? What would you do differently next time? How you going to apply this learning going forward?

Reflection helps you learn from your mistakes, but it also gives you time to figure out the value of your aspirations, and whether you can raise them higher. It allows you the chance to spot great ideas using what you are already doing or things that are going on in your life. Managers are often caught up in the pressures of the moment. A mistake or a high-pressure project can feel overwhelming. But if you take a minute to step back and reflect on these problems, it can provide the space to see what you did right.

Some reflection is more productive than others. Psychologists warn about "rumination," or dwelling on deceptive messages about your own inadequacies or the intractability of problems in a way that reinforces your feeling of being stuck. To avoid this pattern, deliberately give yourself a constructive question to reflect on. For example, what are the capabilities we need to build next? How can we best contribute? Human capital teams can help by training individuals in these practices and ensuring that all managers support their team members who take the time to reflect.

Recognize Leadership Development as an Ongoing Practice

Strategists have the humility and intelligence to realize that their learning and development is never done, however experienced they may be. They admit that they are vulnerable and don't have all the answers. This characteristic has the added benefit of allowing other people to be the expert in some circumstances. In that way, strategic leaders make it easy for others to share ideas by encouraging new ways of thinking and explicitly asking for advice.

Their thirst for learning also gives potential strategists the space to be open to less obvious career opportunities — new industries, different types of roles, lateral moves, stretch assignments, secondments, or project roles — that may help them fulfill their potential.

At some point, you may advance to the point where you are not concerned solely with your own role as a strategic leader, but also with cultivating opportunities for others. This will require a clear-eyed, reflective view of the talent pool around you. It isn't easy for any leader to accept that others in the company may not have what it takes. Or, worse, to learn that the people with the potential to demonstrate leadership feel constrained by current organizational practices, and they are taking their talents elsewhere.

Leadership Strategies to Improve Performance

Leadership strategies that can improve their ability to influence action and improve performance on their team. Others may just need a little reminder to help reignite your use of these important leadership strategies.

Define and Communicate Vision

The eye looks, but it is the mind that sees.

Your vision is a vivid, aspirational leadership strategy that paints a picture of the future of your organization. It is long term and it is measurable. Hopefully, you already have a vision for yourself and your organization; a purpose that drives you to do what you do every day. But are you able to share that vision with others and put it into action to drive results?

When you lead a team without a vision, everyone still ends up working, and often working quite hard, but important goals might not be achieved. Positive results are not achieved. Your vision brings the team together under a common goal so you are not simply working, but performing together toward something. Something that is big and exciting.

Your vision answers the question: Where are we going?

And you need to be crystal clear in your definition of what that destination looks like, even if you do not yet know exactly how you are going to get there. This leadership strategy gives you and your team the ability to know exactly where you are located within the vision at any given time, and whether you are getting closer to or further away from your destination.

Encourage Recognition

Employees want to feel appreciated. They want to feel valued. It instills a sense of commitment and engagement

When individuals and teams work above and beyond expectations to achieve great results, celebration and recognition are how you encourage continued commitment to the organization's vision, mission, and goals. It is how excellence is encouraged over time, and how it stays strong even in times of high production volume and stress.

What gets rewarded gets repeated. This statement has become a business maxim, yet managers still often overlook the positive impact of this simple, yet effective leadership strategy.

Studies have shown that only 60% of adults in the workplace will agree that personal recognition is important to them and that it works well to help keep them motivated. That means that 40% think they do not really need recognition, they are self-motivated enough to work well without recognition. And yet, 96% of the people in that same group responded that when they receive personal recognition, it definitely inspires and motivates them to do more work. The conclusion is that, while your team may not need recognition, recognition does inspire people to do more and better work.

Even better, when you create a culture of gratitude and recognition on your team, they will pick it up and start to recognize each other on their own. This creates a great sense of community and cohesion that motivates everyone to perform at their highest level.

Speak from the Heart

Do you speak about your organization from your heart or from your budget?

Many people mistakenly believe that leadership is something that some people are born with and others are not. The truth is that leadership is a choice. It is a choice that only you can make; leadership can not be given or forced upon you.

When you communicate with your team, they know whether or not you are passionately engaged in being the leader by how you speak about your company's vision, mission, and goals. They can sense in your daily interactions if your commitment to their growth and development is as important to you as your own.

Delegate and Empower

Perhaps the best leadership strategy to engage your team is to empower them by delegating greater responsibility. It can be exciting to be entrusted with a position of responsibility, so if something makes you feel a sense of self-worth, give that self-worth to others on your team. Find areas where you can give people the responsibility and, importantly, the authority to get things done.

Have you ever heard from your team that they can not finish their work because they are waiting for you? Are they waiting for you to take a look at or approve their work? That may be a prime example of an area that you should consider letting go. Empower and, if necessary, train them, coach them, encourage them, and reward them.

Take a minute to do a mental exercise. Imagine you have been given a special assignment which will require you to be out of the office for the next three months. During those three months, all of your work still has to get done, but you are not allowed to hire anybody new. The assignment will only last for three months, and you have thirty days to figure out how you will redistribute your work.

Pick up your pen and, for a few seconds, think about to whom you would start delegating more responsibility. Write down one to three things you would start delegating. The reality is that a leader can not perpetually do everything that needs to get done. You need others who are empowered to complete critical tasks, and you need backup.

Commit to Continued Education

Leadership is a journey with no real destination. Great leaders commit to continued growth and refinement through continued education, practical application of skills, and networking both internally and externally. You are never done growing as a leader.

This includes sharing your knowledge and experiences with others. They say you never learn as much as when you are teaching, and we are truly fulfilling ourselves as leaders when we are in the role of the coach and mentor. Commit to developing your team's leadership skills as much as your own, and you will find not only gratitude and fulfillment but will also lay the foundation for a strong leadership pipeline.

Ohio State Leadership Studies

In 1945, the Bureau of Business Research at Ohio State University initiated a series of studies on leadership. These studies sought to identify independent dimensions of leader behaviour. The studies started with the premise that no satisfactory definition of leadership existed and there was no precise indication of the qualities of a good leader. So it sought to define leadership in terms of performance.

These studies identified two independent leadership dimensions called initiating structure and consideration which meant more or less the same thing as task behaviour and relationship behaviour of a leader.

Initiating structure refers to the extent to which a leader is likely to define and structure his own role as well as the roles of subordinates in the search for goal attainment. It includes behaviour that attempts to organise work, work relationships and goals. The leader characterized as high in initiating structure specifies the task to be performed by each member of his group, sets down deadlines, gives directions and puts pressure on them for its fulfillment.

Consideration refers to the extent to which a leader is likely to have job relationships which are characterized by mutual trust, respect for subordinates' ideas and regard for their feelings. He shows concern for his followers' comfort, well-being, status and satisfaction.

A leader characterized as high in consideration could be described as one who helps subordinates in their personal problems, is friendly and approachable and treats all subordinates as equals.

The Ohio State Studies suggested that the "high-high" leadership style (high in initiating structure as well as in consideration) generally results in positive outcomes but there are exceptions which indicate that situational factors should be integrated into the theory.

The Ohio studies have value for the study of leadership. They were the first to emphasize the importance of both task direction and consideration of individual needs in assessing leadership. This two-dimensional approach lessened the gap between the strict task orientation of the scientific management movement and the human relations emphasis.

Michigan Leadership Studies

The Michigan Leadership Studies was a well-known series of leadership studies that commenced at the University of Michigan in the 1950s, with the objective of identifying the principles and types of leadership styles that led to greater productivity and enhanced job satisfaction among workers. The studies identified two broad leadership styles: an employee orientation and a production orientation. They also identified three critical characteristics of effective leaders: task-oriented behavior, relationship-oriented behavior, and participative leadership.

The studies concluded that an employee orientation rather than a production orientation, coupled with general instead of close supervision, led to better results. The Michigan leadership studies, along with the Ohio State University studies that took place in the 1940s, are two of the best-known behavioral leadership studies and continue to be cited to this day.

Criticisms of the Michigan Leadership Studies

The overarching assertion of the studies was that less direct pressure and control allows employees to be more productive and engaged with their tasks. However, there have been critiques and questions about the methodology and results of the studies. One such critique is that the context of the employees, leadership, and task were not taken into consideration, which raises the possibility that the situation at the organization might warrant one leadership style over another.

Furthermore, the disposition of the workers can be a factor in the leadership approach. The way employees perform may influence a leader to be more hands-on if greater direction is needed due to the complexities of the task. Likewise, if employees prove themselves to be capable and handle their tasks fluidly on their own, there is little need for more overt control. A team of veteran workers who have studied and worked on a task for many years might not require a direct manager to issue directives; thus, in that context, it is more likely for the leader to afford them more autonomy.

The narrow options of the studies also do not consider that one-size does not fit all organizations or circumstances. Using the same leadership at two different companies can still result in failure or success at other due other elements at play. It is common for leaders to adapt their styles over time and as warranted rather than remain committed to a fixed pattern.

Though the Michigan Leadership Studies remain notable, other theories and studies on leadership approaches have developed in more recent years that take into account different dynamics, such as the servant leadership philosophy.

Leadership Pipeline

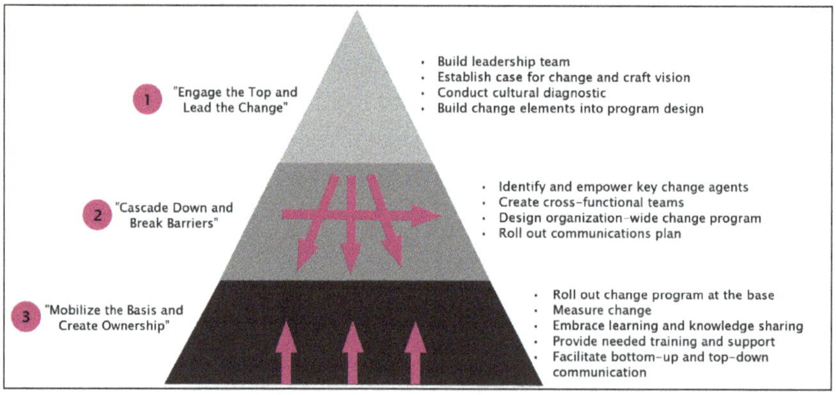

A leadership pipeline is your database of employees at various stages of becoming leadership-ready. As your company grows or transitions occur, do you have a pipeline of people to tap into that you can promote or move cross functionally to fill the gaps?

Many company leaders and human resources managers recognize that their organization's leadership skills gap continues to grow, but most do not have a plan for how they will solve this critical issue. Focusing on your leadership pipeline will help you begin to determine where you currently have talent that can fill gaps and what areas you need to either develop skills or hire additional talent.

Strength of your Pipeline

How do you know whether or not you have a strong leadership pipeline? It's fairly simple. If you have at least two levels of employees that are either ready to fill management and leadership roles now or have the potential to in the future with development, then you have sufficiently managed your leadership pipeline and you are in good shape.

Think about a scenario in which one of your key managers gets in an accident and is suddenly no longer able to take care of their responsibilities at the office. Who on your team can take their place at a moment's notice? Who would be able to fill it, but may need six months or so of training and development to become at least as effective as the person they are replacing? How about a year? How about people on your team who will be prime for promotion in three to five years?

Segmenting your pipeline for all key positions by ready now, ready in one year, and ready 2 – 3 years will help you understand your depth and strength of your pipeline. Starting on structured annual development plans for your leaders will ensure they are ready and stay engaged.

Importance of Leadership Pipeline

You're perhaps wondering at this point why a leadership pipeline is important to you. So what if you don't have someone who can take over? You can just hire someone, right? Wrong. There are certainly times when hiring new talent is advantageous and necessary. However, generally, it is typically less efficient to have to hire, onboard, and train a new manager or leader than it is to have a plan for developing your team over the long run. For example, replacing a salaried mid-range position can cost your company 20% of that person's annual salary. Cost of human capital replacement studies go further to indicate a sharp increase when you need to replace a highly educated, executive-level position – up to 213%. These costs include a number of areas beyond just the cost of recruitment. You also need to consider training and onboarding, decreased engagement rates and lowered morale of those left behind, and the cost of lost productivity.

Focusing your efforts on developing and mentoring your team to build a strong leadership pipeline pays dividends for the bottom line of your company. Companies that invest in leadership development and mentoring programs enjoy higher employee engagement and retention rates. They are better positioned to leverage changing market conditions and have a much stronger market position overall.

Developing depth in your leadership pipeline does not happen overnight. It is a process that you need to map out and identify what strength in leadership means to your organization. Practical leadership programs focused on developing and growing your people will not only strengthen your pipeline, but will also improve retention, motivation, and productivity – generating far greater ROI for your bottom line than any other capital investment in your portfolio.

E-Leadership

E-leadership has been defined as a social influence process mediated by technology to produce a change in attitudes, feelings, thinking, behaviour, and performance with individuals, groups, and/or organizations. A more anecdotal definition is provided by Chan, where e-leadership means challenging the accepted belief that running a business means bringing the staff under one roof from 9-to-5 every day; measuring success differently than in the past; and finding new ways to be a leader, new ways to motivate when you do not see every employee every day.

E-leadership can include one-on-one, to one on-many interactions within and across large units and organizations. It has been suggested that technology will become so ingrained in business practice that soon it will not occur to anyone to add an "e" in front of the word leadership. However, organizations are currently struggling with integrating technology into the management process. This is further complicated by the steep technology learning curve that many employees face.

Often, e-leaders have two employee populations they serve. E-leaders have to balance relationships with "online" versus face-to-face followers. A simple "I'll get back to you" to an e-employee's idea without accompanying verbal cues may be alienating. Frequent communication may offset the lack of non-verbal cues. Several factors impact the quality of e-leadership including the degree of face-to-face interaction, media richness, and team composition.

Face-to-Face

Examining the level of face-to-face interaction associated with e-leadership, Hart and McLeod categorized the content of communication exchanges between 126 pairs of teammates. The communications were divided into task oriented and social-emotional categories. Summarizing the findings, the study indicated that leaders should encourage a variety of task-related communication to foster closer relationships in geographically dispersed teams. Leaders must provide virtual team members with a reason to work together, by promoting interdependence and reliance on one another, by taking such steps as dividing members by tasks or assigning mentoring duties. Hart and McLeod conclude that the results are consistent with a growing body of research that close personal relationships are possible in virtual settings. Leaders can aid in fostering these relationships.

Media Richness

In addition to the level of face-to-face interaction, media richness plays a role in the quality of e-leadership and subordinate relationships. Media richness refers to the capacity of the technology to provide immediate feedback, the number of cues and channels used for the personalization of messages, and the language variety. In the context of e-leadership, media richness becomes a key factor of interaction.

E-leaders have many opportunities, or channels, to be in touch with stakeholders. For example, anonymously clicking into either an employee or a customer related chat room may provide information needed for a same day global teleconference. Leaders need to learn the vividness and interactivity of media to make their presence felt in a positive way.

In a study involving online youth and language style, emergent leaders demonstrated collaboration, sociability, and persuasiveness in the absence of face-to-face interaction. The adolescent talk may be an index of what is to come in the future. A quick look at a text messaging session between teenagers shows that communication takes place in a very truncated style. Given that the frequency of messages, not length, was found to be important for establishing closer relationships, the leader of the future may be better able to form virtual bonds.

Virtual Teams

A large portion of research on e-leadership has involved virtual teams. A virtual team uses information technology and telecommunications to facilitate collaboration between geographically dispersed members who work on the same project. A virtual team can consist of other workers outside of an organization but is usually made up of employees working for the same company. E-teams and traditional teams share many characteristics; what distinguishes e-teams is their frequent geographic dispersion and their time-limited mission or task. E-leaders need to act as liaisons, set and convey team directions, and coordinate team operations in an environment of limited and mediated communication.

References

- Leadership-basics: managementstudyguide.com, Retrieved 2 April, 2019
- Leadership-skills: techtarget.com, Retrieved 12 February, 2019
- Leadership-skills-every-leader-needs-to-success: game-learn.com, Retrieved 17 June, 2019
- What-is-leadership-development: hrzone.com, Retrieved 7 August, 2019
- Guide-to-leadership-development-by-leader-level: flashpointleadership.com, Retrieved 3 July, 2019
- Leadership-development-plan: managementstudyguide.com, Retrieved 13 January, 2019
- Big-benefits-of-leadership-training: elearningindustry.com, Retrieved 20 March, 2019
- Strategic-leadership-guide: cleverism.com, Retrieved 23 July, 2019
- Principles-of-Strategic-Leadership: strategy-business.com, Retrieved 21 January, 2019
- Short-notes-on-the-ohio-state-leadership-studies: yourarticlelibrary.com, Retrieved 16 July, 2019
- How-strong-is-your-leadership-pipeline: crestcomleadership.com, Retrieved 11 March, 2019

2

Types of Leadership Styles

A leader can choose from a large number of behavioral patterns in order to inspire and influence the followers. Some of these styles are transactional or managerial leadership, opinion leadership, innovation leadership, autocratic leadership and executive leadership. All the diverse principles related to the different styles of leadership have been carefully analyzed in this chapter.

Leadership Styles

The Leadership Styles are the behavioral patterns that a leader adopt to influence the behavior of his followers, i.e. the way he gives directions to his subordinates and motivates them to accomplish the given objectives.

The leadership styles can either be classified on the basis of behavioral approach or situational approach. These approaches are comprised of several theories and models which are explained below:

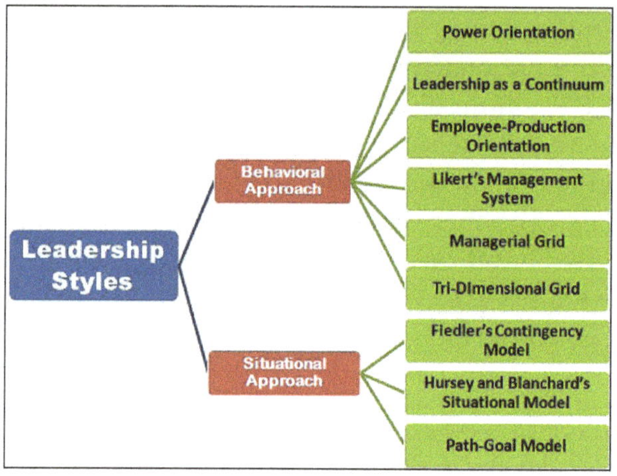

Based on Behavioral Approach

- Power Orientation: The power orientation refers to the "degree of authority" that a leader adopts to influence the behavior of his subordinates. Based on this, the leadership styles can be further classified as:
    - Autocratic Leadership
    - Participative Leadership
    - Laissez-Faire
- Leadership as a continuum: This model is given by Tannenbaum and Schmidt, who believed that there are several leadership styles that range between two extremes of autocratic and free-rein, which are shown below:

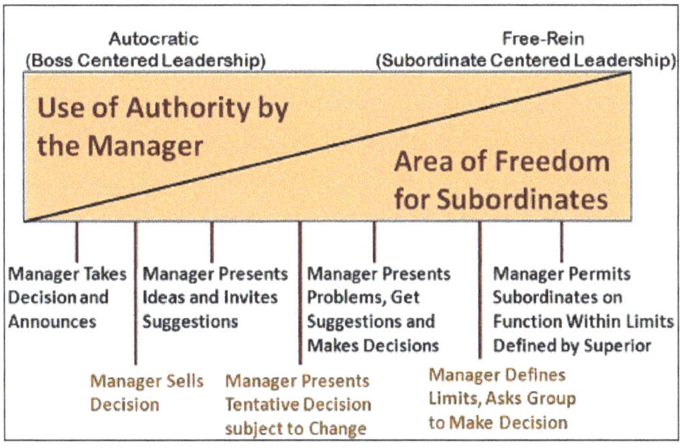

- Employee-Production Orientation: Several types of research were conducted to study the leadership behavior that gets affected by the several characteristics that are related to each other. It was found that employee orientation and production orientation play an important role in determining the leadership style.The employee orientation is based on the premise that an employee is an important part of the group and is in parallel to the democratic leadership style. Whereas the production Orientation focuses on the production and technical aspects of the job and the employees are considered as the tools for accomplishing the jobs. Thus, the production orientation is parallel to the autocratic leadership style.

- Likert's Management System: Rensis Likert along with his associates studied the patterns and behavior of managers to identify the leadership styles and defined four systems of management. These four systems are: Exploitative Authoritative, Benevolent Authoritative, consultative system and participative system.

- Managerial Grid: The managerial grid is the tool designed by Blake and Mouton to determine the leadership style. According to them, the leadership style gets influenced by both the task-oriented and relation-oriented behavior in varying degrees.

- Three Dimensional Grid: The three-dimensional grid is also called as a 3-D leadership model given by W. J. Reddin. Reddin included the effectiveness dimension along with the task-oriented and relationship-oriented dimensions to study how a leader behaves in a given situation and a specific environment.

Based on Situational Approach

- Fiedler's Contingency Model: This theory is given by Fred Fiedler, who, along with his associates identified the situational variables and their relationship to determine the leadership styles. Thus, this model is comprised of three elements, leadership styles, situational variables and the interrelationship between these two.

- Hursey and Blanchard's Situational Model: According to this model, the leader has to adopt the leadership style that matches up with the subordinate's maturity i.e. his willingness to direct his behavior towards the goal.

- Path-Goal Model: The Path-Goal Model is given by Robert House, who, along with his associates tried to predict the effectiveness of leadership styles in varied situations. He believed that the foremost function of any leader is to define the goals to the subordinates clearly and assist them in finding the best path to accomplish that goal.

Thus, a manager behavior and the situational demands give rise to several leadership styles as discussed above.

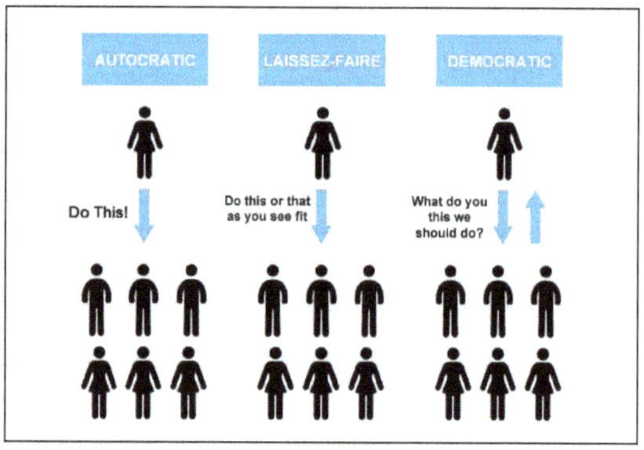

Emotional Leadership Styles

Any leader can use any style, and a good mix that is customised to the situation is generally the most effective approach.

The Visionary Leader

The Visionary Leader moves people towards a shared vision, telling them where to go but not how to get there - thus motivating them to struggle forwards. They openly share information, hence giving knowledge power to others.

- They can fail when trying to motivate more experienced experts or peers.
- This style is best when a new direction is needed.
- Overall, it has a very strong impact on the climate.

The Coaching Leader

The Coaching Leader connects wants to organizational goals, holding long conversations that reach beyond the workplace, helping people find strengths and weaknesses and tying these to career aspirations and actions. They are good at delegating challenging assignments, demonstrating faith that demands justification and which leads to high levels of loyalty.

- Done badly, this style looks like micromanaging.
- It is best used when individuals need to build long-term capabilities.
- It has a highly positive impact on the climate.

The Affiliative Leader

The Affiliative Leader creates people connections and thus harmony within the organization. It is a very collaborative style which focuses on emotional needs over work needs. When done badly, it avoids emotionally distressing situations such as negative feedback. Done well, it is often used alongside visionary leadership.

- It is best used for healing rifts and getting through stressful situations.
- It has a positive impact on climate.

The Democratic Leader

The Democratic Leader acts to value inputs and commitment via participation, listening to both the bad and the good news. When done badly, it looks like lots of listening but very little effective action.

- It is best used to gain buy-in or when simple inputs are needed (when you are uncertain).
- It has a positive impact on climate.

The Pace-setting Leader

The Pace-setting Leader builds challenge and exciting goals for people, expecting excellence and often exemplifying it themselves. They identify poor performers and demand more of them. If necessary, they will roll up their sleeves and rescue the situation themselves.

They tend to be low on guidance, expecting people to know what to do. They get short term results but over the long term this style can lead to exhaustion and decline. Done badly, it lacks Emotional Intelligence, especially self-management. A classic problem happens when the 'star techie' gets promoted.

- It is best used for results from a motivated and competent team.
- It often has a very negative effect on climate (because it is often poorly done).

The Commanding Leader

The Commanding Leader soothes fears and gives clear directions by his or her powerful stance, commanding and expecting full compliance (agreement is not needed). They need emotional self-control for success and can seem cold and distant.

This approach is best in times of crisis when you need unquestioned rapid action and with problem employees who do not respond to other methods.

Executive Leadership

Executive leadership is the ability of those who manage or direct employees in an organization to influence and guide these individuals. Those leading executive leadership processes typically oversee such business activities as fulfilling organizational goals, strategic planning development and overall decision making.

There are several different types of executive leadership, including servant leadership, authentic leadership and paternalistic leadership. Characteristics of strong executive leaders include accountability, motivational leadership skills, problem solving abilities and extensive job experience in their profession. Strong executive leaders also possess analytical skills to determine how to maximize employee productivity and derive the most business benefit from company resources. To do so, executive leaders will use processes such as company and individual employee performance measurement and risk assessment/analysis. Other leadership traits such as empathy, willingness to collaborate and the ability to listen are especially valuable to successful executive leaders.

Executive leaders usually have a mix of soft (interpersonal) skills and hard skills that are used to inspire employees and leverage their attributes to improve business processes. They also play a big role in developing and exemplifying their organization's corporate culture, including the degree of emphasis placed on various defining elements such as hierarchy, innovation, collaboration, competition, community involvement and social engagement.

Executive leadership for CIOs has become both more complicated and important as new concepts such as mobility, IoT and cloud computing have become vital to business success. Executive leaders must make sure these new technologies and concepts are properly integrated into company processes, and in a way that maximizes their business value while avoiding regulatory compliance or security risk.

Some examples of high-profile, successful executive leaders in recent decades include Apple CEO (and Steve Jobs' successor) Tim Cook, Microsoft founder Bill Gates, Amazon CEO Jeff Bezos, Facebook co-founder and CEO Mark Zuckerberg, and Alibaba co-founder Jack Ma.

Transactional or Managerial Leadership

Transactional leadership emphasizes results, stay within the existing structure of an organization and measures success according to that organization's system of rewards and penalties.

Transactional leaders hold the formal authority and positions of responsibility in an organization. And responsible for maintaining routine by managing individual performance and facilitating group performance.

Transactional, or managerial, leaders set the standards for workers and does performance reviews are the most common way to judge employee performance.

Transactional leaders are expected to do the following:

- Set goals and give specific direction about what they demand from the employee and how they will be rewarded for their efforts.
- Provide productive feedback on performance.
- Focus on increasing the efficiency of established routines and procedures and show concern for following existing rules rather than making changes.
- Establish and standardize practices that will help the organization become efficient and productive.
- Respond to deviations from expected outcomes and identify corrective actions to improve performance.

Transactional leadership styles are more concerned with maintaining the normal flow of operations. Transactional leaders use disciplinary power and an array of incentives to motivate employees to perform at their best.

The term "transactional" refers to the fact that this type of leader essentially motivates subordinates by exchanging rewards for performance.

A transactional leader does not look ahead to strategically guiding an organization to a position of market leadership; instead, these managers are solely concerned with making sure everything flows smoothly today.

A leadership style based on the setting of clear goals and objectives for followers and the use of reward and punishments to encourage compliance.

Transactional leaders are those who guide or motivate their followers towards established goals by clarifying role and task requirement.

Transactional leadership sometimes referred to as managerial leadership; focuses on the interactions between leaders and followers. The core of transactional leadership lies in the notion that the leader, who holds power and control his or her employees or followers, provides incentives for followers to do what the leader wants.

Transactional leaders utilize rewards and punishments to motivate .their followers. While it has limitations, it can be effective in certain situations. A transactional style can work well in cases where the problems are clear-cut and simple.

One of the major problems with this style is that it does not encourage group members to look for solutions to problems or to contribute creatively, which is why transactional leadership is not the best choice in complex situations where input from group members is required.

The transactional style of leadership was first described by Max Weber in 1947 and then by Bernard Bass in 1981.

Characteristics of Transactional Leadership

- Revel inefficiency.
- Very left-brained.
- Tend to be inflexible.
- Opposed to change.
- Focused on short-term goals.
- Favor structured policies and procedures.
- Thrive on following rules and doing things correctly.

Advantages and Disadvantages of Transactional Leadership

Transactional leadership works well in organizations where the structure is essential. Transactional leadership is not the right fit for organizations where initiative is encouraged.

Advantages of Transactional Leadership

- Awards those who are motivated by self-interest to follow instructions.
- Gives an unambiguous structure for large organizations, systems requiring repetitive tasks and infinitely reproducible environments.
- Achieves short-term goals quickly.
- Rewards and penalties are defined for workers.

Disadvantages of Transactional Leadership

- Rewards the worker on a practical level only, such as money or perks.
- Creativity is limited since the goals and objectives are already set.
- Does not reward personal initiative.

Examples of Transactional Leadership

The transactional leadership model is likely to succeed in a crisis or in projects that require linear and specific processes.

This model is also useful for big corporations, such as Hewlett-Packard, a company known for its extensive use of management by exception. Many high-level members of the military, CEOs of large international companies, and NFL coaches are known to be transactional leaders.

Transactional leadership also works well with policing agencies and first responder organizations.

Bill Gates is a great example, a transactional leader. Bill Gates was born in Seattle in 1955. In his early teens, he met Paul Allen at the Lakeside School, where they both developed computer programs as a hobby.

When Gates went to Harvard, Allen went to work as a programmer for Honeywell in Boston. In 1975, they started Microsoft, and by 1978, the company had grossed $2.5 million, when Gates was 23. In 1985, Microsoft launched Windows. Bill Gates is now one of the richest and most influential people in the world.

As a transactional leader, he used to visit new product teams and ask difficult questions until he was satisfied that the teams were on track and understood the goal.

Opinion Leadership

Opinion leadership is defined as the process in which one person influences the attitudes or actions of other person informally, who may be identified as opinion leader. They offer informal advice about the product or service. Opinion leaders are part of the social groups. They have social communication network. The communication is informal and interpersonal in nature which happens between those who are not associated with the commercial selling source directly.

The most important thing for the marketer is to understand about the role of 'opinion leadership' in marketing of goods and services. Opinion leadership which is otherwise known as word of mouth communication is an important personal influence on consumers. With the proliferation of cell phone usage and e-mail, many people are always available to friends, family and business associates. Message spreads like virus among people. Opinion leaders offer advice or information about a product, service and how a particular product may be used. Words of mouth takes place through personal or face to face communication.

Examples of Opinion Leadership

The role of opinion leadership could be seen in the following examples.

1. During casual talk, a friend talks about the car he recently bought. He recommends buying it.
2. A person shows a friend photographs of his recent tour abroad. He suggests that by using a particular make of camera, better pictures could be shot.
3. A family wants to have a swimming pool in their spacious house. The family head asks neighbors which pool construction company they should call.
4. A parent wants admission for his child in a particular school. He contacts other parents sending their children to the same school.

Characteristics of Opinion Leaders

Opinion leadership is a dynamic process. It is the most powerful consumer force. As informal communication sources, it effectively influences consumers in their product related decisions. The dynamics of the opinion leadership may be discussed under the following headings.

Credible Source

Opinion leaders are knowledgeable. Their advice about a product or service is considered reliable. As opinion leaders are informal sources of information, it is perceived that they give advice in the best interest of opinion seekers. The first hand information received from opinion leaders helps in reducing perceived risks. It properly tackles the anxiety in buying new products as the opinion is based on the first hand experience.

Provision of Both Positive and Negative Product Information

Marketers provide information which is invariably favorable to the products they are marketing. But opinion leaders are not directly associated with marketers. They provide both favorable and unfavorable information about the product. So, opinion seekers have faith in opinion leaders. They are confident that they are receiving both positive and negative information in an accurate way.

Sources of Information and Advice

Opinion leaders are the source of both information and advice. They simply share their experience about a product or service. Their talk is related to what they know about a product. In their more aggressive talks, they advise others to buy or avoid a specific product. They base their advice on proper reasons.

Two-way Street

Opinion leaders in one product related situation become opinion receivers in another situation even for the same product. For example, a new homeowner thinking of buying a lawn mover seeks information and advice from other people about which brand to select. After purchasing the lawn mover, he may be satisfied with the product (in the post purchase experience). Now he has a compelling need to talk favorably about the purchase to other people to confirm the correctness of his choice. In the first instance, he is an opinion receiver and in the second he is an opinion leader.

Sometimes, an opinion leader is influenced by an opinion receiver. For example, a person may recommend a favorite hotel to his friend. In response the opinion receiver gives his own comments on that hotel. Finally, the opinion leader may come to realize that the hotel is too small, too isolated and offers fewer amenities than other hotels.

Specific Characteristics

Opinion leaders possess distinct personality traits. These include self confidence and gregariousness. They are socially inclined, outspoken and are knowledgeable.

Innovation Leadership

Innovative leadership is the ability to both think and influence others to create "new and better" ideas to move towards positive results.

In the rapidly changing world today, it is crucial for organizations to be innovative in order to stay competitive in the market and ensure continued success. This need for innovation has brought on a requirement for leaders who are capable of influencing and inspiring creative efforts.

Without innovation leadership, it is difficult for modern organizations to survive in the dynamic marketplace. The following are the key characteristics of innovation leadership.

Risk Tolerance

Innovation is synonymous with creativity. And free-flowing creativity involves a great deal of risk. An innovation leader has high risk tolerance, and has the uncanny knack to consider all possible eventualities to make well-calculated bets that often pay off.

Domain Expertise

Innovation leaders are typically required in technology oriented industries that advance rapidly. They must have the required domain expertise to communicate effectively with their team, convey a unified vision, understand the inherent risks and advantages of a creative idea, and also to command respect from the team.

Openness

When team members come up with a new idea, innovation leaders are receptive and are completely open to exploring the idea. This openness to new ideas, even radical ones, significantly contributes to the creation of a highly innovative climate in the organization.

Low Anxiety

A person who is chronically stressed and feels anxious about every little thing will not succeed in a creative and innovative environment. Anxiety is contagious, especially if it comes from a leader. Innovation leaders are typically low on anxiety. This helps them create an environment where people feel comfortable and secure, rather than anxious and threatened.

Emotional Stability

An innovation leader is grounded and has their emotions under control. Huge swings from an elated mood to depression, and then back to elation is not conducive to a workplace that is bustling with ideas. Ideally, an innovation leader is wired to be happy and positive, so they will do what is required to maintain a similar stable environment in the workplace.

Confidence

In swiftly changing fields, the job comes with the requirement of constantly exploring the unknown. It is only natural to feel anxious about stepping into new and unknown territories. But it is necessary to explore the unknown to identify new opportunities. An innovation leader has the confidence in their ability to succeed, and holds the belief that the outcomes are likely to be positive even in the face of unknown risks.

Action Oriented

Effective innovation leaders have the inclination to jump into the fray of action and actively participate. They feel energized by the action, and enjoy the exhilaration of leading change that leads to improvement and innovation.

Collaborative Inquiry

Innovations are not always made by lone geniuses. Creative insights that come from intelligent and non-judgmental sharing of ideas can give rise to continual innovation that propels the organization to greater heights. An innovation leader facilitates the process of collaborative enquiry, and encourages open dialogue between people who are involved in the situation.

Serious Play

All work and no play makes Jack a dull boy, and dullness rarely sparks innovation. These leaders understand that routine work and traditional way of thinking can become rigid and put people in a rut. Innovation requires having fun, and bending rules. Innovation leaders seek to generate insight and knowledge through non-traditional ways such as experimentation, free exploration, improvisation, and rapid prototyping.

Paying Attention

Paying attention means being a keen observer, looking deeply at the situation, and perceiving new patterns and details. The ability to notice things that may have gone unnoticed will help innovation leaders make accurate assessments and figure out the best solution to a problem.

Autocratic Leadership

Autocratic leadership, also known as authoritarian leadership, is a leadership style characterized by individual control over all decisions and little input from group members. Autocratic leaders typically make choices based on their ideas and judgments and rarely accept advice from followers. Autocratic leadership involves absolute, authoritarian control over a group.

Like other leadership styles, the autocratic style has both some benefits and some weaknesses. While those who rely on this approach to heavily are often seen as bossy or dictator-like, this level of control can have benefits and be useful in certain situations. When and where the authoritarian style is most useful can depend on factors such as the situation, the type of task the group is working on, and characteristics of the team members.

If you tend to utilize this type of leadership with a group, learning more about your style and the situations in which this style is the most effective can be helpful.

Characteristics of Autocratic Leadership

Some of the primary characteristics of autocratic leadership include:

- Little or no input from group members.
- Leaders make almost all of the decisions.
- Group leaders dictate all the work methods and processes.
- Group members are rarely trusted with decisions or important tasks.
- Work tends to be highly structured and very rigid.
- Creativity and out-of-the box thinking tend to be discouraged.
- Rules are important and tend to be clearly outlined and communicated.

Benefits

- Can make decisions quickly, especially in stress-filled situations.
- Clear chain of command, oversight.
- Good where strong, directive leadership is needed.

Drawbacks

- Discourages group input.
- Can impair morale and lead to resentment
- May impair or ignore creative solutions and expertise from subordinates.

Benefits of Autocratic Leadership

The autocratic style tend to sound quite negative. It certainly can be when overused or applied to the wrong groups or situations. However, autocratic leadership can be beneficial in some instances, such as when decisions need to be made quickly without consulting with a large group of people. Some projects require strong leadership to get things accomplished quickly and efficiently.

When the leader is the most knowledgeable person in the group, the autocratic style can lead to fast and effective decisions.

The autocratic leadership style can be useful in the following instances:

1. It can be effective in small groups where leadership is lacking.

Have you ever worked with a group of students or co-workers on a project that got derailed by poor organization, a lack of leadership and an inability to set deadlines? If so, the chances are that your grade or job performance suffered as a result. In such situations, a strong leader who utilizes an autocratic style can take charge of the group, assign tasks to different members, and establish solid deadlines for projects to be finished.

These types of group projects tend to work better when one person is either assigned the role of leader or simply takes on the job on their own. By setting clear roles, assigning tasks, and establishing deadlines, the group is more likely to finish the project on time and with everyone providing equal contributions.

2. It can also be used well in cases where a great deal of pressure is involved.

In situations that are particularly stressful, such as during military conflicts, group members may prefer an autocratic style. This allows members of the group to focus on performing specific tasks without worrying about making complex decisions. This also allows group members to become highly skilled at performing certain duties, which is ultimately beneficial to the success of the entire group.

3. Manufacturing and construction work can also benefit from the autocratic style.

In these situations, it is essential that each person have a clearly assigned task, a deadline, and rules to follow. Autocratic leaders tend to do well in these settings because they ensure that projects are finished on time and that workers follow safety rules to prevent accidents and injuries.

Downsides of Autocratic Leadership

While autocratic leadership can be beneficial at times, there are also many instances where this leadership style can be problematic.

People who abuse an autocratic leadership style are often viewed as bossy, controlling, and dictatorial. This can sometimes result in resentment among group members.

Group members can end up feeling that they have no input or say in how things or done, and this can be particularly problematic when skilled and capable members of a team are left feeling that their knowledge and contributions are undermined.

Some common problems with autocratic leadership:

This Style Tends to Discourage Group Input

Because autocratic leaders make decisions without consulting the group, people in the group may dislike that they are unable to contribute ideas. Researchers have also found that autocratic leadership often results in a lack of creative solutions to problems, which can ultimately hurt the group from performing.

Autocratic leaders tend to overlook the knowledge and expertise that group members might bring to the situation. Failing to consult with other team members in such situations hurts the overall success of the group.

Autocratic Leadership can also Impair the Morale of the Group in some Cases

People tend to feel happier and perform better when they feel like they are making contributions to the future of the group. Since autocratic leaders typically do not allow input from team members, followers start to feel dissatisfied and stifled.

Ways Autocratic Leaders Thrive

The autocratic style can be beneficial in some settings, but also has its pitfalls and is not appropriate for every setting and with every group. If this tends to be your dominant leadership style, there are things that you should consider whenever you are in a leadership role.

- Listen to team members: You might not change your mind or implement their advice, but subordinates need to feel that they can express their concerns. Autocratic leaders can sometimes make team members feel ignored or even rejected, so listening to people with an open mind can help them feel like they are making an important contribution to the group's mission.
- Establish clear rules: In order to expect team members to follow your rules, you need to first ensure that these guidelines are clearly established and that each person on your team is fully aware of them.
- Provide the group with the knowledge and tools they need: Once your subordinates understand the rules, you need to be sure that they actually have the education and abilities to perform the tasks you set before them. If they need additional assistance, offer oversight and training to fill in this knowledge gap.
- Be reliable: Inconsistent leaders can quickly lose the respect of their teams. Follow through and enforce the rules you have established.
- Recognize success. Your team may quickly lose motivation if they are only criticized when they make mistakes but never rewarded for their successes.

Bureaucratic Leadership

The Bureaucratic Leadership is the management system a couple of large corporations are using till today. If you are dealing with a highly regulated business environment, this leadership style may have a massive impact. This style of management is also very efficient when used in companies that do not require much innovations or creativity from the employees. This post talks about the meaning of bureaucratic leadership, examples, and disadvantages.

Bureaucratic leadership is one of the leadership styles postulated by Max Weber in 1947. It is a system of management whereby employees are made to follow specific rules and lines of authority created by the superiors. In other words, these set of leaders function based on official regulations fixed by higher authorities within the organization.

The bureaucratic leadership pattern focuses on the administrative needs an organization has. Teams and departments of various private and public sector employ this system of management. But it is used mostly in the public sector, which relies heavily on consistency and adherence to rules and regulations to get whatever results they seek.

However, there are unique features that differentiate the Bureaucratic style of Leadership from others practiced by organizations across the globe. Leaders in this leadership setting create a form of separation for the labor requirements which teams need to complete. In this case, there is a line of command with each leader having separate powers in their jurisdiction. They also do not like laws that are more flexible. Instead, they prefer to have rigid rules and regulations to govern people.

Examples of Bureaucratic Leadership

As one can deduce from the definition, bureaucratic style of leadership is strictly centered on a structure and depends largely on a framework to support its function. But unlike other leadership styles like charismatic leadership, one can set up and follow the structure of the bureaucratic system of management with ease.

But the point is this style of leadership has been applied in different aspects of business and organizations which includes religion, business, and politics throughout the globe. A significant number of high profile personalities have also recorded tremendous achievements owing to the rigid framework of this leadership style. Here are a few examples of leaders whose leadership style were purely bureaucratic.

- Harold Sydney Geneen – ITT

  Harold was a Bureaucratic Leader who served as president of the ITT (International Telephone and Telegraph Corporation). As the CEO of the organization, Harold recorded enormous success and accredited with helping the company develop into a multinational corporation.

  However, Harold's Bureaucratic style of Leadership is quite evident on how he structured and led ITT as the president. ITT's accountability structure followed a hierarchical outline that was clear to everyone in the organization. Each department where formed on a hierarchical pattern, with the framework of the firm set on a macro-level. Also, smaller teams had the privilege to make micro decisions where necessary.

- Winston Churchill

  Winston Churchill also exhibited Bureaucratic Leadership during his reign as a leader. He was once a British Prime Minister and credited with leading Britain to victory during the Second World War. As a leader, he had great charisma and had a structured system to ensure that individuals carry out their tasks as planned.

  Churchill was a very decisive leader and one that is so difficult to persuade. He showed persistence at all levels to carry on with his plans against all the odds. He created the plan which helped Britain to conquer the enemies during the war. Churchill is also a leader that is highly detail-oriented and meticulous, which are traits possessed by bureaucrats. He always wanted to know what was going on in all aspect of government and military efforts on the battlefield, especially during the war.

- Collin Powell

  Collin is another famous personality that used the Bureaucratic Leadership Style in politics. His leadership model is rooted deeply in the military, a public establishment known for the steady use of the bureaucratic system of leadership. Collin exhibited rare leadership qualities which earned him the position of general in the US army and Secretary of State.

  The military is an organization that likes to follow due process in the handling of its affairs. And that was where Collin drew his knowledge and understanding of the bureaucratic leadership style. He is one of the few leaders that enjoy following procedures in doing things.

Advantages and Disadvantages

There are some unique elements which distinguish this leadership style from others that are commonly practiced. Bureaucratic leaders create a defined separation for the labor requirements which a team must complete. It is defined on a clear chain-of-command, with each leader having a defined structure for their power.

Bureaucratic leaders also tend to prefer rules, laws, or regulations that are rigid. When flexibility can be removed from the equation, then there are fewer unexpected consequences which may occur. With greater predictability comes more opportunities for personal growth for everyone.

Here are some of the key advantages and disadvantages of the bureaucratic leadership style to discuss.

List of the Advantages of Bureaucratic Leadership

1. It removes Favoritism from the Equation

Bureaucratic leaders create relationships that are impersonal. The goal of each relationship is to ensure that the best possible results can be achieved. That means a friendship or family relationship doesn't affect the process. The dynamics of these relationships are set aside for the good of the team and the company. That is why a bureaucratic leader is often part of a family-run business.

2. It Centralizes Duties and Roles within a Team

Bureaucratic leaders prefer to have team members that have defined roles. Although people with the right experience may be asked to fill multiple roles on occasion, the goal of this leadership style is to create siloed experts. Each team member is responsible for a specific task. That allows each person to focus their strengths toward what they do best, including the leader, who helps to ensure that all questions are answered by the correct people.

3. It Promotes Higher Levels of Creativity

For some, bureaucratic leadership looks like a mess of red tape. With numerous rules, regulations, and expectations, the responsibility appears to involve conformity, not creativity. The opposite is actually true. The people who tend to thrive while working for a bureaucratic leader tend to have a college degree, can work independently, and use their own creative influences to improve their workflow.

4. It Creates a Stronger Level of Job Security

Bureaucratic leaders work toward rules and regulations which reinforce the need to keep teams around. Although their positions are often governed by the rules they create, this also generates a lifestyle they can enjoy. Most bureaucratic leaders are in service positions, which means the focus tends to be less on the salary and more on the benefits, like vacation time or a pension.

5. It is a Predictable form of Leadership

Bureaucratic leaders thrive in an environment where predictability is present. They create rules which are intended to help their teams create consistent results. Everyone is expected to follow the regulations which govern the work in the same way. Although this does place a limit on how creative influences can sometimes be applied, it does allow for an organization to have confidence in the results a bureaucratic leader may promise.

6. It Always seeks to Create Best Practices

There are reasons why work is completed in one specific way for many organizations. That is because the best practices for a project are based on the fastest, cheapest way to do things without compromising the quality of the final work. Every leadership style has some level of innovation which must be built into the best practices over time. With these items in place, however, the outcomes are consistent enough that they can be used to create budget expectations for the future.

7. It is a Leadership Style which Offers upward Scalability

Bureaucratic leaders work within a style which allows for scalability on an almost infinite level. Companies can keep adding teams to their structure to take on more work because they are confident that each project will be completed to the same skill and quality levels. Over time, an economy of scale can be built within an organization, allowing for team members to enjoy upward mobility, which has the side effect of lowering the overall churn rate.

8. It is a Style of Leadership which Encourages Familiarity

The chain-of-command that is followed within the bureaucratic leadership style is one that is followed by most households, companies, and public service structures in some way. That makes it easy for new leaders to fit right into the company structure. Team members can identify their roles and meet expectations right away. When there is familiarity, there is confidence, and that can lead toward higher productivity levels.

List of the Disadvantages of Bureaucratic Leadership

1. It has a Structure which has Limited Forward Movement

The issue with a bureaucratic leadership style is that the focus tends to be on specialization and consolidation. Leaders tend to stay in their positions until another position with a better salary opens up. Team members become specialists who stay in their position until the bureaucracy requires them to be in a leadership position. The only way that the chain-of-command functions well is if everyone involved is invested into the structure. If not, then one team member can disrupt the productivity of an entire team.

2. It can be a Challenge to Increase Productivity

Bureaucratic leadership may have scalability built into its style, but that does not mean productivity comes along for the ride. The structure can limit productivity because bureaucratic leaders use rules and regulations to create consistency. As more rules are added into the mix, workers are forced to slow down to ensure they are meeting required standards. For many teams, the best result is to maintain current productivity levels with better quality over time. At worst, bureaucratic leaders can create sharp drops in productivity.

3. It is often based on a System of Quotas

One of the reasons why team members become uninspired by a bureaucratic leader is that most systems are based on a series of quotas. If you meet the quota, then you've done your job. If not, then you're not doing your job and are subject to possible disciplinary action. This can become an issue if one team member is extremely efficient and another is not. Most workers will not work beyond their quota either, which places another limit on the productivity levels that are available.

4. It is a Leadership Style which bases Decisions on Cost Structures

Bureaucratic leaders tend to be more concerned about what their teams and projects look like on paper instead of what is happening with each person. That means appearance takes a priority over reality. That perspective can cause changes in budget line expenditures, project availability, and even which demographics are targeted for consumers. In some ways, bureaucratic leaders encourage wasting money instead of saving it.

5. It does not offer Freedom for Creativity

Workers are permitted to use their creativity with bureaucratic leaders within the context of meeting their quotas. Stepping outside of their job assignments is not permitted. Leaders will not usually listen to the advice of their team in this style either, though they might solicit for new ideas from time to time. Because of this lack of freedom, there can be low levels of morale frequently found on teams run by a bureaucratic leader.

6. It is not Always a System that is Efficient

Although the goal of a bureaucratic system is to create consistency, this system can be highly inefficient in some instances. If workers are paid on a fixed salary and are asked to work extra hours, then their work productivity levels invariably decline. Completing repetitive tasks may lead to expertise in a specific specialty, while also creating fewer cross-over opportunities if a labor shortage occurs. If circumstances change quickly, the structures of bureaucracy can make it difficult to adapt.

7. It can be Difficult for Bureaucratic Leaders to Adapt to change

A bureaucracy is built on the idea that what worked yesterday will also work today. That is a repetitive structure which continues on until someone forces it to change. In today's world, markets can evolve on a daily basis. Opportunities may only be available for a moment or two. A bureaucratic leader may be able to recognize these opportunities, but be able to do nothing about them, because the organizational structures in place do not offer the flexibility required to act.

The advantages and disadvantages of the bureaucratic leadership style show that it can be a useful structure for companies which need consistency on a large scale. It creates rules and regulations which make it possible for multiple people to complete the same work in the same way. It can also be the foundation for numerous inefficiencies, especially when the focus of the leader is to consolidate their own position.

Laissez-Faire Leadership

Laissez-faire leadership is based on trust. People who enjoy a wide degree of latitude in making decisions and working on projects autonomously are often most comfortable with laissez-faire leaders.

At the opposite end of the spectrum, people who work well in a rigid environment with clear directives and routine goals typically prefer authoritarian leaders.

The short version of laissez-faire leadership: Do what you want as long as you get the job done right.

From a laissez-faire leader's perspective, the key to success is to build a strong team — and then stay out of the way.

Loosely translated from its French origins, laissez-faire means "let it be" or "leave it alone." In practice, it means leaders leave it up to their subordinates to complete responsibilities in a manner they choose, without requiring strict policies or procedures.

Although laissez-faire leadership does not fit every organization, industry or situation, some workplaces thrive under laissez-faire leaders. It's all a matter of finding the right match.

Kurt Lewin is often credited with developing the concept of laissez-faire leadership. Lewin was an early contributor to the study of social psychology. He was one of the first experts to research group dynamics and organizational psychology. Human resource experts still rely on Lewin's research to assess and manage workplace productivity.

Although Lewin recognized laissez-faire leadership as one of three primary management styles, he did not subscribe to it as his preferred leadership method. Lewin simply identified laissez-faire leadership as the opposite of autocratic leadership.

Along with researchers Ronald Lippitt and Ralph K. White, Lewin identified the laissez-faire leadership style in the 1930s study "Leadership and Group Life." They recognized laissez-faire leadership as requiring the least amount of managerial oversight.

Laissez-faire is the antithesis of centralized leadership, whereby a CEO — or military general — makes most of the decisions and relies on subordinates to carry out instructions. Lewin and his research partners deduced that neither laissez-faire nor autocratic leadership styles were ideal. Instead, they concluded that democratic leadership was the optimal style.

Laissez-faire Economics

Laissez-faire economics and laissez-faire leadership share free-market traits, but they are not identical.

Within the field of economics, the term laissez-faire came into vogue in the 1980s during the Reagan administration with the rise of libertarian theories. Laissez-faire economic policies are frequently associated with Alan Greenspan, U.S. Federal Reserve chairman from 1987 to 2006. But it was Greenspan's mentor, economist Milton Friedman, who popularized the term laissez-faire. Both men espoused macroeconomic theories that reduce government's role in regulating private industry, international trade and monetary policy.

Because of their hands-off philosophy, people often misinterpret laissez-faire leaders as absent from the decision-making process. Although some absentee owners may take such an approach, most laissez-faire leaders are more involved in policy decisions than people realize.

Examples of Laissez-faire Leadership

People don't often associate laissez-faire leadership with government. However, there are many historic examples of large-scale endeavors led by political leaders that required delegating authority and decision-making to experts. Most of these examples entailed massive infrastructure projects that would not have been successful without some form of laissez-faire leadership.

Examples of large-scale projects led by a laissez-faire leadership style:

- Transcontinental Railroad: No single individual was responsible for building the North American railway system, but it serves as an example of laissez-faire leadership in action. The combination of presidential directives, congressional cooperation and private enterprise coming together during the second half of the 19th century to lay thousands of miles of track from coast to coast and across U.S. territories remains unprecedented.
- Panama Canal: Led by President Theodore Roosevelt, the Panama Canal was one of the

most ambitious projects in history when construction began in 1904. Although it was beset by accidents and geographic challenges, completion of the Panama Canal in 1914 was an engineering marvel. It could not have been accomplished without Roosevelt's willingness to delegate authority to experts.

- Hoover Dam: The Hoover Dam involved three U.S. presidents and was built by hundreds of leaders. Initiated in the early 1920s by Secretary of Commerce Herbert Hoover under President Calvin Coolidge, the project was finished the following decade under President Franklin D. Roosevelt. Although he is rarely associated with laissez-faire leadership, Roosevelt could not have completed the many infrastructure projects built during his presidency had he not delegated authority to others.
- Interstate Highway System: Recognizing the importance of the automobile and trucking industries to America's future, President Dwight D. Eisenhower led the charge to build a state-of-the-art highway system. The massive public works project provided jobs for tens of thousands of Americans and would not have been possible without Eisenhower's hands-off approach. His decision to delegate authority to civil engineers, contractors and specialized workers is a prime example of laissez-faire leadership.

Laissez-faire Leadership Case Study: Intel

When Intel was launched in the late 1960s, the leadership style of Robert Noyce helped inspire other Fairchild employees to join him. Initially, Noyce's laissez-faire management style appealed to the brilliant engineers who founded Intel, including Andrew Grove and Gordon Moore, who coined Moore's Law of exponential growth.

As Intel and the semiconductor industry matured, Noyce's laissez-faire management style was no longer optimal for a company increasingly dependent on perfecting quality assurance processes and scaling costs. Eventually, Noyce was succeeded by Grove, whose management style was more refined and autocratic — better-suited for Intel's long-term survival.

Today, similar transformations are occurring among social media companies that thrived under the dynamic, personal leadership styles of their founders. As innovative startups mature, from the incubator stage to full-fledged companies with narrow profit margins, their leaders must adapt. For such companies, this means changing from a laissez-faire management style to other forms of leadership, such as autocratic or democratic.

Famous Laissez-faire Leaders

Here are some famous leaders who adopted the laissez-faire management style or blended it with other leadership styles, such as autocratic, transformative and servant:

- Andrew Mellon embodies the 20th-century laissez-faire American leader. Mellon was a brilliant innovator, as comfortable in banking and commerce as he was in politics and philanthropy. Mellon is credited with helping build America's manufacturing industries, including behemoth U.S. aluminum, steel and oil refineries. Mellon epitomizes the laissez-faire leader because he not only believed in selecting talented experts to run businesses, but also opposed government intervention in the form of regulations and tariffs.

- Ronald Reagan was known for allowing his subordinates to complete their responsibilities in the manner they saw fit, without autocratically looking over their shoulders. Most of Reagan's high-level leadership selections were experienced captains of industry from Wall Street, engineering and aerospace contractors. During his two terms as U.S. president, Reagan delegated unprecedented authority to his chief of staff, Cabinet secretaries and others — sometimes to his peril. However, Reagan earned a reputation as a strong but hands-off leader.

- Warren Buffett may be the most surprising name among successful laissez-faire leaders. Buffett is known for taking a hands-off approach toward leadership of the many companies he owns, or in which he invests after actively canvassing the industries he favors. Once he makes an investment decision, though, Buffett trusts his managers to know how to achieve the performance he expects.

- Lou Holtz, former head football coach for Notre Dame University, represents a blend of leadership styles. This is uncommon for gridiron coaches, who typically exhibit dominant authoritarian traits. Although he was one of collegiate football's most successful coaches, Holtz emphasized principles over winning. Because of his devotion to personal responsibility, his coaching style was part laissez-faire, part autocratic. Holtz expected all his college players — from redshirt freshmen to senior quarterbacks — to behave as mature leaders.

- John F. Kennedy is rarely considered a laissez-faire leader, especially among U.S. presidents. However, Kennedy's space exploration program would have failed had he not entrusted the Apollo project to experts. Kennedy inspired an entire nation with his "moon shot" speech. His executive style persuaded Congress to commit financial resources toward putting a man on the moon within 10 years. Kennedy's laissez-faire management style motivated NASA to accomplish the goal.

- Jack Welch, CEO of General Electric for more than two decades, adopted many leadership styles. He epitomized the autocratic leader with his quest for 99.99 percent quality control tolerances in all manufacturing facilities. Yet Welch mentored executives by giving them wide latitude to run their operations without interference. Welch earned a reputation as a hard-driving perfectionist who paid close attention to GE's expansion. However, he succeeded at increasing GE's value 4,000-fold by delegating authority to experts — once he made the decisions to acquire subsidiaries or launch new operations.

- Donna Karan, founder of DKNY jeans and apparel, enjoys a reputation as an attentive but hands-off leader who follows fashion trends while keeping her eyes on profits. The Center for Association Leadership noted in a 2013 article that Karan trusts managers to make good decisions while monitoring their performance and offering ongoing feedback. Karan reportedly believes firmly in autonomy, which leads to strong job satisfaction and increased productivity.

- Paul Allen, co-founder of Microsoft, epitomizes the laissez-faire leader who is challenged by new ideas but maintains a hands-off managerial style. Allen's decision to leave Microsoft early in its history demonstrates a trait often found among laissez-faire leaders, who tend to dislike the mundane but vital processes that accompany all successful enterprises.

Allen has funded dozens of successful ventures. They range from the NFL's Seattle Seahawks and NBA's Portland Trail Blazers to the Living Computer Museum and the Allen Institute for Brain Science.

- Sebastián Piňera, president of Chile from 2010 to 2014, led the rescue operations of 33 miners trapped 2,300 feet underground in a collapsed mine. As documented in a 2013 issue of Harvard Business Review, Piñera's decisiveness is an example of laissez-faire leadership at its finest. Piñera made decisions common to laissez-faire leaders. He immediately recognized that past assumptions did not apply to the 2010 mine collapse. He was open to suggestions and sought advice from engineers and mechanics, deep-sea operators, doctors and psychologists. Piñera selected key players and approved their rescue plans. Then he gave them latitude to save the day using unconventional methods.

Quotes about Laissez-faire Leadership

Here are some quotations from leaders who embody the laissez-faire model while managing people effectively through a combination of leadership styles.

- Warren Buffett: "Pick out associates whose behavior is better than yours and you'll drift in that direction."
- Andrew Mellon: "Strong men have sound ideas and the force to make these ideas effective."
- Donna Karan: "You can design from instinct. It's the only way you know how to live. What feels good. What feels right. What is needed. Give me a problem and you will be approach it creatively, from my gut."
- Ronald Reagan: "Surround yourself with the best people you can find, delegate authority, and don't interfere as long as the policy you've decided upon is being carried out."
- Lou Holtz: "It's a fine thing to have ability, but the ability to discover ability in others is the true test."
- Paul Allen: "While you sign off on trades or free agents, you've rarely overruled my basketball people's decisions. But you not shy about steering the discussion or pushing deeper if something doesn't make sense to me."
- Jack Welch: "If you pick the right people and give them the opportunity to spread their wings, and put compensation as a carrier behind it, you almost don't have to manage them."

Laissez-faire Leadership Style Requirements

Laissez-faire leadership entails giving managers and staff wide latitude in carrying out their responsibilities.

People who work for laissez-faire leaders are responsible for completing tasks and identifying issues. Moreover, they are expected to anticipate near-term problems and spot upcoming opportunities. Laissez-faire leaders usually allow staff to capitalize on opportunities without having to check in with their superiors.

To succeed, laissez-faire leaders need to:

- Closely monitor group performance.
- Employ highly skilled, well-educated staff.
- Treat people as motivated self-starters.
- Use the laissez-faire style only with experienced staff.
- Give consistent feedback to team members.

Laissez-faire Management Style Explained

Within organizations — from private companies and nonprofit entities to government agencies — laissez-faire leadership starts at the top of the organizational hierarchy.

For example, a CEO or executive director with laissez-faire leadership characteristics typically hires or appoints senior executives and department heads with considerable experience in their respective fields. Those individuals are expected to know how to run their departments. They are entrusted to do so with minimal supervision.

Effectiveness of Laissez-faire Leadership

Expert merchandizing managers and retail buyers are good examples of people who often work well under a laissez-faire leadership structure.

Within fast-moving markets, purchasing and promotional decisions are based on fluctuating factors — from consumer trends and supply-chain bottlenecks to price increases and severe weather patterns. Product managers who work under laissez-faire leaders are given autonomy to pivot fast and make quick decisions without waiting weeks for an approval process to begin.

In business parlance, this is called being nimble. It does not mean laissez-faire leaders are reckless or blasé. On the contrary, successful laissez-faire leaders are observant. They reward people for their successes and hold them accountable for their mistakes.

Benefits of Laissez-faire Leadership

Managers who adopt a laissez-faire leadership style expect accountability from people who report to them. Whether the laissez-faire leader is a CEO, department director or group manager, he or she expects positive results.

Some people prefer working under autocratic managers because they don't want to be held responsible for failures. For these people, a laissez-faire leadership style is a mismatch.

Future Laissez-faire Leaders

To be successful in an age of daily productivity metrics reporting, laissez-faire leaders need to establish milestones for staff. This means today's laissez-faire leaders can no longer be completely hands off.

Contemporary laissez-faire leaders must:

- Observe group and individual performance.
- Track results and stay on top of issues and problems.
- Give credit where credit is due and encourage individual responsibility.

In summary, today's laissez-faire leaders must delegate authority without losing sight of group objectives and individual performances.

Main Principles of Laissez-Faire Leadership

A Strict Hands-off Approach

Laissez-faire leaders are there to give their workers the tools they need to solve problems on their own. They do not try to push the group in a particular direction, but they allow them to create their objectives and criteria for decision-making.

Training and Support

Leaders leave a lot of responsibility in the hands of their workers. As a result, they are very concerned with the experience and educational level of employees. Therefore, many laissez-faire leaders will step into the role of support and provide the training, educational opportunities, and resources that workers need to make to perform and make decisions.

Trust in those they Hired

Laissez-faire leaders are relaxed in their approach, but this should not be mistaken for lack of caring: they care deeply about the direction of the team and show this by hiring the best people for the job. They search for those with specialized expertise in the duties they will assign to them. Therefore, these leaders feel they have a team they can trust because they have handpicked the talent.

Decisions are Left to Employees

Laissez-faire leaders recognize how important it is to hire the right people because those individuals will be making the decisions about how they work. Leaders assume the role of support and help employees come together to consult one another or others about decisions. They act as consultant and mentor when needed.

Comfortable with Mistakes

Laissez-faire leaders establish an environment of creativity where it is alright for employees to make mistakes in the pursuit of innovation. Employees feel comfortable knowing that they can pursue innovation freely since they will not receive a reprimand for mistakes. Instead of everything resting on "getting it right," the atmosphere shifts to learning.

The Qualities of Laissez-Faire Leaders

- Laissez-faire leaders are good at showing compassion and keeping the big picture in perspective.

- They are also resourceful and creative in how they approach situations.
- They are good at using what they have, taking advantage of technology, and creatively solving problems.
- These leaders are excellent at putting teams together. They look for the best and brightest and do their part in examining whether someone would work in their environment.
- As a result, they can take a page from the charismatic leader in inspiring others to want to be a part of what they are doing.
- All in all, laissez-faire leaders are confident and thoughtful individuals who bring those qualities to leadership.

Advantages and Disadvantages of Laissez-Faire Leadership

The qualities of this leadership style may seem positive, especially for employees. However, there are some elements that leaders and their subordinates need to be aware of if they decide to implement this style.

Advantages

- Gives Employees the Chance to Succeed: Since leaders are hands-off in their approach to leading employees, this leadership style allows them the opportunity to show what they can do. If they have always wanted to try a new idea, or collaborate on a particular project, this style gives them the opportunity to do that.
- A Freeing Atmosphere: As stated above, employees value workplace autonomy. People enjoy when their employers do not micromanage and trust them enough to allow them to control their work environment. For highly-skilled employees that are engaged in the work they do, this leadership style can be an excellent way to acknowledge their talent.
- Can Facilitate New Ideas: The company can significantly benefit from laissez-faire leadership. If employees are given the opportunity to be creative and come up with new ideas, then this can benefit the organization. These ideas can help promote better processes, policies, or a more streamlined work environment for everyone. Giving highly talented people the opportunity to stop their regularly scheduled work day to figure out problems can benefit everyone.
- Frees the Leader up to Handle Other Issues: If leaders are not always having to stand over employees and provide constant guidance, then they can be engaged in other pertinent matters. Leaders who engage in micromanaging are likely unable to get to managerial duties that need their attention. Laissez-faire leaders bypass this issue by letting employees handle the work they need to so they can handle more pressing situations.
- Faster Decision-Making: Since there is no micromanagement, workers do not have to wait around for feedback from management on each and every small step. In a fast-paced work environment, this means the frustration of needing a “yes” from everyone is non-existent.

Disadvantages

- Lack of Role Clarity: There may come a time when employees do not know what is expected of them. If a new project is being entered into, a laissez-faire leader may not provide all the details needed for teams to get started. Therefore, employees can become frustrated with not being in the know regarding what they are supposed to accomplish.
- Everyone May Not Be Able to Handle the Responsibility of This Style: Some employees may take advantage of this method and slack off or miss critical deadlines. Others might not break the rules, but they need more guidance than what is given. Laissez-faire leaders can only work with a specific personality type that is comfortable with this arrangement.
- Indifference: If leaders are seen as not caring about the work because of their lack of involvement in day-to-day happenings, then workers could take on the same attitude. Laissez-faire leaders could come off as uncaring and unconcerned about the happenings they are supposed to be managing. It is important for a successful laissez-faire leader to maintain a healthy level of involvement, usually by providing guidance and coaching.
- An Increase in Conflict: Without a guiding voice, different groups of employees might engage in interdepartmental conflict. Employees can start acting in their own self-interest and begin to fight over resources. Without something to manage these disputes, departments could start to descend into chaos.
- Lack of Accountability: While these leaders are supposed to take accountability for the group, some may use this as a means to shirk their responsibility for outcomes. As a result, employees could bear the brunt of the blame for unfavorable issues, making them fearful of trying anything new. Productive laissez-faire leadership is possible when laissez-faire leader takes accountability and accepts mistakes.

Laissez-Faire Leadership Best Practices

Closely Monitor Employees and their Performance

These leaders should not go to the extreme of micromanaging employees, but they should take an active role in making sure tasks are done. This can look like a weekly check-in, a weekly meeting where everyone updates the leader and the group on progress, or updates on a company intranet. Either way, leaders need to be aware of how the team is progressing.

Set-up Regular Feedback Sessions

Every employee might not benefit from the laissez-faire leadership style. Therefore, leaders should have regular meetings with individual employees to see what they could do to support them better.

Make a Personality Assessment a Part of the Hiring Process

It takes a particular kind of person to be comfortable with a hands-off leadership style. Therefore, leaders should employ a personality assessment where they can see what potential employees are satisfied with as far as autonomy, self-monitoring, and minimal guidance.

Find Ways to Thank and Congratulate Employees

While employees do value autonomy, they also enjoy being acknowledged for a job well done. Laissez-faire leaders need to make sure they are engaged in showing recognition privately and publicly to engage and motivate employees.

While this leadership style supports employee self-monitoring, leaders need always to keep an eye on performance and have the lines of communication open so they can stay current on project updates and employee needs. As a result, laissez-faire leaders can instill a balance between autonomy and guidance.

Effective leadership is all about communicating effectively.

Importance of Laissez-Faire Leadership

As with most of the other leadership styles, there are pros and cons to this approach to leading employees. However, there is one quality from it that will likely be a favorite of any worker: autonomy.

Workers enjoy feeling as if their decision-making is trusted enough to where they do not have to be continuously monitored by leaders. A 2013 Workplace survey conducted by Gensler, an architectural firm, revealed that when employees are allowed to utilize choice in their work environment, workplace satisfaction was 12 points higher than those who did not have a choice. A survey conducted by Trinity Solutions further solidified this statistic by revealing the effects of micromanaging. Seventy-nine percent of respondents experienced micromanagement, and 69 percent considered changing jobs because of it. Ultimately, 36 percent transitioned to other positions. While there are statistics that reveal that workers like to have some involvement from their bosses, many enjoy the feeling of freedom. Therefore, it is essential to understand that while all of the methodologies of laissez-faire leadership might not be favorable for workplaces, the level of autonomy that it promotes is something all employers should consider implementing in their work environment.

Charismatic Leadership

Charismatic leadership is basically the method of encouraging particular behaviors in others by way of eloquent communication, persuasion and force of personality. Charismatic leaders motivate followers to get things done or improve the way certain things are done. This is accomplished by conjuring up eagerness in others to achieve a stated goal or vision. In essence, the charismatic leadership style has its basis in a form of heroism. This leadership style is almost of divine origin.

Charismatic and Transformational Leadership

Transformational leadership can be viewed as guidance that goes beyond charisma, given that two of the elements of transformational leadership involve charisma. These elements are:

Idealized Influence

This is basically the capacity of the leader to be a moral and positive role model to their followers.

In addition, the transformational leader practices what he or she preaches and is always there in the trenches with the followers. A good example of this leadership style is Dr. Martin Luther King, Jr. These leaders are known to make the same sacrifices that they want the followers to make. In an organizational setting, the charismatic and transformational leader occasionally becomes the "face" of the organization. The late, great Steve Jobs is a prime example of this.

Inspirational Motivation

This is the other element of transformational leadership and charismatic leaders are renowned for it. This is their capacity to motivate and inspire followers to execute at higher levels and to be totally dedicated to the cause or the organization.

Similarities and Differences between Charismatic and Transformational Leadership

There are a number of similarities between charismatic and transformational leadership. For example, the transformational leader is typically charismatic as well. The primary dissimilarity is the basic focus of these two leadership styles. For example, the basic focus of the transformational leader is transforming the organization and the followers during the process, while the charismatic leader could be quite satisfied with the status quo.

Transformational leadership involves the use of charisma; however, transformational leaders are well-known for leading groups and teams that perform excellently. In addition, they are noted for their ability to identify and foster leadership capacity in the followers. They also devise methods of assisting the organization or group to innovate and change.

The Flip Side of Charismatic Leadership

In spite of the apparent concern and charm, charismatic leaders could very well be self-involved; thinking more about themselves than the people they are supposed to be leading. A classic experience with charismatic leaders is that while having a conversation with them, the experience is similar to being bathed in a pleasant, warm glow and what they are saying is extremely convincing. However, afterwards when their attention is focused somewhere else, you may start to question what was said or if there was any significance in what was said.

Charismatic leaders have values that are highly significant; however, this is only useful when these leaders are well-intentioned towards their followers and can transform and elevate the entire group. If charismatic leaders are Machiavellian and selfish, they have the power to form cults and in effect rape the minds and even the bodies of the individuals they are leading.

The self-belief of charismatic leaders is quite high and some are of the belief that they are infallible and can blindly lead their followers into an abyss. This elevated sense of self can result in psychotic narcissism as well. This occurs when the need for worship and admiration and self-absorption result in followers being perplexed about the leadership.

Creating Good Charismatic Leaders

Teams require effective leadership from leaders who must be able to project an inspiring and clear vision. In an economic climate that is extremely challenging, it is that much more essential to keep the motivation and determination of team members on a high.

Charismatic leaders are formed and shaped by their gallant deeds and they need to be associated with historical figures that exemplify their aspirations. There should be specialized training for individuals who are aspiring to become charismatic leaders. Training for charismatic leadership aspirants should delve into the great ambitions and vivid imaginations of current exemplary charismatic leaders and those from the past.

Charismatic leaders should not only want to stand out within an organization; they should have the overwhelming desire to transform the industry. There is a great requirement for these leaders to possess exceptional communication skills that involve active listening, motivation and paraphrasing. Charismatic leaders can use their superior communication skills to evoke certain emotions within followers and to transform initiatives via direct action from employees.

Similar to other leadership development programs, the curriculum for charismatic leadership should be designed to invigorate and motivate aspiring charismatic leaders to thrive where their greatest strengths are exhibited.

Task-Oriented Leadership

Task-oriented leadership often is contrasted against relations-oriented leadership. One emphasizes the tasks needed to achieve goals, and the other focuses on relationships required to keep employees satisfied with their work.

Students of leadership will find that the task-oriented style fits the definition of a manager while the people-oriented style focuses on the characteristics of a leader. According to the Center for Leadership Development, "The manager's job is to plan, organize and coordinate. The leader's job is to inspire and motivate."

Leadership students need to understand the difference between task- and relations-oriented styles because they are likely to encounter both over the course of their careers. Which leadership style is better? Which style would you prefer as a future leader or future employee?

What is task-oriented leadership? Perhaps the most concise definition of task-oriented leadership is "doing whatever it takes to get the job done." The approach tends to be autocratic and emphasizes completing tasks required to meet organizational goals.

While it has its place in a modern workplace, task-oriented leadership can lack attention to the well-being of team members, which can prove to be a deficiency in many leadership scenarios.

Qualities and Examples of Task-oriented Leadership

A task-oriented leader places a heavy emphasis on structure, plans, and schedules for getting things done. The task-oriented leadership style might include:

- Step-by-step planning and reward/punishment systems.

- Constantly defining structure and goals.
- Prioritizing achievement of specific outcomes..
- Sticking to rigid schedules.
- Requiring employees to set process-oriented goals and formulate plans to achieve them.

When should this type of leadership be used? Why does task-oriented leadership work? One prudent principle of modern leadership theory is that leaders should base their approach on each unique situation they face. If certain team members have poor time management skills, task-oriented leadership is a possible solution. Also, a workplace with tight deadlines can benefit from task-oriented leadership.

Apparently William Shakespeare advocated this leadership approach centuries ago with his observation, "Better three hours too soon than one minute too late."

Potential Drawbacks of task-oriented Leadership

Because task-oriented leadership is essentially an autocratic style, it can lead to retention and motivation problems.

Jim Collins, author of the leadership classic "Good to Great," summed up what's at stake for most leaders: "Those who build great companies understand that the ultimate throttle on growth for any great company is not markets, or technology, or competition, or products. It is one thing above all others: the ability to get and keep enough of the right people."

Contemporary leadership studies have illustrated that both task-oriented and relations-oriented leadership models are too simplistic for many modern workplace environments. Additionally, the increased prominence of individuals and "knowledge workers" (a term popularized by Peter Drucker) has made the leadership process more complicated.

As a result, task-oriented leadership as a distinct leadership style often has been replaced by more specialized approaches such as situational and transformational leadership.

Relationship-Oriented Leadership

Relationship-Oriented Leadership focuses on creating success as a result of building lasting relationships with employees and the motivation, job satisfaction and work-life balance of their employees. They still care about getting tasks done, however they believe that work culture is more important.

Relationship-oriented leaders are primarily focused on supporting, motivating and developing individuals and teams. They seek to establish meaningful relationships with their staff and aim to utilise this emotional connection to maximise staff performance.

Advanced levels of emotional intelligence are required for effective relationship-oriented leadership enabling them to easily empathise with their staff and understand their point of view when making decisions. This style of leadership encourages effective teamwork and collaboration through enhanced relationships that exist between team members. Understanding the needs and requirements of each individual person is vital for relationship-oriented leadership to be effective.

Relationship-oriented leaders are very personable, their door is always open and they have a genuine interest in the wellbeing of their staff. People are supported and looked after in way that enables them to perform to the best of their ability, free from distractions and emotional burdens. Harmony within the workforce is often good as social cohesion is promoted.

Key Strengths

By focusing on the emotional needs of the staff, relationship-oriented leaders ensure they have a positive and motivated workforce. Staff will be enthused and inspired to work and will feel valued and appreciated.

In a well-supported team of staff, personal conflicts, dissatisfaction and boredom will be minimised resulting in a happy and productive team. Free from personal issues the staff will be able to work more productively and at a higher standard.

Staff may also be more inclined to work creatively and innovatively, taking risks and challenging key operations. Risks can be taken because staff are aware that the leader will provide support if they are unsuccessful. This is essential for development and improvements in organisational performance.

Key Criticisms

The major criticism to this style of leadership is that with a focus on the relationships between the leader and the staff the actual task at hand can sometimes be overlooked. Not wanting to work staff too hard, to much, in a way they don't enjoy, etc. can risk not getting the job completed in the timeframe that has been set.

Another key criticism of relationship-oriented leadership is that some employees may take advantage of a people-focused leader. If staff see the leader accommodating their every need they may start to take liberties to see how far they can push the leader with what they will get away with.

While risk taking was a key strength it can also be considered a criticisms as well. While risk is essential for progressing an organisation the risk also needs to be calculated. Too much risk taking, at the wrong time and in the wrong place can result in irreversible errors which the leader will find difficult to repair.

Participative Leadership

Participative leadership, also known as democratic leadership, is one of the four participative decision-making styles where employers invite employees to take a part in organizational decision-making. While this leadership style is not as common in the corporate world, some professions require this type of attitude, e.g., social workers, arbitrators, group therapists, and facilitators. Some of the most famous examples of participative leaders in the corporate world include Donald Trump, Bill Gates, Bob Diamond, James Parker, Jim Lentz, and John Stahl.

Working

Here is how participative leadership works:

While participative leadership comes in several flavors, there is a common pattern that is present in most of these types:

- The leader facilitates the conversation;
- The leader openly shares information and knowledge necessary for decision-making;
- The leader encourages people to share their ideas;
- The leader synthesizes all the available information and solutions suggested by the team;
- The leader comes up with the best possible solution and communicates it back to the group.

Four Types of Participative Decision-Making

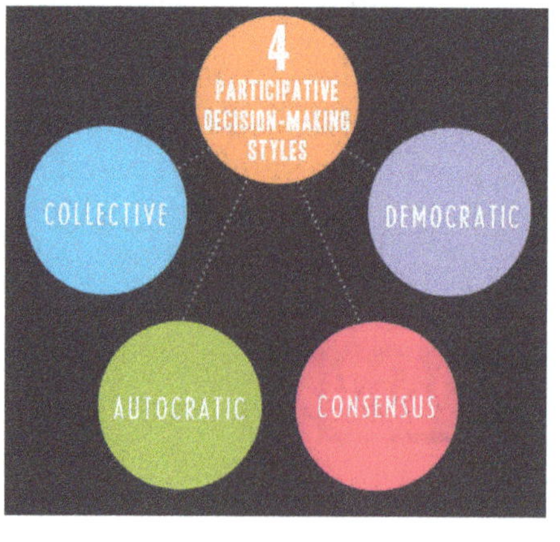

There are four types of participative decision-making with democratic (or participative) leadership being only one of them. All of these styles are somewhat similar and have similar advantages and disadvantages. They are:

- Collective,
- Democratic,
- Autocratic,
- Consensus.

Collective decision-making is a form of leadership style where all decisions are taken by the group, and the responsibility for these decisions are also entirely on the group. One of the characteristics of collective leadership is that during the decision-making process the group must develop clear lines of authority that define the responsibilities of each member.

Democratic or participative leadership encourages participation of all members, but the final decision is taken by the leader. Once the decision is taken, the leader has to communicate it back to the group and resolve possible objections if any.

Autocratic participative decision-making implies that while possible solutions are brainstormed collectively, the responsibility of taking the final decision is still on the leader alone. Autocratic leadership style allows the organization to benefit from the collective input provided by all employees while making decisions reasonably fast.

Democratic and autocratic styles of participative leadership may seem to be very much alike, but the difference is that while autocratic leadership is more goal oriented, i.e. to get results and meet deadlines, democratic leadership is more people-oriented and quality-oriented. The advantage of autocratic decision-making over democratic is that the results are obtained much faster.

Consensus decision-making is a leadership style where the leader gives up control and responsibility of decision-making, leaving it entirely to the group. The decision has to be approved by the majority of the group while the minority of those who don't agree initially have to agree to go along. In other words, the decision has to be modified to remove any objectionable features so that the minority can agree with it.

Pros and Cons of Participative Leadership

PARTICIPATIVE LEADERSHIP	
ADVANTAGES	**DISADVANTAGES**
People feel valued.	Social pressure to confirm to group domination.
People perform well even When the leader is absent.	Decision – making may take a lot time.
People are more committed to achieving The goals and objectives of the organization.	High cross .
	Inefficiency.
	Incompetence.
	Indecisiveness

Participative leadership model is very much in vogue these days with many supporters promoting its advantages:

- All of the members of the team feel valued and in control;
- The team tends to perform better because the members are more committed to achieving the goals and objectives of the organization;
- The team performs well even when the leader is absent;
- Increased group morale;
- Decreased competitiveness.

However, there is a number of serious disadvantages to be considered as well:

- The members may feel social pressure to conform to group domination;
- Decision-making may take a long time;
- High unnecessary costs;
- Incompetence;
- Indecisiveness;
- Inefficiency.

Ethical Leadership

Ethical leadership is a form of leadership in which individuals demonstrate conduct for the common good that is acceptable and appropriate in every area of their life. It is composed of the following three major elements:

- Be the Example:

  A noble quality of a leader is leading by example. As an ethical leader, it's important to remember that actions often speak louder than words. People are more likely to judge someone based on how they act, rather than what they say. By practicing and demonstrating the use of ethical, honest and unselfish behavior to subordinates, ethical leaders may begin to earn the respect of their peers. People may be more likely to follow a leader who respects others and shows integrity.

- Champion the Importance of Ethics:

  One role of an ethical leader is focusing on the overall importance of ethics, including ethical standards and other ethical issues, and how these factors can influence society. As an ethical leader, it's important to teach peers about ethics, especially in cases where they are faced with an ethical issue in the workplace.

- Communicate:

  Successful ethical leaders tend to be good communicators. People communicate in different ways. Some may feel comfortable speaking in public, regardless of personnel or situation, while others may be hesitant to speak with a leader because of fear, anxiousness or simply not knowing how to articulate what they are trying to say. They might be better talking via email, rather than in person. It's an ethical leader's job to communicate with each member of the team, but also allow for open conversation, as some people may have questions and concerns that need addressed. It's important for leaders to build camaraderie with their team. Quality relationships tend to be built on trust, fairness, integrity, openness, compassion and respect.

Impacts of Ethical Leadership

Ethical leaders can help establish a positive environment with productive relationships over three levels: the individual, the team and the overall organization.

Nurturing the relationships at each of these levels can lead to the following outcomes and benefits:

- The Well-Being of the Individual:

  Maintaining a positive working atmosphere is an important responsibility of a strong ethical leader. Ethical leaders who lead by example may influence others to do the same. Generally, people are affected by the interactions that occur around them. Positive communication among co-workers may help influence job productivity and attitude.

- The Energy of the Team:

  Ethical leadership can also involve the management of conduct and collaboration within a team. Typically, morale is higher in the workplace when people are getting along with each other. When co-workers are working as a team, it can help build relationships in the workplace and help the overall performance of the group. Generally, strong leaders lead by example.

- The Health of the Organization:

  The importance of maintaining a positive attitude in the workplace has a lot to do with improving the overall health of the organization. When people can show respect for one another, and can value other's opinions, it may help create a productive working environment. An ethical organization can occur when communities of people work together in an environment of mutual respect, where they can grow personally, build friendships and contribute to the overall goal.

The 4-V Model of Ethical Leadership

The 4-V model helps align the internal beliefs and values with the external behaviors and actions for the purpose of the common good. The four V's stand for Values, Vision, Voice and Virtue, the characteristics that help create a strong ethical leader. In the end, the main goal of an ethical leader is to create a world in which the future is positive, inclusive and allows the potential for all individuals to pursue and fulfill their needs and meet their highest potential.

Authentic Leadership

Authentic Leadership is a modern and more inclusive approach to leadership.

Authentic Leadership works on the principle that a leader can prove their legitimacy by nurturing sincere relationships with their subordinates and giving importance to their input.

An authentic leader encourages their subordinates to be more open; they appreciates their support in the success of the organization. Their leadership style promotes both individual and team performance.

Self-awareness

An authentic leader reflects upon all of their actions and decisions and examines their own strengths and weaknesses without any bias. They put in a lot of effort to overcome their fears and uses their strengths to the maximum.

Lead with Heart

An authentic leader is all heart. They are not afraid to dig deep, and they lead their team with a courage and empathy that only comes from listening to the heart.

Focus on Long-term Results

Authentic leaders don't waste precious time unnecessarily worrying over temporary setbacks, or less than stellar results in the previous quarter. Their focus is always long-term. They know that patience and hard work do take time but yield rich results in the long run.

Integrity

Strength of character is essential for an authentic leader. They don't say things which they don't mean, and they earn respect because of this quality. People trust them because they keep their word, no matter what it takes.

Lead with Vision

Authentic leaders lead with purpose and vision. They always add value to people they interact with and help them realize higher professional goals which lead to better personal lives as well. They push themselves and others around them to raise the bar and aim for excellence.

Listening Skills

An authentic leader is always a good listener, even when someone else contradicts their views. In fact, they are even willing to consider those ideas with an open mind and change their opinion if the arguments make sense.

Transparency

Authentic leaders believe in open communication and combine their directness with empathy, which more often than not brings success. The image they project in public is not drastically different from how they really are in private. They don't hide their mistakes and weaknesses, and have the courage to actually be who they really are.

Consistency

Consistency is another hallmark of authentic leaders. They aren't fickle and they stick to their principles. Their behavior is consistent, and they are not easily swayed by superficialities.

Share Success with the Team

This is something that sets an authentic leader apart from other leaders. They not only build a good team, but also give credit where it is due and shares success and achievements with the entire team.

Drawing on Experience

There is no better teacher than life, and these leaders draw from lessons learnt from their life experiences. Their stellar leadership skills slowly evolved from real-world experiences and life stories.

Self-leadership

Self-leadership is the ability to consciously influence your own thoughts and behavior in order to achieve your personal goals or an organization's objectives.

Self-led people mostly take their own decisions and set personal targets. This ability is typical of entrepreneurs, mentors, top managers etc.

We say a person has self-leadership skills when he has foresight, makes the right decisions and choices on his own, and exhibits dedication towards achieving his goals.

Aside goal setting, self-awareness is another factor that helps make people great self-leaders. Every manager must possess self-leadership skills.

Importance of Self-leadership

Self-leadership is the first stage or level of leadership. For employees, whether mangers or ordinary subordinates, self-leadership is of great importance.

As a manager, you receive very little or no supervision. This means you should be able to plan and set your objectives on your own, as well as influence your own self to follow those plans.

As lower level employee, you can never be sure the kind of management or leaders you will meet in the course of tour career. Despite whatever leadership you may come across –whether laissez faire, democratic or autocratic – you should be able to exhibit self-leadership. Employers like workers who can take great decisions on their own and are able to influence themselves to work effectively.

Self-leadership helps make the individual proactive, disciplined, and an independent decision maker. People who have no strong sense of self-leadership tend to feel they are not in control of themselves, often lack focus and get overwhelmed easily.

Ways to Improve on Self-leadership

Self-leadership is indisputably a lovable skill. Here are four tips that should help you improve on self-leadership skills.

- Clarity of purpose: Every leadership or leader has a vision. Being your own leader, your purpose or vision will be the foundation upon which you will build self-leadership. Without properly scripted objectives or purpose for your life, you will be at peril – trying to follow people's plans or ideas for your life – and you end up stuck in the middle of nowhere.
- Aim at success and take reasonable risks: Risk taking is an essential aspect of life. Challenge yourself to take on daring projects. Don't discourage yourself with past failures of yourself or others – focus on success. However, they should be reasonably calculated risks that are relevant to your purpose.
- Spend time to reflect on your life: While you remain the active doer of the things you do, you may see things from your perspective only. Take some time off to reflect on your life – compare the past to the present and the present to future goals. Until you take a break to analyze yourself, you may never identify certain petty shortcomings. Reflections can also mean allowing someone to make an objective assessment of you.
- Don't tolerate just anything: You cannot put your vision at risk. You should learn to be intolerant of any suggestion or ideas which are not in line with your vision. This intolerance is not towards others only but yourself too. It includes not tolerating negative aspects of your nature such as laziness, fear, timidity etc.

References

- Leadership-styles: businessjargons.com, Retrieved 2 June, 2019
- Laissez-Faire-Leadership: cleverism.com, Retrieved 11 March, 2019
- Six-emotional-styles, leadership: changingminds.org, Retrieved 20 February, 2019
- Executive-leadership: techtarget.com, Retrieved 22 April, 2019
- Transactional-leadership: iedunote.com, Retrieved 12 July, 2019
- Opinion-leadership-meaning-definition-characteristics: accountlearning.com, Retrieved 13 January, 2019
- Innovation-leadership-characteristics: yscouts.com, Retrieved 28 August, 2019
- What-is-autocratic-leadership: verywellmind.com, Retrieved 19 March, 2019
- Bureaucratic-leadership-guide-definition-pros-cons-examples: managementstudyhq.com, Retrieved 10 July, 2019
- Bureaucratic-leadership-style-advantages-and-disadvantages: futureofworking.com, Retrieved 12 February, 2019
- What-is-laissezfaire-leadership: stu.edu, Retrieved 14 January, 2019

- Laissez-faire-leadership: status.net, Retrieved 5 May, 2019
- Charismaticleadership: teamworkdefinition.com, Retrieved 15 March, 2019
- What-is-task-oriented-leadership: stu.edu, Retrieved 27 January, 2019
- Relationship-oriented-leadership: jonathansandling.com, Retrieved 2 May, 2019
- Participative-leadership: psychologia.co, Retrieved 18 April, 2019
- What-is-ethical-leadership, leadership: villanovau.com, Retrieved 8 February, 2019
- Authentic-leadership-characteristics: yscouts.com, Retrieved 7 June, 2019
- Self-leadership, skills-and-tools: cleverism.com, Retrieved 6 August, 2019

3

Leadership: Philosophies, Models and Theories

The leadership philosophy is an important factor which has a profound impact on the success or failure of any person as a leader. Some of the different philosophies and theories related to leadership are authentic leadership, servant leadership, path-goal leadership theory and evolutionary leadership theory. This chapter discusses in detail these theories and methodologies related to leadership.

Leadership Philosophies

A leadership philosophy contains value-based ideas of how a leader should be and act and the sources of their power. Any leadership philosophy is a way of thinking and behaving. It is a set of values and beliefs. A philosophy is a series of reference points or a foundation upon which processes, decisions, actions, plans, etc. can be built, developed and applied. Ultimately, a leadership philosophy connects leadership with humanity, morality and ethics, and crucially, trust. Leadership philosophies help us to understand how a leader comes to power and stays in power. They are not 'designed' to be applied like a model or a style, but they do enable much greater insight into the wider causes of, and effects upon, leadership from the widest possible human viewpoint. although the combination of leadership and philosophy might sound rather odd. On the face of it, the terms don't seem to have much in common.

Development of Leadership Philosophy

The Components of a Leadership Philosophy

When you combine philosophy, the guiding principles, and leadership, which is the model behavior for inspiring others, you create a theory or an attitude, which provides the norms for behavior and action. The definition is brought to life with four key components, which are:

- A theory: The way you define leadership and what's it about.
- An attitude: Your mindset in regards of approaching leadership.
- Guiding principles: The principles and values you hold dear when you are thinking about leading others.
- Behavior: The behaviors you showcase in your journey to reach the desired results and outcomes.

You could view leadership philosophy as a compass – it helps define your expectations, your values and provide the roadmap for actions. With a clear leadership philosophy, you create a focused thought system surrounding your leadership, and you define the behaviors and attitudes you want to cultivate in yourself, but also in others. Leadership doesn't just provide focus for you personally, but it can allow the people around you to know what to expect from your leadership.

Examples of Leadership Philosophies

Just as there are differences in what philosophers think and divergence in how leadership is defined, leadership philosophies also come in a number of different flavors and styles. Since the framework is based on personal values, leaders can approach it from different angles. There are plenty of options to choose from, but we've selected three unique frameworks to provide you an idea of the divergence.

Laissez faire leadership philosophy:

- Leader believes followers should have the power to make decisions.
- Leader believes in empowering followers through increased responsibilities.
- The framework is effective when followers are knowledgeable.

Democratic leadership philosophy:

- Leader believes that everyone should have equal say within the team.
- Leader values participation, consultation and consideration.
- Leader emphasizes co-operation and support.

Autocratic leadership philosophy:

- Leader believes results are best achieved in a controlled system.
- Leader has clear vision, including how and when things should be done.
- Leader is accountable for the decision-making.

You can use these generalized models as guidance for defining your own leadership philosophy. Nonetheless, you shouldn't try to copy a specific leadership philosophy. While learning about other philosophies can be a solid way to identify useful qualities, you need to adopt an approach that comes from your heart.

Reasons why Should you have a Leadership Philosophy

Leadership philosophy has a foundational element to it. The different components included create a strong basis on which to build on and take your leadership forward. You are better-equipped to lead and to succeed in your leadership with a leadership philosophy due to three core benefits: character, consistency and collaboration.

Character

Drafting a leadership philosophy will provide clarity and focus in your character. Character matters because it influences your everyday decision-making and communication with other people. Without a proper understanding of your character and the traits you truly value, you are more likely to fall into bad habits and to let emotions control you.

By making a conscious decision with the help of a leadership philosophy, you outline the characteristics you want to strive for and which you value in other people as well. In a way, you become better at controlling your behavior and you strengthen the qualities required of a successful leader.

Consistency

The above benefit directly relates to the second advantage of creating a leadership philosophy: consistency. The most important aspect of the philosophy is setting out and defining your values and objectives.

Once you define these, you immediately create more consistency to your behavior and actions. You have guidelines, which help you make decisions and take action. You'll always use the same defining values at the heart of your decision-making. Let's assume your leadership philosophy is defined by sustainability.

Whenever you are faced with a decision, you will evaluate the options based on how they relate to the value of sustainability – Will it hinder or enhance it? This assures your actions and behaviours are consistent. You don't flip-flop from one value to another, but you stick to your principles.

Collaboration

Leadership always requires a level of collaboration. Since you need followers to voluntarily to follow you, you can't expect to achieve much without an understanding and focus on teamwork. Getting along with people will become much easier if you have a clear leadership philosophy to follow.

Among the things you need to define with your philosophy is your approach to collaboration. The framework requires careful consideration of engagement, communication and accountability. Defining these, you create more consistency and improve your chances of more meaningful collaboration.

People will know what your values are, they understand your approach to teamwork and thus they feel more comfortable because you follow these well-defined patterns of behavior. Essentially, people can trust you because they don't need to constantly be on their toes.

Overall, leadership philosophy will provide clarity to your leadership. Business strategist and author John Spence used the famous quote by Walt Disney to make a point about why successful leaders need to define the framework for action.

The quote says, "When values are clear decisions are easy." Spence flipped it around stating, "When values are not clear decisions are difficult." By defining your leadership philosophy, you clarify your decision-making by enhancing your focus on the values and actions that truly matter.

The Steps to Developing a Leadership Philosophy

Hopefully, the above would have convinced you about the importance of having a leadership philosophy. We've talked about the characteristics of the framework, but how do you develop it? Here are the four steps you need to take in order to draft a proper leadership philosophy, which will guarantee you succeed as a leader.

Step 1: Define your Values and Priorities

The first, and perhaps the most important part of the process is defining your values and priorities. You need to look deep inside you to discover the values you want to highlight and which you think make leaders great. You need to be able to answer the following questions as part of this step:

- What are the values I think are the most important in life and business?
- What are my personal strengths and weaknesses when it comes to values and behaviors?
- What do I feel are the priorities of a leader?

But how do you define the core values and priorities? It's easy to create a list of things you think are important, but you need to dig deeper when it comes to a leadership philosophy. First, you need to actually understand why you think a specific value has value. Second, you can't have a list of 20 values as this doesn't truly clarify your position, but instead, you must focus on just a few core priorities. Entrepreneur and author Kevin Daum has written a great post on Inc. on how to define your values. Daum suggests taking the following steps:

- Identifying the following moments from your life and describing them in detail:
    - Three greatest accomplishments.
    - Three greatest moments of efficiency.
    - Three greatest failures.
    - Three greatest moments of inefficiency.
- Consider the above moments and examine the possible common themes between them.
- Using these common themes, identify the advice/tips you would give yourself. For example, if you find yourself avoiding conflict situations, your advice might be "Don't walk away from difficult situations."
- Refine your advice into a value. For instance, the above advice could become "Confront difficulties".

Furthermore, once you have these core values and themed outlines, it's auspicious to take a moment to define them properly. Let's say you realized 'authenticity' is a value you cherish. Define what you mean by it by writing down a few sentences. You can use the formula:

"Authenticity to me means"

You can do this with all of your values, whether the value is 'communication', 'family', or 'competitiveness'. It is definitely worthwhile doing this all on paper because it will help you better communicate your ideas to yourself.

When you've selected your values, you need to prioritize them further. If you have around 3-7 values selected, you should consider which ones resonate the most with you or which you think are the most essential in terms of leadership. An effective way to prioritize your values is by comparing them with each other. You can do it by simply taking two values, such as 'authenticity' and 'respect', and make the following statements with your chosen values:

- Authenticity but NO respect,
- Respect but NO authenticity.

Would you pick the first or the second sentence? The value you choose is the one you rank as more important. You can do this prioritization with all of your values by comparing them against each other. You should eventually have a value on top that beat all the others in comparison.

Step 2: Define the Desirable Outcomes you want to Achieve

As well as defining your values, you also need to examine the outcomes you wish to achieve as a leader. In order to do this, you need to study the outcomes you want to achieve in the light of your chosen values. First, you should identify the goals for your leadership and the possible operational goals your organization is looking to achieve.

What are the actions you want to or should achieve as a leader? An auspicious way to set goals is by using the SMART method, described in the image below:

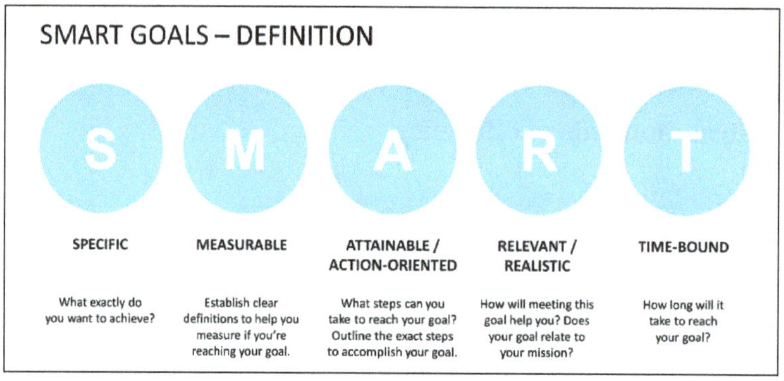

Furthermore, once you've identified the objectives, you need to outline and write down the actions required to achieve these goals. The actions can range from finding tools to motivate your team to enhance innovation.

When you have the goals defined, you must reflect on the ways your values relate to and impact these objectives. You can do this by answering the following questions:

- How do my values support the key goals of leadership? Remember leadership was about influencing others to follow your vision. You need to pick each value and examine how it would help inspire others and move you closer to your vision. If you value '*honesty*', then you want to consider how it is demonstrated in influential leadership.

- How do my values support the operational goals? You should consider the same in terms of the specific organizational objectives you've identified.
- How can my values strengthen the actions required to achieve the objectives? Look at each action and consider the different ways your values would have a positive impact on it. '*Honesty*' could be seen as a way to strengthen trust, which in turn would boost motivation, for example.
- How do my values show in the way I communicate with my teams? Think about the above and the positive or negative impact your values, actions and objectives will have on the team. You want to identify the routes that uphold your values, but create a meaningful partnership with your followers.
- What are the behaviors and actions I expect from my followers? Your followers don't necessarily have to subscribe to the exact same values as you do or prioritize the values the same way. Nonetheless, you need to consider the behaviors and actions, which are in conflict with the objectives you want to achieve as a leader and as an organization, and the behaviors, which are not sustainable in terms of your own values.

The above helps you to clarify what your leadership philosophy should look like in action. It makes the values turn into concrete examples in terms of behaviors and actions.

Step 3: Write down your Leadership Philosophy

With the above steps concluded, you can start putting your leadership philosophy on paper. We briefly mentioned the importance of having a written statement in the previous section. Writing down your philosophy helps clarify your ideas and makes it all just a bit more concrete. It can improve your focus and help you keep yourself more accountable, since you can always go back and read what you've created.

To help you write down your leadership format, we propose using the format below, although you can always just write a document in your own style. The format is based on the four core elements of leadership philosophy: theory, attitude, principles and behavior.

Theory: I believe in ____________________.

Write the specific elements of leadership you believe are at the heart of being a good leader; the values you prioritize. An example sentence could be: I believe in confronting issues head-on is the key to better communication.

Attitude: My thoughts will ______________ and my words will ________________.

These sentences refer to the attitudes you want to foster in the workplace; the example you want to set with your own attitude. The aim is to focus on the attitude you think will boost your success as a leader and help to achieve the objectives you've set out. You might say, "My thoughts will focus on finding solutions and my words will be based on honesty and integrity."

Principles: I will lead by/with _______________.

The focus is on writing down the guiding principles you will use as part of your leadership. These are the top priorities to you as a leader; the principles you won't negotiate on and which you'll consider each time you make decisions. You'll most likely end up writing a few of these and an example sentence might be: I will lead by understanding and embracing change and how situations and people can change over time.

Behavior: I expect to ____________ and ______________ in situations.

Finally, you need to write down how you will behave and react in the workplace, no matter what the situation is. The behaviors should reflect your leadership philosophy and highlight the core ideas in action. The identification of your past successes and failures during Step 1 will help with the last point. You could state, "I expect to consider the different options and listen to feedback in challenging situations."

When it comes to drafting the document, there are a few things to keep in mind. First, keep it concise; you don't want the document to be more than one page. You should be able to state the essence of your leadership philosophy in a few sentences. The other crucial point is to aim for clarity and this is why you also want someone else to have a look at your philosophy.

You need to define the philosophy in a manner that will help others to understand it without the need to ask multiple questions. Even if you decide not to publish it, you want at least one person to view it. Aiming for clarity will guarantee you truly understand what you are looking for with your philosophy and this will guarantee you are focused on your intentions.

Step 4: Evaluate your Leadership Philosophy

Finally, it's not enough to write your leadership philosophy and continue with your daily activities; you need to actively evaluate how well you are holding on to your ideals. You must regularly reflect on how well your actions and behaviors follow your statements. Essentially, you need to hold yourself accountable.

Take time to review your leadership philosophy and go back to your previous actions. Are you practicing what you preach? What are the things you excel in and which behaviors and actions do you struggle to follow? You could look at these questions each week or every month. Write a list of the major actions you took that week; for example, consider the three successes for the weak and the three possible failures for the week.

Reflect on which principles you held on to and which actions or behaviors went against what you believe in. As you identify the actions and behaviors where you didn't follow your leadership philosophy, consider what were the reasons leading to this situation. Why didn't you remember your philosophy at that moment or why did you reject it? This will help you understand what are the areas where you need to work harder on or even identify the values and priorities that might be unattainable for you.

Furthermore, you should occasionally have a chat with people who know you or who work with you. Finding out what they think your guiding principles are can reveal a great deal to you about how they view you and whether your philosophy shows in action. If your followers identify values that are counter to everything you've written in your statement, then you are properly doing something wrong as a leader. On the other hand, if people relate values to you, which are at the heart of your philosophy, you get confirmation you are on the right path and achieving success as a leader.

As eluded to earlier, evaluating your leadership philosophy will help you realize whether your philosophy is working or not. If it's not, you need to carefully think about the reasons behind the failure. It might be that you are simply failing in staying true and you need more time to instill these values deeper into your actions. Just continue to be more mindful of your philosophy and think more about the ways you can stick to your principles. But your failures might not be due to lack of motivation.

It could well be the actions and behaviors you chose are not truly you and do not fit into your leadership strategy. Therefore, you might have to re-evaluate each value and principle, adding in new ones and removing the ones that don't reflect your philosophy. Successful leadership is a fluid strategy and the philosophy shouldn't be too rigid either. As you gain more experience, both in business and in life, you will develop and grow as a person. This personal development might well change the way you approach leadership and therefore, you should be willing to make small changes to your philosophy if you feel like it.

Authentic Leadership

Authentic leadership is a type of management style in which people act in a real, genuine and sincere way that is true to who they are as individuals. Proponents of authentic leadership say this type of leader is best positioned to inspire trust, loyalty and strong performances from employees.

The belief that leaders who are authentic produce good and sometimes the best results is a long-standing idea that has been documented as part of modern management studies for at least two decades. However, this leadership philosophy has not always been identified specifically using the term *authentic leadership*, as its roots trace back thousands of years.

History of Development into a Working Philosophy

Authentic leadership has its roots in ancient Greek philosophy, which examined the development of cardinal virtues, such as prudence, temperance, justice and fortitude, in a leader.

Leadership theorists say that an authentic leader rejects the idea that they have to adopt a persona different than their own. Authentic leaders also don't believe their professional self is different than their personal or private self. Instead, authentic leaders are self-aware and know their strengths and weaknesses.

Other characteristics of authentic leaders include:

- They are focused on delivering results, particularly in the long term.
- They are driven by the organization's mission and needs and not their own ego.
- They have integrity and are guided by morals, while also displaying strong ethical characters.

- They are disciplined and committed to their own improvement and growth.
- They possess a healthy amount of emotional intelligence and are empathetic to others' needs.

Measures

Proponents of authentic leadership say that these characteristics not only inspire trust and loyalty in employees but, when taken together, they give leaders the ability to influence others and contribute to an organization's success.

Assessments such as the Authentic Leadership Inventory (ALI) and the Authentic Leadership Questionnaire (ALQ) exist to help individuals and organizations measure these traits. Authentic leadership development courses are available, as well.

Servant Leadership

Servant leadership is a leadership philosophy in which an individual interacts with others—either in a management or fellow employee capacity—with the aim of achieving authority rather than power. The system embodies a decentralized organizational structure.

The authority figure intends to promote the well-being of those around him or her. Servant leadership involves the individual demonstrating the characteristics of empathy, listening, stewardship, and commitment to personal growth toward others.

How Servant Leadership Works

Servant leadership seeks to move management and personnel interaction away from "controlling activities" and toward a more synergistic relationship among parties. The term "servant leadership" was coined by Robert Greenleaf, a twentieth-century researcher who was skeptical about traditional leadership styles that focused on more authoritarian relationships between employers and employees.

According to Greenleaf's observations, the servant leader approaches situations and organizations from the perspective of a servant first, looking to lend their presence to answer the needs of the organization and others. They seek to address wants and requirements as their priority, with leadership to be pursued secondarily. This contrasts with the leader-first perspective, wherein a person aims to gain control quickly often driven by the desire and prospects for material gain or influence.

Developing and mentoring the team who follow their instructions, or the clients' and customers' needs, take precedence over personal elevation. Even upon attaining a position of governance, a servant leader typically encourage their subordinates to look to serve others as their priority over focusing on personal gains. A servant leader may aim to share power with others and encourage the development and growth of others. This trait can extend to listening to followers carefully to better understand their needs, but it also involves leaders holding themselves and others accountable for their words and actions.

Servant Leadership Example

Where the leader-first dynamic is oriented to appease a personal desire for power, the servant leader looks first to how their service benefits others. For example, a servant leader might question how their efforts uplift those who are underrepresented or are from lower economic standing before seeking to attain a position of control. Their progression to a position of leadership comes after their commitment to service.

This can be seen in the healthcare world, for instance, as medical practitioners work to benefit their patients and assist their peers and teammates in providing that care. In the business world, this can mean seeing that employees, customers, and all other stakeholders can prosper through their service.

These ten characteristics include:

Listening

Leaders have traditionally been valued for their communication and decision- making skills. Although these are also important skills for the servant leader, they need to be reinforced by a deep commitment to listening intently to others. The servant leader seeks to identify the will of a group and helps to clarify that will. He or she listens receptively to what is being said and unsaid. Listening also encompasses hearing one's own inner voice. Listening, coupled with periods of reflection, is essential to the growth and well-being of the servant leader.

Empathy

The servant leader strives to understand and empathize with others. People need to be accepted and recognized for their special and unique spirits. One assumes the good intentions of co-workers and colleagues and does not reject them as people, even when one may be forced to refuse to accept certain behaviors or performance. The most successful servant leaders are those who have become skilled empathetic listeners.

Healing

The healing of relationships is a powerful force for transformation and integration. One of the great strengths of servant leadership is the potential for healing one's self and one's relationship to others. Many people have broken spirits and have suffered from a variety of emotional hurts. Although this is a part of being human, servant leaders recognize that they have an opportunity to help make whole those with whom they come in contact. In his essay, *The Servant as Leader*, Greenleaf writes, "There is something subtle communicated to one who is being served and led if, implicit in the compact between servant-leader and led, is the understanding that the search for wholeness is something they share.

Awareness

General awareness, and especially self-awareness, strengthens the servant-leader. Awareness helps one in understanding issues involving ethics, power, and values. It lends itself to being able to view most situations from a more integrated, holistic position. As Greenleaf observed: "Awareness is not a giver of solace—it is just the opposite. It is a disturber and an awakener. Able leaders are usually sharply awake and reasonably disturbed. They are not seekers after solace. They have their own inner serenity.

Persuasion

Another characteristic of servant leaders is reliance on persuasion, rather than on one's positional authority, in making decisions within an organization. The servant leader seeks to convince others, rather than coerce compliance. This particular element offers one of the clearest distinctions between the traditional authoritarian model and that of servant leadership. The servant leader is effective at building consensus within groups. This emphasis on persuasion over coercion finds its roots in the beliefs of the Religious Society of Friends (Quakers)—the denominational body to which Robert Greenleaf belonged.

Conceptualization

Servant leaders seek to nurture their abilities to dream great dreams. The ability to look at a problem or an organization from a conceptualizing perspective means that one must think beyond day-to-day realities. For many leaders, this is a characteristic that requires discipline and practice. The traditional leader is consumed by the need to achieve short-term operational goals. The leader who wishes to also be a servant leader must stretch his or her thinking to encompass broader-based conceptual thinking. Within organizations, conceptualization is, by its very nature, a key role of boards of trustees or directors. Unfortunately, boards can sometimes become involved in the day-to-day operations—something that should be discouraged—and, thus, fail to provide the visionary concept for an institution. Trustees need to be mostly conceptual in their orientation, staffs need to be mostly operational in their perspective, and the most effective executive leaders probably need to develop both perspectives within themselves. Servant leaders are called to seek a delicate balance between conceptual thinking and a day-to-day operational approach.

Foresight

Closely related to conceptualization, the ability to foresee the likely outcome of a situation is hard to define, but easier to identify. One knows foresight when one experiences it. Foresight is a characteristic that enables the servant leader to understand the lessons from the past, the realities of the present, and the likely consequence of a decision for the future. It is also deeply rooted within the intuitive mind. Foresight remains a largely unexplored area in leadership studies, but one most deserving of careful attention.

Stewardship

Peter Block —author of Stewardship and The Empowered Manager—has defined stewardship as "holding something in trust for another. Robert Greenleaf's view of all institutions was one in which CEO's, staffs, and trustees all played significant roles in holding their institutions in trust for the greater good of society. Servant leadership, like stewardship, assumes first and foremost a commitment to serving the needs of others. It also emphasizes the use of openness and persuasion, rather than control.

Commitment to the Growth of People

Servant leaders believe that people have an intrinsic value beyond their tangible contributions as workers. As such, the servant leader is deeply committed to the growth of each and every individual within his or her organization. The servant leader recognizes the tremendous responsibility to do everything in his or her power to nurture the personal and professional growth of employees and colleagues. In practice, this can include (but is not limited to) concrete actions such as making funds available for personal and professional development, taking a personal interest in the ideas and suggestions from everyone, encouraging worker involvement in decision-making, and actively assisting laid-off employees to find other positions.

Building Community

The servant leader senses that much has been lost in recent human history as a result of the shift from local communities to large institutions as the primary shaper of human lives. This awareness causes the servant leader to seek to identify some means for building community among those who work within a given institution. Servant leadership suggests that true community can be created among those who work in businesses and other institutions. Greenleaf said: All that is needed to rebuild community as a viable life form for large numbers of people is for enough servant-leaders to show the way, not by mass movements, but by each servant-leader demonstrating his or her unlimited liability for a quite specific community-related group.

Contingency Theory of Leadership

Contingency theories primarily focus on the context of leadership. They look at the effects of the situation on the success of a leader. Put differently, the propose that a leader's effectiveness is heavily determined by the situation he is in.

This does not mean that they completely disregard the leader's personality. They consider it but not as the most important factor determining the success of the leader.

Factors Determining the Style of Leadership

Given the different perspectives of the contingency theory, it is obvious that there are factors which make one more applicable than the other in a given situation. These are what you will first have to consider before deciding which one of the four styles to use.

Whereas you cannot preempt all factors beforehand, here are some of the most common ones.

Maturity Level of the Followers

Leaders and followers are never at the same level of thinking, understanding or acting. By and large, regardless of the leadership theory applied, this is one of the reasons the leader stands out as different from the followers.

The maturity level of your followers greatly determines how you interact with them. For example, highly mature followers understand responsibility. As such, you can rely on the job being done once the instructions are given.

On the other hand, less mature followers may not have grasped the importance of this. For this reason, they may not be very diligent in their work thus prone to produce low quality work. For optimum results, you may need to get involved in the work being done.

The Organization's Culture

The organization's culture dictates everything—from communication styles to individual behaviors. It is the leader's responsibility to create a good culture at the workplace which will make the environment conducive for work.

However, an organization's culture is also affected by the individuals working in it. People bring in their learned habits and influence the work environment. This is something which the leader has to consciously work on controlling.

For example, if the organization's culture is one which encourages competition, team work may not be an easy thing to achieve. In such a situation, a leader who works well with teams may have a difficult time operating in this environment, thereby possibly being unsuccessful.

Amount of Time Available to Complete the Task

Some tasks have time constraints attached to them. This is especially so in competitive industries. When such tasks are before the organization, then the best way to handle them is to focus on them.

This makes a task-oriented leader very effective because he is mainly concerned in achieving goals. If there is an issue raised which does not directly affect the outcome of the work being done, then the issue may not receive much attention.

Amount of Personal Power held by the Leader

Personal power is the ability to control the situations around you which can hinder you from achieving your goals. It is easily seen in the ability to change from bad habits to productive ones.

Having personal power gives you a good perspective of the situations around you. You are able to understand them in ways others are not. As a result, the kind of interaction you seek with your followers will rely on this insight which you have.

This influences the response you get from your followers when you ask them to do certain jobs. With personal power, you will have an easy time convincing people to do something. Being respectful towards your followers is part of this and helps achieve your goals.

Amount of Positional Power held by the Leader

Positional power is the one exercised by someone by virtue of the position held. If he is a supervisor, he has power over those reporting to him directly.

Positional power can only be practiced depending on the amount of authority you have. A manager will have and exercise power over the employees directly reporting to him but a CEO will have power over all the employees in the organization.

When it comes to leadership however, things can go south if you abuse your authority. And as much as you may still be the manager (positional power), you may have lost the ability to influence and direct people after they lose their trust in you.

Type of Relationship between the Leader and Followers

The relationship which you have with your followers is key in determining how the situation will be handled. If the relationship is positive, then it becomes easy for you to get input from your followers.

It will also be easier to direct your followers when you have something that needs to be done. A positive relationship between a leader and his followers will provide a conducive environment for the leader's success regardless of the situation arising.

Clarity of Task at Hand

Some tasks are simple while others are complex. If the task is easy enough, then you can use a style which focuses on delegation without much concern. If however it is complex, you may need to be more involved in the execution of the tasks.

This is also related to the technical expertise of your followers. If the followers are technically or intellectually skilled, then dealing with situations will be easier as opposed to when they lack these skills.

Strengths of Contingency Theories

The contingency theory of leadership gives much attention to the situations surrounding the leader. It gained much acceptance and was hailed for several reasons. Some of them are:

1. It has brought better understanding to the study of leadership – this theory does not attempt to explain leadership as something that can be handled using a particular style. In fact, there is no best style of leadership. With this theory, the situations determine the kind of leadership required.

As such, it recognizes that different situations bring about different demands which are the ones that determine whether a particular style of leadership will be effective or not.

2. It helps know what kind of leaders are needed for various situations – these theories give the understanding of how situations affect the success of a leader. In order to achieve success in a particular situation, an organization could easily check the leadership styles of various candidates then pick one for the position.

This gives the contingency theory the ability to predict who could become a suitable leader in certain situations. All that is needed is an understanding of the situation and the leadership styles of the candidates.

3. Can help organizations in human resource planning – this theory is based on a lot of research and as such, can provide organizations with a lot of information to help them build leadership profiles.

This is very helpful because as different situations occur, an organization will know who exactly to put in a position that can steer a project into success.

Weaknesses of Contingency Theories

Like all other theories, the contingency theory is not without its fair share of criticism. The below considerations are some of the arguments by critics.

- It doesn't account for the position of the leader– although this theory is a leadership theory, it focuses too much on the situation and does not consider the leader himself. This means that it doesn't really look at what it's meant to explain the leader.
- Can be too rigid to practice – for example, the LPC scale proposed by Fiedler can be used to decide that a leader is not a good leader based on his LPC score. However, in some cases, it may actually be that the situation itself is what needs to change.
- It doesn't offer opportunities to improve leaders – with no set traits to develop but only focusing on the situation, it becomes difficult to groom leaders. The theory primarily proposes specific types of styles which all leaders are supposed to fall under.

Fiedler's Contingency Theory

Fiedler's contingency theory is one of the contingency theories that states that effective leadership depends not only on the style of leading but on the control over a situation. There needs to be good leader-member relations, task with clear goals and procedures, and the ability for the leader to mete out rewards and punishments. Lacking these three in the right combination and context will result in leadership failure. Fiedler created the least preferred co-worker (LPC) scale, where a leader is asked what traits can be ascribed to the co-worker that the leader likes the least. As an example:

Uncooperative	1	2	3	4	5	6	7	8	Cooperative
Unfriendly	1	2	3	4	5	6	7	8	Friendly
Hostile	1	2	3	4	5	6	7	8	Supportive
Guarded	1	2	3	4	5	6	7	8	Open
……..	1	2	3	4	5	6	7	8	……..

Fiedler's contingency theory is a qualification or type of contingency theory. Contingency theories in general state that the effectiveness of leadership depends upon the situation, and there are numerous factors, such as the nature of the task, leader's personality, and make-up of the group being led.

To provide meaning to Fiedler's contingency theory it is necessary to focus on at least one aspect of the leader-led situation, although such a focus only highlights an issue, rather than giving a complete description of the situation.

Fiedler's contingency theory emphasized the leader's personality, or psychological disposition, is a main variable in her/his ability to lead, and said that how the group receives the leader, the task involved, and whether the leader can actually exert control over the group are the three principle factors that determine how successful the leader-led arrangement will be. Thus, the values from the least preferred co-worker (LPC) are added and then averaged to produce the score. A high LPC score, as can be seen from the example, exhibits a positive orientation towards human relations. S/he gets along with people. The nature of the task is less important and issues in doing it may be compensated for with good human relations. When the environment is such that each group member is independent, such as in a scientific setting, tasks may not be all that well defined, and a leader must rely more on her or his personality to accomplish goals.

On the contrary side, the low LPC score, the respondent relies on the nature of the task to drive leadership. The task has to be well defined or manageable, or the leader will be in trouble. In natural disasters or survival situations, tasks are not always well defined or prioritized well. Human relations are vital. A classic scenario is depicted in William Golding's Lord of the Flies, where kids are stranded on a deserted tropical island and ultimately fall into fighting with each other. While they are youth, they exhibit many basic human qualities that emerge under duress. Situations, where tasks are structured such as in most blue collar environments or the military, a personable leader isn't as much of a required. Orders come to "do it, or else", and while cultivating a following based on personality never hurts, it is not a requisite, except when authority becomes overbearing, such as in tyrannical situations.

Leaders who have a low LPC scoring (task-oriented) are effective, regardless of whether the factors are highly favorable or not. Also, they will act in a more assertive manner. With high LPC scores (relations-oriented) are more effective when the three factors are middle-of-the-road. Fiedler claimed that the LPC scores could be used to identify the appropriate leader for a situation. If a leader is able to control the tasks to be done, leader-led situations, and have power, the leader can create a favorable leadership environment.

Critique

The vagueness of the parameters in the LPC scale makes them open to interpretation and they are context-free. For example, "supportive" could mean anything. Giving criticism can be supportive, but in whose eyes? A leader who is egotistical may not see any criticism as supportive. As with any surveys, one must ask how dynamic are they? Personalities and judgments of them change over time and with circumstances. Survey research is notoriously inaccurate, as Gabriel Almond found four decades ago, and modern survey techniques are very sophisticated, albeit fraught with problems. The proof of a theory is its ability to predict, but if the terms are vague enough, just about any prediction will do. As somewhat of a sidebar, controversies about "prophets" such as Nostradamus abound, but the fact is that his predictions were so general that many could be deemed accurate. Horoscopes are beset with the same difficulties, as the traits are so general that just about anyone would qualify as having those about any day and in the right circumstances - which also are usually described in vague terms.

Future of Theory

The LPC model appears very much like a Bayesian weighting scheme that might be integrated into a social networking model to test organizational integrity. However, the parameters would need to be quantified, and a research instrument tested. The ways in which such models can emerge is suggested by the diagrams of those giving their renditions of Fiedler's contingency theory and applications.

As with any theory, research awaits concerning how this theory might be compared or integrated with others, such as the Leader-Member Exchange, where a leader maintains leadership through working with her or his supporters. This involves more of an analysis of the particulars of group dynamics. There can be a refinement of the LPC with the Leadership Participation Inventory which identifies characteristics of a leader that followers admire and would cause them to follow.

Pro's

- The theory is extremely well researched, given the stated parameters.
- For a "thumb-in-the-wind" approach to identifying leaders, Fiedler's contingency theory can assist enormously:
    - Leaders with good personal relations are matched to a poorly structured task environment.
    - For leaders who are impersonal, they are placed in well task structured environment.
- Because this is a contingency theory, it is inherently more flexible than a "one takes all" theory.

Con's

- LPC scale is subjective, and characteristics are relative in contexts.
- Even according to Fiedler, the LPC score is valid only for groups that are closely supervised and does not apply to "open ones" such as teams.
- It is questionable whether Fiedler's contingency theory is valid in all situations, such as when neither the task is well defined and no choice of leaders is to be had, except ones with bad personalities.

Situational Theories of Leadership

Situational theories of leadership work on the assumption that the most effective style of leadership changes from situation to situation. To be most effective and successful, a leader must be able to adapt his style and approach to diverse circumstances.

For example, some employees function better under a leader who is more autocratic and directive. For others, success will be more likely if the leader can step back and trust his team to make decisions and carry out plans without the leader's direct involvement. On a similar note, not all types of industries and business settings require the same skills and leadership traits in equal measure. Some fields demand a large measure of innovation, whereas in others, personal charisma and relational connection with clients are far more important.

Different theories have been developed that recognize the situational aspects of leadership. Each theory attempts to provide its own analysis of how leadership can be most successful in various situations. Let's consider a few of the key theories.

Hersey and Blanchard's Situational Leadership Theory

The term "situational leadership" is most commonly derived from and connected with Paul Hersey and Ken Blanchard's Situational Leadership Theory. This approach to leadership suggests the need to match two key elements appropriately: the leader's leadership style and the followers' maturity or preparedness levels.

The theory identifies four main leadership approaches:

- Telling: Directive and authoritative approach. The leader makes decisions and tells employees what to do.
- Selling: The leader is still the decision maker, but he communicates and works to persuade the employees rather than simply directing them.
- Participating: The leader works with the team members to make decisions together. He supports and encourages them and is more democratic.
- Delegating: The leader assigns decision-making responsibility to team members but oversees their work.

In addition to these four approaches to leadership, there are also four levels of follower maturity:

- Level M1: Followers have low competence and low commitment.
- Level M2: Followers have low competence, but high commitment.
- Level M3: Followers have high competence, but low commitment and confidence.
- Level M4: Followers have high competence and high commitment and confidence.

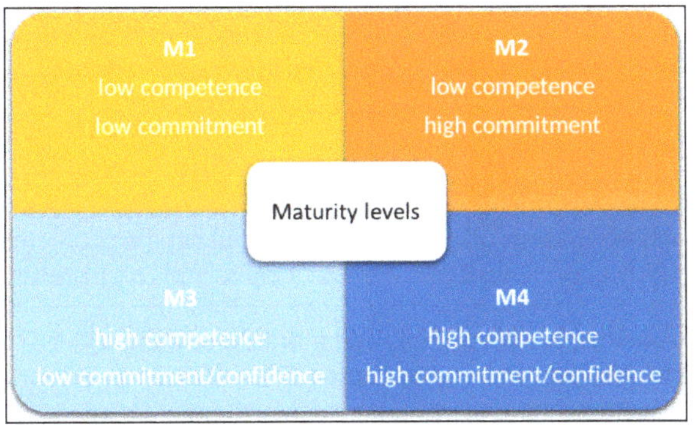

In Hersey and Blanchard's approach, the key to successful leadership is matching the proper leadership style to the corresponding maturity level of the employees. As a general rule, each of the four leadership styles is appropriate for the corresponding employee maturity level:

- Telling style works best for leading employees at the M1 level (low competence, low commitment).
- Selling style works best for leading employees at the M2 level (low competence, high commitment).
- Participating style works best for leading employees at the M3 level (high competence, low commitment/confidence).
- Delegating style works best for leading employees at the M4 level (high competence, high commitment/confidence).

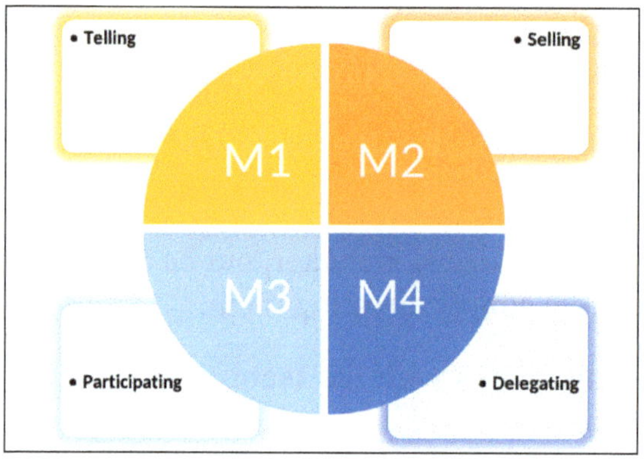

Maturity levels and leadership styles

Identifying the employee maturity level becomes a very important part of the process, and the leader must have the willingness and ability to use any of the four leadership styles as needed.

Goleman's Model of Situational Leadership

Another situational theory of leadership has been developed by Daniel Goleman. His theory incorporates his development of the concept of emotional intelligence. He develops that idea into six categories of situational leadership, describing the leadership style and suggesting when each style is most appropriate and likely to be successful:

Pacesetting Leader	The leader sets aggressive goals and standards and drives employees to reach them. This works with highly motivated and competent employees, but can lead to burnout due to the high energy demands and stress levels.
Authoritative Leader	The leader authoritatively provides a direction and goals for the team, expecting the team to follow his lead. The details are often left up to the team members. This works well when clear direction is needed, but can be problematic if the team members are highly experienced and knowledgeable and might resent being dictated to.
Affiliative Leader	A positive reinforcement and morale-boosting style. The leader praises and encourages the employees, refraining from criticism or reprimand. The goal is to foster team bonding and connectedness, along with a sense of belonging. This approach works best in times of stress and trauma or when trust needs to be rebuilt. It is not likely to be sufficient as a long-term or exclusive strategy.

Coaching Leader	The leader focuses on helping individual employees build their skills and develop their talents. This approach works best when employees are receptive to guidance and willing to hear about their weaknesses and where they need to improve.
Democratic Leader	The leader intentionally involves followers in the decision-making process by seeking their opinion and allowing them a voice in the final decision. This works well when the leader is in need of guidance and/or the employees are highly qualified to contribute and there are not strenuous time constraints that require quick decisions.
Coercive Leader	The leader acts as the ultimate authority and demands immediate compliance with directions, even applying pressure as needed. This can be appropriate in times of crisis or disaster, but is not advisable in healthy situations.

Normative Decision Theory

One final theory we will look at is Vroom and Yetton's Normative Decision Theory. This approach is intended as a guide in determining the optimum amount of time and group input that should be committed to a decision. A leader has a number of options available to him in this regard:

- He can make a decision entirely by himself.
- He can use information from team members to make decisions.
- He can consult team members individually and ask their advice before making the decision.
- He can consult team members as a group before making the decision.
- He can consult the team as a group and allow the team as a whole to make the decision.

Victor Vroom and Phillip Yetton provide a model that helps leaders decide when to use each approach. The model walks leaders through a series of questions about the decision to be made, and the answers will lead the decision maker to the suggested approach. The questions focus on a few key factors:

- Is decision quality highly important?
- Does the leader have sufficient information to make the decision?
- Is it highly important for team members to accept the decision?
- Are the team members likely to accept the leader's decision if he makes it individually? What if he makes it with their consultation?
- Do the team members' goals match those of the leader and organization?
- Is the problem structured and easily analyzed?
- Do team members have high levels of expertise in the matter to be decided?
- Do team members have high levels of competence in working together as a group?

Leaders are challenged not only to make good decisions, but to decide who decides. At times, the best choice is to involve others in the decision.

Vroom-Yetton-Jago Decision Model

No business will be successful without quality decision making. At the heart of all business success stories is a series of quality decisions that kept the organization pointed in the right direction. There are always opportunities to go off track when you are managing any kind of organization, so making quality decisions all along the way is critical for your success.

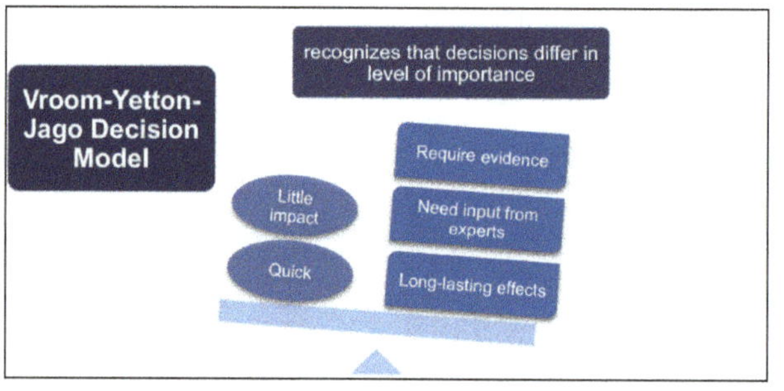

Of course, making good decisions is not always an easy task, so it is helpful to have models available that you can use to guide your process. The Vroom-Yetton-Jago Decision Model is one such tool.

At the heart of this decision model is the fact that not all decisions are created equal. Some decisions are extremely important and will require input from many people, while other decisions can be made quickly as they won't have long-lasting effects on the company as a whole. Understanding this basic concept is important, because you aren't going to use the same decision making process for all choices that you have to make. With the assistance of this model, you can customize your approach to decision making based on the situation at hand.

Three Factors

Right off the top, this model asks you to think about three specific factors with regard to the decisions you are facing. Once you think about your upcoming decisions in reference to these three factors, you will have a much better idea of how to proceed.

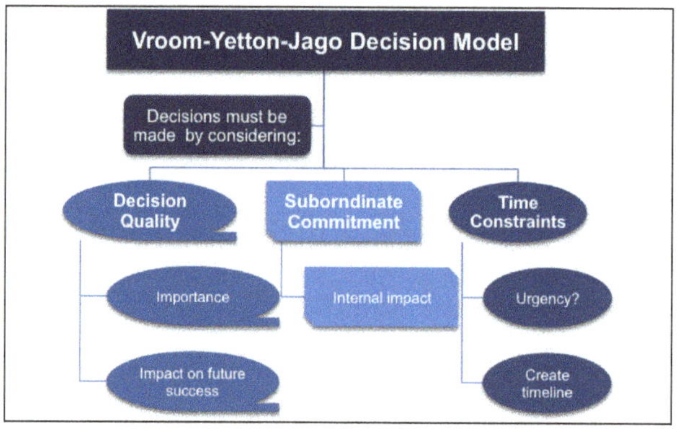

Decision Quality

Simply put, this is where you think about how important it is to come up with the right decision.

Sure, you always want to make the right choice, but some circumstances are more important than others in the context of business as a whole. Committing a large number of resources to each and every decision you make would be inefficient, as many decisions just are not important enough to warrant that kind of investment. Pick and choose your spots and only invest a large amount of time and energy into the decisions that are truly going to shape your organizational future.

Subordinate Commitment

Some decisions that you make are going to have a strong impact on your team, while others will not affect them at all. When thinking about each decision, consider how much of an affect it is going to have on your team and others within and around the organization.

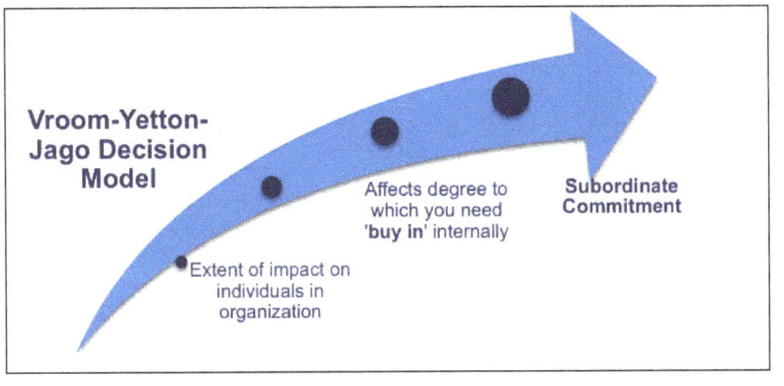

If you it essential that you have 'buy in' from the people on your team, you will be more inclined to include them in the decision making process. If not, you may be able to make the decision on your own with very little input from others below you.

Time Constraints

Obviously, the timeline that you have in front of you for a given decision is going to impact the process that you can use to make your choice. If you are in no particular rush to make the decision, there will be plenty of time to include others, conduct research, and more.

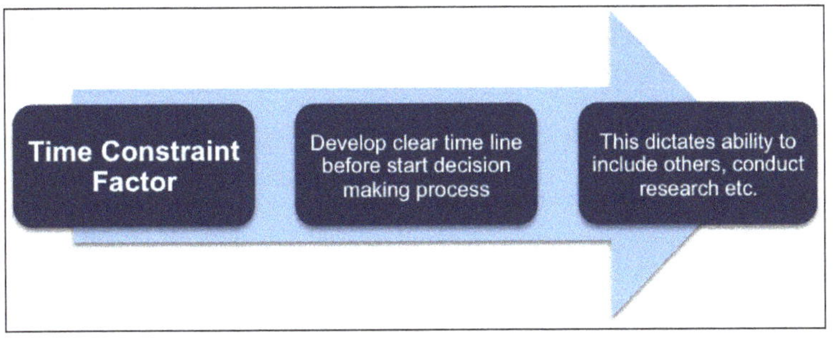

On the other hand, if the matter if time sensitive, you might not really have the option of going to others for help. Develop a clear timeline right up front for your decision and then chart out whether or not you are going to have time to get input from various areas.

In order to determine the influence each of these three factors will have on a decision, Vroom, Yetton, and Jago defined the following eight questions.

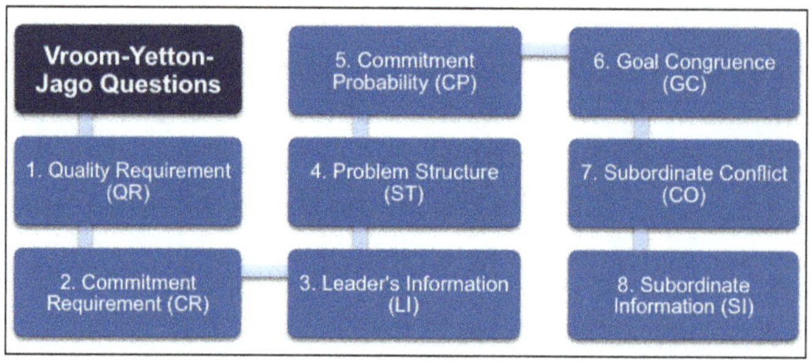

They must be asked in a specific sequence so that you are able to accurately identify the correct style of leadership that a particular decision must be presented and managed in.

This sequence is outlined below:

1. Quality Requirement (QR): How important is the technical quality of the decision?
2. Commitment Requirement (CR): How important is subordinate commitment to the decision?
3. Leader's Information (LI): Do you (the leader) have sufficient information to make a high quality decision on your own?
4. Problem Structure (ST): Is the problem well structured (e.g., defined, clear, organized, lend itself to solution, time limited, etc.)?
5. Commitment Probability (CP): If you were to make the decision by yourself, is it reasonably certain that your subordinates would be committed to the decision?
6. Goal Congruence (GC): Do subordinates share the organizational goals to be attained in solving the problem?
7. Subordinate conflict (CO): Is conflict among subordinates over preferred solutions likely?
8. Subordinate information (SI): Do subordinates have sufficient information to make a high quality decision?

For each of the questions, your answer will take you through this decision tree to an appropriate decision making option.

These options are shown on the right (AI, AII, CI, CII and GII) and are described below.

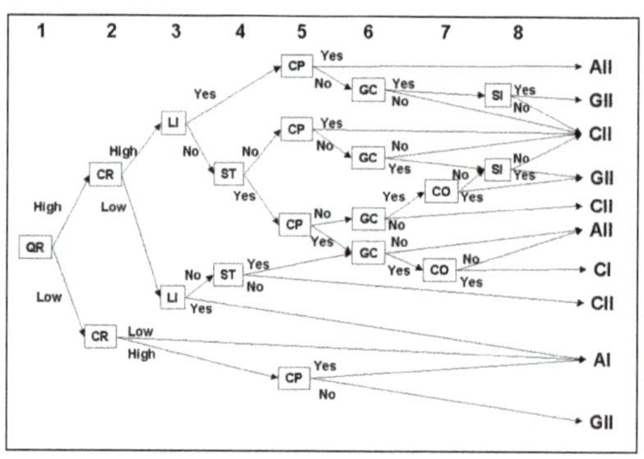

The new leadership: Managing participation in organizations

Three General Leadership Options

At this stage you know how your decision compares to the three factors listed above and where it lies on the decision tree of optional leadership styles. The Vroom-Yetton-Jago model then goes onto explain how each leadership style directs the making of your decision.

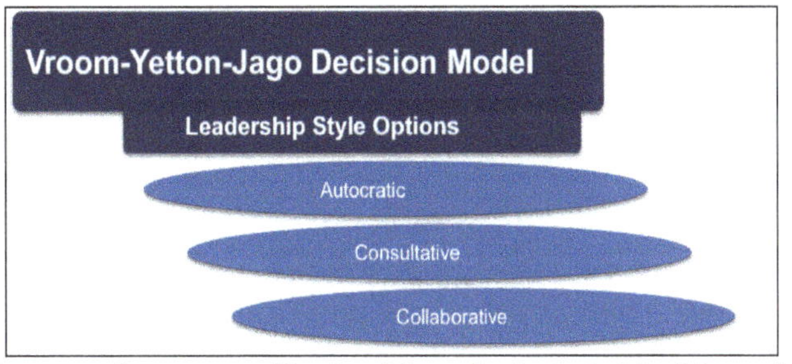

There are three general leadership styles included in this model

Autocratic AI and AII

When you make a decision in an autocratic style, you simply make the decision and then tell others what you have decided. That's it. There are no long meetings to deal with, no back and forth conversations with team members, etc. You simply use the information available – either information you already have, or information you acquire – and make the choice you feel best. In the model, these are defined as:

- Autocratic AI – Leader solves the problem along using information that is readily available to him/her.
- Autocratic AII – Leader obtains additional information from group members, then makes decision alone. Group members may or may not be informed.

Consultative CI and CII

This type of leadership is something of a 'softer' style of autocratic decision making. Ultimately, you are still going to make the decision on your own – but you will first consult with others to gather opinions and input. The decision remains completely your responsibility, but you are going to work through the process of gather information from your team and other related parties before making your final choice. In the model, these are defined as:

- Consultative CI – Leader shares problem with group members individually, and asks for information and evaluation. Group members do not meet collectively, and leader makes decision alone.
- Consultative CII – Leader shares problem with group members collectively, but makes decision alone.

Collaborative GII

As the name would indicate, this is a type of decision making where you are going to work together with your team to make a choice. The decision is no longer yours alone at this point – rather, it is a collaborative effort among those who have been selected to work on the decision. Naturally this is going to be a more time-consuming operation when you make a decision this way, but it can lead to well thought out choices in the end.

In the model, this is defined as:

- Leader meets with group to discuss situation.
- Leader focuses and directs discussion, but does not impose will.
- Group makes final decision.

Decision making is an important part of running any organization, so you don't want to go into the decision making process without a plan. The use of a model such as this one is a great way to prepare yourself to make any decision in the best possible manner. By treating each decision as a unique proposition, and using the method of decision making that is best suited to its characteristics, you will optimize your chances for positive outcomes.

Social Identity Theory of Leadership

A social identity theory of leadership is described that views leadership as a group process generated by social categorization and prototype-based depersonalization processes associated with social identity. Group identification, as self-categorization, constructs an intragroup prototypicality gradient that invests the most prototypical member with the appearance of having influence; the appearance arises because members cognitively and behaviorally conform to the prototype. The appearance of influence becomes a reality through depersonalized social attraction processes that make followers agree and comply with the leader's ideas and suggestions. Consensual social attraction also imbues the leader with apparent status and creates a status-based structural differentiation within the group into leader(s) and followers, which has characteristics of unequal status intergroup relations. In addition, a fundamental attribution process constructs a charismatic leadership personality for the leader, which further empowers the leader and sharpens the leader-follower status differential.

Social Identity and Self-Categorization

The social identity perspective contains a number of compatible and interrelated components and emphases, in particular an original emphasis by Tajfel and Turner and their associates on social identity, social comparison, intergroup relations, and self-enhancement motivation and a later cognitive emphasis by J. C. Turner and his associates on the categorization process. Social identity theory and self-categorization theory have been extensively overviewed as an integrated whole elsewhere.

Social Identity and Intergroup Relations

Tajfel Introduced the idea of social identity to theorize how people conceptualize themselves in intergroup contexts, how a system of social categorizations "creates and defines an individual' s own place in society". He defined social identity as "the individual' s knowledge that he belongs to certain social groups together with some emotional and value significance to him of this group membership". Because groups only exist in relation to other groups, they derive their descriptive and evaluative properties, and thus their social meaning, in relation to these other groups.

Furthermore, because social identity is self-evaluative and derives its value from the evaluative properties of the in group, social comparisons between groups are focused on establishing evaluatively positive distinctiveness for one's own group. Intergroup relations involve a process of competition for positive identity in which groups and their members strive to protect or enhance positive distinctiveness and positive social identity. The specific way this occurs is governed by people's subjective understanding of the psychological permeability of group boundaries and the stability and legitimacy of status relations between groups. This aspect of social identity theory has had a significant impact on social psychology.

Self-Esteem Hypothesis

The drive for evaluatively positive social identity through positive distinctiveness is underpinned by a basic human need for positive self-esteem, a self-enhancement motive. The implication is that self-esteem motivates social identification and group behavior, and social identification satisfies the need for self-esteem. Reviews of research on this self-esteem hypothesis reveal inconsistent findings that suggest a distinction between individual and group membership based self-esteem, and that the relationship between self-esteem and group behavior may be affected by other variables such as self-esteem extremity, identity strength, and group threat. Crocker and her colleagues have explored self-esteem processes in intergroup behavior extensively and have developed a collective self-esteem scale that some researchers employ as a measure of social identity.

Self-Categorization, Prototypicality and Depersonalization

The cognitive dimension of social identity is specified by self-categorization theory in terms of the causes and consequences of social categorization of self and others. The process of social categorization perceptually segments the social world into in groups and out groups that are cognitively represented as prototypes. These prototypes are context specific, multidimensional fuzzy sets of attributes that define and prescribe attitudes, feelings, and behaviors that characterize one group and distinguish it from other groups. Social categorization of other people perceptually assimilates them to the relevant ingroup or outgroup prototype and thus perceptually accentuates prototypical similarities among people in the same group and prototypical differences between people from different groups; there is an accentuation effect that underpins stereotyping. This overall process is called depersonalization because people are not viewed as unique and multifaceted individuals but as matches to the relevant ingroup or outgroup prototype; prototypicality, not individuality, is the focus of attention. Depersonalization refers to change in the basis of perception; it does not have the negative connotations of deindividuation or dehumanization.

Social categorization of self, self-categorization, has the same effect but more so. It not only depersonalizes self-perception but goes further in actually transforming self-conception and assimilating all aspects of ones attitudes, feelings, and behaviors to the ingroup prototype; it changes what people think, feel, and do. Depersonalization is the basic process underlying group phenomena; it perceptually differentiates groups and renders perceptions, attitudes, feelings, and behaviors stereotypical and group normative.

Prototypes are often stored in memory to be "called forth" by social categorization in a particular context to guide perception, self-conception, and action. However, they are almost always modified to varying degrees, and they can be entirely constructed by specifics of a particular social context. Prototypes are contextually responsive, and the principle governing this contextual sensitivity is metacontrast. New prototypes form, or existing ones are modified, in such a way as to maximize the ratio of perceived intergroup differences to intragroup similarities; prototypes form to accentuate similarities within a category and differences between categories.

Social Attraction Hypothesis

Depersonalization affects people's feelings about one another. They become based on perceived prototypicality (called social attraction) rather than idiosyncratic preferences or personal relationships (called personal attraction), which is the social attraction hypothesis. Ingroup members are liked more than outgroup members because the former are perceptually assimilated to a relatively positive ingroup prototype, or because their prototypical similarity to self is perceptually accentuated, or because self-liking (self-esteem) is extended to embrace people who are to some extent now viewed as prototypical extensions of self. Within the ingroup there is consensual liking that is stronger for more prototypical than for less prototypical members; there is a prototype-based social attraction gradient.

Uncertainty Reduction Hypothesis

It has recently been suggested that social identity processes are not only motivated by self-enhancement (the self-esteem hypothesis) but also by an epistemic or self-evaluative motive to reduce subjective uncertainty. This motive is closely tied to social categorization.

Subjective uncertainty about important, usually self-conceptually relevant matters is aversive; thus, subjective uncertainty reduction is a powerful human motive. The processes of self-categorization and prototype-based depersonalization reduce uncertainty because perceptions, attitudes, feelings, and behavior are now prescribed by an ingroup prototype that usually has consensual validation from other group members. Groups with high entitativity with clear, unambiguous, and consensual prototypes, and which are located in a clearly delineated intergroup structure, are most effective at reducing subjective uncertainty.

Salience

A key question for social identity theory is what causes social identity (as defined earlier) as opposed to personal identity (self-conception in terms of unique properties of self or of one's personal relationships with specific other individuals), or one social identity rather than another, to become the contextually salient basis of perception, thought, and behavior? Theory and research suggest that there is an interaction between category accessibility and category fit that operates within the motivational framework provided by self-esteem and uncertainty reduction.

People, influenced by self-enhancement and uncertainty reduction motives, categorize the social context in terms of categories, represented as prototypes, which are chronically accessible in memory or rendered accessible by the immediate context, or both. That categorization becomes salient, which best accounts for relevant similarities and differences among people in the context (structural or comparative fit), which best accords with the social meaning of the context (normative fit), and which best satisfies self-enhancement and self-evaluative concerns. Situational cues or personal agenda, or both, cause people to “try out” different categories or prototypes to make sense of the social field in ways that also evaluate self relatively favorably. This is a fast and relatively automatic cognitive perceptual iterative process that stabilizes when fit is optimized. Only then does self-categorization occur, in the sense of depersonalized self-conception, cognition, and behavior.

Social Identity, Intragroup Processes and Structures

Social identity theory originally focused on intergroup behavior in the context of large social categories: intergroup social comparisons, positive distinctiveness, stereotypes, discrimination, and intergroup relations. Intragroup behavior was generally treated as an unproblematic by-product of intergroup relations; in groups were largely treated as homogenous and undifferentiated. In contrast, the recent emphasis on self-categorization and depersonalization has prompted recognition that groups are internally structured with respect to prototypicality. Within a group, some people are more prototypical than others. Therefore, depersonalized social identity processes within groups may involve differentiation among people that is not interpersonal but is genuinely grounded in common category membership.

Initially, this idea was explored in the context of group cohesion and social attraction and group polarization, but it has subsequently produced other research on social identity-based intragroup processes for example, structural differentiation into subgroups within groups and deviance and the “black sheep effect. However, perhaps the most basic and pervasive structural differentiation within groups is into leader(s) and followers.

Social Identity, Self-Categorization and Leadership

Leadership is about how some individuals or cliques have disproportionate power and influence to set agenda, define identity, and mobilize people to achieve collective goals. The differential ability of some people to stamp their mark on attitudes, practices, decisions, and actions is endemic to all social groups-for example, nations, communities, organizations, committees, cliques, and families. Leaders are people who have disproportionate influence, through possession of consensual prestige or the exercise of power, or both, over the attitudes, behaviors, and destiny of group members. Leadership is very much a group process. We propose that there are three core processes that operate in conjunction to make prototypicality an increasingly influential basis of leadership processes as a function of increasing social identity salience: prototypicality, social attraction, and attribution and information processing. These processes are described mainly in terms of emergent leadership in new groups. However, they also apply to situations in which established leadership roles are structurally assigned; this is explicitly addressed later.

Prototypicality

We have seen that when group membership is psychologically salient, social categorization of self and other ingroup members depersonalizes perception, cognition, affect, and behavior in terms of the contextually relevant ingroup prototype. The more salient the group the more profound is the effect. Group members conform to, and thus are influenced by, the prototype. Those people who are more prototypical to begin with will be less influenced than those who are less prototypical to begin with; the former make fewer changes than the latter to approximate the prototype. In salient groups, people are highly sensitive to prototypicality, as it is the basis of perception and evaluation of self and other group members. Thus, they notice and respond to even very subtle differences in how prototypical fellow members are; there is a clearly perceived gradient of prototypicality within the group, with some people perceived to be more prototypical than others. Within a salient group then, people who are perceived to occupy the most prototypical position are perceived to best embody the behaviors to which other, less prototypical members are conforming. There is a perception of differential influence within the group, with the most prototypical member appearing to exercise influence over less prototypical members. In new groups, this is an "appearance" because the most prototypical person does not actively exercise influence; it is the prototype that he or she happens to embody that influences behavior. In established groups the appearance is backed up by actual influence.

We have seen that prototypes are contextually sensitive to the intergroup social comparative context (the metacontrast principle). Thus, if the context remains unchanged, the prototype will remain unchanged, and the same individual group member will occupy the most prototypical position. It follows that the longer a particular individual occupies the most prototypical position, the stronger and more entrenched will be the appearance that he or she has actively exercised influence over others. In new groups this person is perceived to occupy an embryonic leadership role, although leadership has not been exercised. There is an embryonic role differentiation into leader and followers.

As group membership becomes more salient, and members identify more strongly with the group, prototypicality becomes an increasingly influential basis for leadership perceptions. People also, of course, rely on general and more task-specific schemas of leadership behaviors. However, the importance of these schemas is either unaffected by self-categorization, or they become less important as group prototypicality becomes more important. In either case, leadership schemas should become less influential relative to group prototypicality as group membership becomes psychologically more salient.

Social Attraction

Leadership is more than passively being a prototypical group member; it involves actively influencing other people. One way in which this is made possible is through the social attraction process. We have seen that self-categorization depersonalizes the basis of attraction within groups, such that more prototypical members are liked more than less prototypical members, and that where there is a consensual prototype this has the effect of producing consensually greater liking for prototypical members .The person occupying the most prototypical position may acquire, in new groups, or possess, in established groups, the ability to actively influence because he or she is socially attractive and thus able to secure compliance with suggestions and recommendations he or she makes.

A well-researched consequence of liking is that it increases compliance with requests. If you like someone you are more likely to agree with them and comply with requests, suggestions, and orders .In this way, the most prototypical person is able to exercise leadership by having his or her ideas accepted more readily and more widely than ideas suggested by others. This empowers the leader and publicly confirms his or her ability to exercise influence. Consensual depersonalized liking, particularly over time, confirms differential popularity and public endorsement of the leader. It imbues the leader with prestige and status and begins to reify an intragroup status differential between leader(s) and followers.

Social attraction may also be enhanced by the behavior of highly prototypical members. More prototypical members tend to identify more strongly and thus display more pronounced group behaviors; they will be more normative, show greater ingroup loyalty and ethnocentrism, and generally behave in a more group serving manner. These behaviors further confirm their prototypicality and thus enhance social attraction. A leader who acts as "one of us" by showing strong ingroup favoritism and intragroup fairness is not only more socially attractive but is also provided with legitimacy. Indeed, research on justice considerations in group contexts confirms that although distributive justice is complicated (intragroup fairness conflicting with intergroup bias), intragroup procedural justice is critical. According to the group value model of procedural justice, members feel more satisfied and more committed to the group if the leader is procedurally fair.

Attribution and Information Processing

Prototypicality and social attraction work in conjunction with attribution and information processing to translate perceived influence into active leadership. As elsewhere, attribution processes operate within groups to make sense of others' behavior. Also as in other contexts, attributions for others' behavior are prone to the fundamental attribution error or correspondence bias a tendency to attribute behavior to underlying dispositions that reflect invariant properties, or essences, of the individual's personality. This effect is more pronounced for individuals who are perceptually distinctive (e.g., figural against a background) or cognitively salient.

We have seen that when group membership is salient, people are sensitive to prototypicality and attend to subtle differences in prototypicality of fellow members. Highly prototypical members are most informative about what is prototypical of group membership and so, not surprisingly, in a group context they attract most attention. They are subjectively important and are distinctive or figural against the background of other less informative members. Research in social cognition shows that people who are subjectively important and distinctive are seen to be disproportionately influential and have their behavior dispositionally attributed.

We have also seen how highly prototypical members may appear to have influence due to their relative prototypicality, and may actively exercise influence and gain compliance as a consequence of consensual social attraction. Together, the leadership nature of this behavior and the relative prominence of prototypical members is likely to encourage an internal attribution to intrinsic leadership ability, or charisma. This attribution will be facilitated if cultural theories of the causes of leadership favor the belief that leadership reflects personality.

In groups, then, the behavior of highly prototypical members is likely to be attributed, particularly in stable groups over time, to the person's personality rather than the prototypicality of the position occupied. The consequence is a tendency to construct a charismatic leadership personality for that person that, to some extent, separates that person from the rest of the group and reinforces the perception of status-based structural differentiation within the group into leader(s) and followers. This may make the leader stand out more starkly against the background of less prototypical followers, as well as draw attention to a potential power imbalance, thus further fueling the attributional effect.

The fact that followers do tend to focus on the leader and make dispositional attributions for that person's behavior has some empirical support. Fiske showed how followers pay close attention to leaders and seek dispositional information about leaders because detailed individualized knowledge helps redress the perceived power imbalance between leader and followers. Conger and Kanungo described how followers attributionally construct a charismatic leadership personality for organizational leaders who have a "vision" that involves substantial change to the group. Meindl, Ehrlich, and Dukerich showed that simplified dispositional attributions for leadership were more evident for distinctive leadership behaviors and under crisis conditions.

Emergence and Endurance of Leaders

Social identity processes associated with leadership do not only apply to emergent leaders but also to enduring and structurally designated leaders. Whether you are an emergent or an established leader, prototypicality processes influence leadership perceptions and effectiveness when group membership salience is elevated.

Under conditions of depersonalization, prototypicality becomes a significant basis for all leadership perceptions. In new groups, the associated processes of social attraction and prototype-based attribution and information processing can translate these perceptions into proactive leadership behavior. The longer an individual remains in a leadership position the more they will be socially liked, the more consensual will be the social attraction, and the more entrenched will be the fundamental attribution effect. Having acquired effective influence in these ways, the person occupying the prototypical position can, just like an established leader whose position is structurally designated, adopt more active aspects of being a leader, including the ability to actively maintain his or her leadership position.

Although an established leader has the power base simply to maintain his or her position, it is often advantageous if the group continues to view them as highly prototypical. However, as we have seen, social contextual changes impact prototypicality. Thus, over time and across contexts, the leader may decline in prototypicality whereas other members become more prototypical, opening the door, particularly under high salience conditions, to a redistribution of influence within the group. An established leader is well placed in terms of resources to combat this by redefining, usually through rhetoric and polemic, the prototype in a self-serving manner to prototypically marginalize contenders and prototypically centralize self. This can be done by accentuating the existing ingroup prototype, by pillorying ingroup deviants, or by demonizing an appropriate out group. Generally all three tactics are used, and the very act of engaging in these tactics is often viewed as further evidence of effective leadership. National leaders often engage in these tactics. During the Falklands War between Britain and Argentina, Margaret Thatcher, the British Prime Minister, accentuated her nationalistic prototype of Britain, pilloried deviant groups within Britain who did not represent her prototype, and demonized the Argentinian outgroup. Her leadership ratings rose significantly.

Leadership endurance also benefits from consensual prototypicality because of the effect of consensual popularity on social attraction. In groups with less consensual prototypes, there is less consensus of perceptions of and feelings for the leader, and thus the leader may have less power and may occupy a less stable position. It is in the leaders's interest to maintain a consensual prototype. Simple and more clearly focused prototypes are less open to ambiguity and alternative interpretations and are thus better suited to consensuality. In addition, ingroup deviants serve an important function; by creating and rejecting such deviants the leader is well able to clarify the self-serving focus of the prototype. Another strategy is to polarize or extremitize the ingroup relative to a specific "evil" outgroup. Leaders can also accentuate or create intergroup conflict to achieve these ends. These processes clearly operate in extremist groups with all-powerful leaders. For example, in Cambodia in the 1970s, Pol Pot constructed a simple and orthodox national prototype; he engaged in a campaign of prototypical purification that involved exterminating deviants, and he polarized from and demonized the "decadent" West.

Path-Goal Leadership Theory

The Path-Goal model is a theory based on specifying a leader's style or behavior that best fits the employee and work environment in order to achieve a goal. The goal is to increase your employees' motivation, empowerment, and satisfaction so they become productive members of the organization.

Path-Goal is based on Vroom's expectancy theory in which an individual will act in a certain way based on the expectation that the act will be followed by a given outcome and on the attractiveness of that outcome to the individual. The path-goal theory was first introduced by Martin Evans and then further developed by House.

The path-goal theory can best be thought of as a process in which leaders select specific behaviors that are best suited to the employees' needs and the working environment so that they may best guide the employees through their path in the obtainment of their daily work activities (goals).

While Path-Goal Theory is not a detailed process, it generally follows these basic steps as shown in the graphic below:

- Determine the employee and environmental characteristics.

- Select a leadership style.
- Focus on motivational factors that will help the employee succeed.

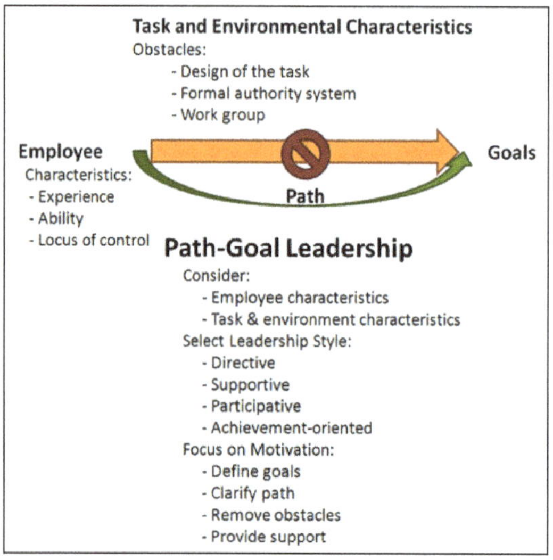

Employee Characteristics

Employees interpret their leader's behavior based on their needs, such as the degree of structure they need, affiliation, perceived level of ability, and desire for control. For example, if a leader provides more structure than what they need, they become less motivated. Thus, a leader needs to understand their employees so they know how to best motivate them.

Task and Environmental Characteristics

Overcoming obstacles is a special focus of path-goal theory. If an obstacle becomes too strong, then the leader needs to step in and help the employee select a path to work around it. Some of the more difficult task characteristics that often arise are:

- Design of the task - The design of the task might call for the leader's support. For example, if the task is ambiguous, then the leader might have to give it more structure or an extremely difficult task might call for leader support.
- Formal authority system - Depending upon the task authority, the leader can provide clear goals and give the employee some or all control.
- Work group - If the team is non-supportive, then the leader needs to be cohesiveness and espouse esprit-de-corps that provides comradeship, enthusiasm, and devotion to all team members.

Leader Behavior or Style

The independent variables of Path-Goal Theory are the leader's behavior — the leader adjusts her style of behavior to the employee and task characteristics so that the employee's motivation is to excel at their goal.

House and Mitchell defined four types of leader behaviors or styles: Directive, Supportive, Participative, and Achievement .They are based on two factors that were identified by an Ohio State University study behaviors.

- Consideration - relationship behaviors, such as respect and trust.
- Initiating Structure - task behaviors, such as organizing, scheduling, and seeing that work is completed.

The first behavior listed below, Directive, is based on initiating structure. The other three (achievement, participative, and supportive) are based upon consideration.

The four path-goal types of leader behaviors are:

- Directive: The leader informs her followers on what is expected of them, such as telling them what to do, how to perform a task, and scheduling and coordinating work. It is most effective when people are unsure about the task or when there is a lot of uncertainty within the environment.
- Supportive: The leader makes work pleasant for the workers by showing concern for them and by being friendly and approachable. It is most effective in situations in which tasks and relationships are physically or psychologically challenging.
- Participative: The leader consults with his followers before making a decision on how to proceed. It is most effective when subordinates are highly trained and involved in their work.
- Achievement: The leader sets challenging goals for her followers, expects them to perform at their highest level, and shows confidence in their ability to meet this expectation. It is most effective in professional work environments, such as technical, scientific; or achievement environments, such as sales.

The leaders' behavior is not set in stone, as there are other leadership styles that may be used depending upon the situation. For example, House defined four other behaviors:

- Work Facilitation,
- Group Oriented Decision Process,
- Work Group Representation and Networking,
- Value Based.

Application

As noted earlier, the independent variables of Path-Goal Theory are the leaders' behavior, thus the path–goal theory assumes that people (leaders) are flexible in that they can change their behavior or style, depending upon the situation. This coincides with the research that while nature (genes) may be our internal guide, nurture (experience) is our explorer that has the final say in what we do.

Evolutionary Leadership Theory

Evolutionary leadership theory (ELT) argues that humans possess specialized psychological mechanisms for solving coordination problems through leadership and followership. We discuss the evolutionary functions and psychological processes underlying leadership, and how to study leadership and followership from an integrated evolutionary perspective. An evolutionary perspective offers novel insights into major barriers to leadership effectiveness in organizations. These obstacles include (a) mismatches between modern and ancestral environments, (b) evolved cognitive biases affecting leader selection and decision-making and (c) innate psychological mechanisms designed to dominate and exploit other individuals. Understanding the evolved psychological mechanisms underlying leadership, in terms of adaptive functions, mismatches, and psychological processes, is critical for the development and integration of leadership theory, research, and practice.

The Evolutionary Psychology of Leadership: Theory and Assumptions

Evolutionary leadership theory (ELT) studies leadership from the perspective of evolutionary psychology, which applies the principles of evolutionary biology and behavioral ecology to better understand human psychology. The core assumption underlying evolutionary psychology is that the human mind is the product of a process of evolution through natural selection. As such, evolutionary psychology contends that over many thousands of years the human mind has been shaped in the same way as has the human body, as well as the bodies and minds of all organisms.

Evolutionary psychology further proposes that the human mind contains many specialized psychological mechanisms that have enabled early humans to solve recurrent problems affecting their chances of survival and reproduction. Adaptations for foraging, self-protection, mating, parenting, collaboration, and conflict resolution are but a handful of these mechanisms. One could conceive of these evolved psychological mechanisms as "if-then" decision rules or psychological heuristics that evolved because they provided reproductive benefits to individuals adopting these rules. For instance, a decision rule to "follow an individual that one trusts" is clearly superior to a decision rule to "follow any one individual. Such decision rules need not be conscious, and in fact much of our behavior is guided by highly automated decision rules. Furthermore, because bio- logical evolution is a slow and gradual process, decision rules that provided adaptive benefits in past environments may no longer produce adaptive outcomes in environments if they underwent rapid change. This idea is referred to as mismatch and it has special implications for studying leadership.

Inspired by evolutionary psychology we pro- pose that leadership and followership evolved in humans, and in other species too, to solve recur- rent coordination problems. We define leadership in terms of the coordination of the actions of two or more individuals to accomplish joint goals. The classic coordination problem that gave rise to the emergence of leadership is group movement. Social animals stay alive by moving together. But how do group members decide where to go and when? Such coordination problems can be solved easily by some individuals seizing the initiative and others following them. Such leadership has been observed in a long list of social species, including honeybees, guppies, hyenas, dolphins, and baboons. A deceptively simple decision rule such as "follow the individual that moves first" can produce something akin to leadership.

Furthermore, if we assume individual differences in the likelihood to move first this will then automatically produce consistent leaders and followers.

Evolutionary leadership theory proposes that in addition to group movement, leadership also served additional functions in ancestral human groups, including conflict resolution, punishment, leading in warfare, teaching, and promoting social cohesion. As humans started to live in increasingly large, socially complex societies perhaps some 200,000 years ago, conflicts between genetic strangers became paramount and this required some form of conflict management in which leaders may have taken on the role of punishers. Our closest relatives, the great apes, all practice some form of conflict resolution and therefore it is almost certain to be a feature of human leadership too. As population densities started to rise in human history, intensifying contact between groups, leadership became useful in managing intergroup relations too. This paved the way for the emergence of war and peace chiefs which have been documented in various traditional societies such as the Navajo Indians. Finally, ancestral leaders played a role in hunting and food sharing practices. Within traditional societies Big Men leaders often take on such roles. For a large part of human evolutionary history, leadership was informal and based on charisma and personalized influence—what we regard as weak leadership. The transition from weak to strong leadership where leaders have formalized, coercive powers is a relatively novel phenomenon in human history.

The Evolutionary Toolkit

To test evolutionary hypotheses about leader- ship we can work with a diversity of methods, research tools, and analytical approaches. Evolutionary psychology is a diverse field, attracting behavioral scientists with an unusually diverse range of scholarly backgrounds, including psychology, evolutionary biology, primatology, anthropology, economics, sociology, organizational and political sciences. As it is impossible to collect data in ancestral environments to track the evolution of alleged adaptations for leadership and followership, evolutionary minded researchers must rely on a multitude of indirect sources of evidence to test their hypotheses.

General evolutionary theories can be invoked to guide attention towards potential psychological adaptations for leadership. Common theories include kin selection theory, multilevel selection theory, parental investment theory, life-history theory, reciprocal altruism theory, and costly signaling theory. If a hypothesized psychological mechanism for leadership flows directly from a theory under the general paradigm of evolution, then we can have some confidence in its existence. For instance, a higher parental investment from females leads to the hypothesis that women are interested in male partners who signal social dominance. This then leads to the prediction that men in leadership positions are deemed more (sexually) attractive by women and that men will be more likely to assume leadership positions in the presence of women—both predictions have received support.

In addition, we can employ mathematical and evolutionary game theory models to study the evolution of leadership and compliment the insights gleaned from these models with computer simulations. Evolutionary game theory shows that genes coding for leadership and followership traits can stabilize in a population at a relative frequency. Mathematical models show that democratic decision-making processes work better than despotic decision making—where one leader makes the decision on behalf of the group—when many individuals possess unique information. Simulation data reveal that a few informed agents can coordinate the actions of a large group of uninformed individuals, producing something akin to leadership.

Experimental methods from behavioral economics and social psychology can be used to further test evolutionary hypotheses about leadership. The experimental games method reveals basic principles of leadership through studying interactions between players in standard games such as the prisoner's dilemma, the ultimatum game, the dictator game, and the public good game. For instance, a recent study suggests that in pure coordination games pro- social personality types are more likely to emerge as leaders than selfish personality types.

Neuroscience methods may be used to identify proximate leadership and followership mechanisms. Brain imaging studies provide data attesting to the specific physiological structures involved in leader decision-making. For instance, fMRI research shows that there is activation in the reward areas of the brain when bystanders witness leaders being punished when they behave unfairly. Transcranial magnetic simulation (TMS) can be used to disrupt activity in specific brain areas and might therefore be used to reveal which brain regions are involved in, for instance, successful coordination between actors.

Hormone data can identify the hormonal correlates of particular leadership experiences. For instance, Josephs, Sellers, Newman, and Mehta showed in an experimental study that high testosterone individuals perform better on cognitive tasks when in a high status position, whereas low testosterone individuals perform better in low status positions. In addition, research suggests that individuals higher up in the hierarchy of an organization produce less cortisol than those at lower levels of the hierarchy. Behavioral genetics studies may help to provide an indication of whether leadership carries a substantial heritable component. A high heritability suggests that there may be important individual differences in these traits. Although there is unlikely to be a single gene responsible for leadership, several studies show a substantial heritable component underlying general personality and ability differences predicting leadership such as extraversion, conscientious- ness, and intelligence.

Developmental psychology studies could examine if cognitive leadership prototypes are culturally learnt or perhaps innate. A recent study found that children as young as 5 years old can pick the winners of political elections based only on information about the faces of the candidates. Cross-cultural data are also useful. For instance, surveys from societies around the globe show that some traits— vision, integrity, and trustworthiness—are universally linked to good leadership, whereas other traits such as generosity and status conscious are culture specific.

Anthropological and ethnographic databases may provide further evidence for the universality of leadership mechanisms. This kind of evidence is necessary to differentiate between phenomena that are evolutionary adaptations, and those that are more superficial, culture-specific manifestations. Research on existing hunter-gatherer societies such as the Kung San or the Hadza can tell us more about leadership in environments in which humans evolved.

Finally, cross-species evidence is instrumental in testing speculations about the evolutionary history of any alleged adaptation such as leadership.

In elephants, for instance, the oldest individual in the herd takes on a leadership position during group movement to a waterhole that only she can remember. In humans too there is an age bias in leadership. This finding implies that the underlying evolved heuristic—"follow a more experienced individual if you are uncertain what to do"—may be the result of convergent evolution.

When considered in conjunction, the findings emerging from these diverse lines of inquiry can produce new insights into the evolutionary functions of leadership. Although no single finding will allow us to accept or refute a hypothesis derived from ELT, together through a process of comparative analysis they may point to the existence of specialized psychological mechanisms underlying leadership and followership in humans.

Barriers to Improving Leadership

Evolutionary leadership theory produces several novel insights into obstacles that need to be overcome to improve the quality of leadership in modern work organizations. These include (a) discrepancies between modern and ancestral environments (mismatch), (b) evolved cognitive decision-making biases of leaders, and (c) evolved psychological mechanisms designed to dominate and exploit other individuals. In this topic we look at each of the obstacles through the lens of ELT, and discuss ideas for future research and application.

Mismatches between Modern and Ancestral Environments

The modern work environment has provided many benefits to humans in recent history. Our better health, greater wealth, and superior technology are all products of an intensification and diversification of labor that started several millennia ago and which culminated in the creation of large-scale corporate structures after the Industrial Revolution. At the same time the modern organizational structures that we live and work in have also produced many social problems such as stress and alienation among employees, inequalities in access to wealth and health care, crime and overpopulation, and threats to global environmental sustainability.

Evolutionary leadership theory argues that this discrepancy between modern and ancestral organizational environments is the result of an evolutionary mismatch. All organisms, animals and plants, possess physical and behavioral traits that have been passed down through generations, preserved by natural selection because of their adaptive function in a given environment. However, over time environments change, and so all organisms face the risk of finding themselves perfectly equipped to deal with challenges that may no longer exist, and ill-equipped to deal with a host of new challenges. Traits that were at one time adaptive can be "mismatched" to the environment in which the organism currently resides. Because evolution through natural selection is a slow, cumulative process mismatches are particularly likely if environments undergo rapid change.

Such is the case for humans. The environment that most of us live in is very different from the environment that our ancestors lived in only some 13,000 years ago, before the advent of agriculture. From 2.5 million years ago— when the first hominids appeared in Africa— until the agricultural revolution humans lived in relatively small nomadic band societies of around 150 individuals, leading a hunter- gatherer life style. Further, fossil evidence indicates that human brain size has remained remarkably stable for at least the last 200,000 years. This leads some evolutionary psychologists to conclude that "our modern skulls house a Stone Age mind" with the potential for significant mismatches.

One mismatch example is the widespread availability of sweet and fatty foods in modern society. Human bodies evolved to respond to the taste of fat and sugar by feeling immense pleasure. Our ancestors evolved to quickly devour all available sweet or fatty foods because such foods were perpetually scarce and perishable in an ancestral world. Yet, now that these foods are widely and cheaply available in supermarkets our evolved tendencies to take in calories produce all sorts of health problems such as obesity, diabetes, and cardio-vascular problems. Needless to say, modern environments do not only pose mismatches for humans but for many other species too. Many of the environmental changes caused by human intervention such as overfishing, deforestation, and climate change create new selective environments which many species are not adapted for.

Thus, the discrepancy between modern and ancestral environments potentially creates mismatches between aspects of human evolved psychology and the challenges of modern society. This may well be the underlying cause of a wide range of problems causing failures in leadership and organizational management. Mismatches can pertain to both the selection of leaders and to their functioning and effective- ness in modern organizations. Consider the selection of leadership in modern organizations. This is often a top-down process in which man- agers at a lower level are appointed by managers at levels higher up in the hierarchy. Or individuals are "flown in" from outside the organization to be appointed as managers. The selection process for leaders consists of an assessment of an individual candidate's personality, skills, and competencies based on some formalized tests, their CV, and an interview, usually with individuals higher up the hierarchy rather than with the subordinates whom they may lead.

This is very much at odds with leadership emergence in ancestral human groups. Extrapolating from the anthropological evidence of past and present hunter-gather societies such as the Kung San in Southern Africa, the Hadza in Tanzania, and the Ache in Paraguay we have a fairly good idea of what leadership may have looked like in the environment in which humans evolved. Such bands do not have formalized leadership. Instead there are individuals of influence who emerge as leaders when they embark on some specialized activity such as hunting, making weapons, defending the group, or preparing a new campsite for which they have some specialized expertise and need to recruit other individuals to cooperate. These individuals have no overall authority over the group, rather they exercise influence in narrowly defined areas of expertise and only through persuasion are they able to emerge as leaders in a temporary group activity. With the next activity leadership selection begins again.

This bottom-up approach selects for leaders with certain characteristics that are universally valued. Universally positive leader characteristics—which are also prominent in hunter- gatherer groups—include such qualities as integrity, persistence, humility, competence, decisiveness, and vision. It is noteworthy that so-called "derailed" executives—bright, ambitious, and talented managers who nonetheless fail—are often described as lacking these traits. Their selection may be due primarily to their ability to please their superiors. In modern industrial and bureaucratic organizations, however, leaders are accountable to, and often appointed by, managers senior to them in the organizational hierarchy and subordinates have little power to sanction their bosses. Modern organizational ethnographers report that most managers implicitly understand that pleasing superiors is more important to career success than pleasing subordinates. It is noteworthy that executives are more likely to succeed if subordinates are included in the selection process.

A different mismatch pertains to what we are we looking for in our leaders. Implicit leadership theories (ILT) argue that humans possess certain prototypes about what constitutes good leadership based on learning and individuals who match these prototypes are more likely to emerge as leaders. Unlike ILT, evolutionary leadership theory assumes that these leadership prototypes have evolved features and that different prototypes are automatically activated in adaptively relevant environments. Yet because the environment in which these prototypes evolved looks so different from the modern world, there remains the potential for a mismatch. Leadership in ancestral humans was often a physical activity such as in hunting or warfare. Leaders led by example and often from the front, and so there would have been selection on cues of health, stamina, and an imposing physique. Although it may have been beneficial for groups in the past to endorse a more physically formidable leader, this might not be the case in a modern environment in which individuals are often leading from the back—e.g., the president in the Oval Office.

There is some evidence that we are still stuck with these biases for ancestral leader proto- types. For example, height is one of the more consistent predictors of leadership emergence in business and politics. Taller individuals are perceived as higher in status, have higher levels of educational achievement, higher starting salaries, earn more money across their careers, and occupy higher positions in organizations. Height even predicts the outcome of presidential elections where taller candidates get more votes and are more likely to get reelected. In terms of psychological properties, taller individuals are seen as more intelligent, healthier, and socially dominant, perhaps explaining why they are seen as more leader-like. A recent experimental study suggests that the height-leadership bias applies more strongly to male candidates than to female candidates. There is no obvious reason why height and physical formidability would still gain individuals a leader- ship advantage in modern organizations. So selection on these cues seems to represent a mismatch.

Another mismatch may provide clues to the controversial issue of gender biases in leader- ship. Because of the physical aspects involved in ancestral leadership, masculine leaders were the norm. This gender bias remains the case in most modern organizations. For instance, although women make up half of the American labor force, in 2009 only 12 of the Fortune 500 companies had a female CEO, a meager 2%. It remains to be seen how beneficial the male leadership bias is in a global economy that emphasizes communication skills and net- working. For instance, there is evidence that women have better verbal memory, empathy, and social skills than men. Thus, women should perform better as leaders where these skills are important. It has been shown that women in executive functions adopt a more transformational leadership style than their male counterparts, and are more effective leaders as a result. Yet this effect might be due to self-selection forces where only the most talented females make it to the top. Nevertheless, this "think leader, think male bias" may be a vestige of our ancestral past which is hard to overcome with socialization practices.

For instance, when women and men work together on group tasks, men are quicker to claim leadership roles even if the women are better qualified. Regardless of their talent, men are also more likely to assume leadership roles when being observed by women perhaps because women prefer high status in potential mates. In inter- group conflicts both men and women prefer a male or masculine leader. Recent studies show that during war people prefer to vote for a leader who has more masculine facial features such as a strong jawline and narrow eyes. This male leadership bias might also occur in highly competitive business environments that our minds may process as situations resembling wars between groups. Finally, there is a consistent but subtle bias in the way many executives—including those who espouse diversity—evaluate women leaders.

The scale and complexity of leadership also provides the potential for a mismatch. The small hunter-gatherer band societies of our ancestral past were essentially extended families: Members knew each other, understood their interdependencies, and had a genetic investment in one another's fate. These groups were held together by kinship and norms of fairness and reciprocity, which require that individuals can depend on each other for assistance and will return in kind. There was room for particularly charismatic individuals to emerge as leaders. Charismatic leadership works in part by influencing followers to identify with a collective enterprise and internalize group aspirations. Charismatic leaders change the way followers see themselves— from self-interested individuals to members of a cohesive group—through emphasizing the similarity and shared fate among group members as if they are kin. However, charismatic leadership is an exception in the modern world. In traditional societies the Big Men leaders are often extremely charismatic. Being inspiring, persuasive, and visionary are important attributes of aspiring leaders in small face-to-face groups. In modern organizations it is extremely hard to get the same levels of intimacy between leaders and followers. Yet even in large bureaucratic organizations we still prefer leaders to adopt an inspirational and personalized leadership style, and such leaders tend to be more effective.

In past environments humans knew their leaders personally and there was no distinction between people's private and public lives. As a consequence, our minds may have difficulties separating the role of the leader from the person occupying this role in modern organizations. In the past, information about people's personality and their personal norms, values, and ambitions were critical in determining whether they should get the chance to lead the group because this was the only information available. In the modern world we crave this information but we do not often get it. We are quite aware that, for instance, middle-level managers have only limited influence because they are following orders of senior management. Because our psychological machinery is not very well adapted to these complex multilayer hierarchies, we hold them personally accountable for any decisions that are harmful to our interests ("My boss is a nasty per- son"). Making trait inferences about leaders is called the "leader attribution error" and it might well be another aspect of our evolved leadership psychology, resembling a possible mismatch.

Finally, leadership in the ancestral environment was fluid, distributed, and situational. The individual most qualified for the task at hand had the greatest influence on collective actions. Rarely would one individual coordinate all group activity and make all group decisions. However, with modern bureaucracies and formal leadership roles, one individual—the "leader"—is responsible for managing all these functions. Leader versatility—the ability to perform multiple, even competing, roles—is increasingly associated with leadership effectiveness, but few leaders have the range of skills needed to perform such a wide array of duties.

This may contribute to the high failure rate of senior managers. Modern societies attribute enormous importance to leadership and often hold leaders personally responsible for organizational success or failure even if this is not always warranted or fair. Thus, the so- called "romance of leadership" may well be a vestige of our ancestral past.

These are just some examples that suggest that discrepancies between modern and ancestral conditions can impede leadership selection and effectiveness. Other possibilities for a mismatch include the sense of powerlessness modern humans feel in large anonymous organizations, the opportunities for toxic leaders to move between organizations, and the prejudice and suspicion against out-group leaders. These discrepancies between modern and ancestral environments may interfere with the quest for good leadership. More research is needed to study potential leadership mismatches and the extent to which they affect organizational functioning.

Biases Underlying Leaders' Selection and Decision-making

Leaders often make decisions on behalf of their group and any biases in their decision-making will have great implications for the organizations that they lead, both positive and negative. There is a large body of work documenting how decision- making biases affect human judgments. The question of why such cognitive biases should exist is one that has been explored by evolutionary psychologists through the lens of error management theory. The crux of EMT is that any cognitive mechanism can risk the possibility of two types of errors—a false positive (assuming a false belief), and false negative (failing to assume a belief that is true). Critical to the theory is that the two types of errors may not always be equivalent in terms of their costs. For instance, falsely recognizing a stick to be a snake may produce a moment of unpleasant anxiety, but failing to recognize a snake when one is actually present can have far more costly and long-lasting consequences. Thus, humans have evolved to make more errors of the former variety than the latter. We suggest that this core principle of EMT has important implications both for who is being selected into leadership positions and the types of decision-making biases that leaders may be especially prone to.

Both historically and today one of the most critical problems faced by groups is how to best assess whether aspiring leaders possess the talents and skills necessary to lead the group towards their goals. As such, people are highly sensitive to displays of competence and one such display is that of confidence. Beyond confidence in one's actual abilities, overconfidence too appears to offer advantages to aspiring leaders, resulting in higher social status, and contributing to the selection of overconfident team leaders, and even CEOs. Although there are potential costs associated with overconfidence, there may also be fitness benefits that arise from self- and group- enhancement. For instance, overconfidence is adaptive insofar as it motivates people and groups to enter competitions they would not otherwise contest. Thus, for many thousands of years overconfidence would have been less costly than an accurate appraisal of one's competence.

ELT suggests however that within contemporary organizations the cost to benefit ratio associated with overconfidence in leadership selection is such that modern leaders are likely to be particularly prone to this self-evaluative bias. Within ancestral environments, the costs associated with falsely attributing confidence to competence (i.e., overconfidence) would have been kept in check. Overconfidence in leadership would have been a regulated problem, as individuals could easily cease following overconfident leaders who provided more harm than benefit to groups. Thus, for ancestral groups, the opportunity cost of failing to assume competence from displays of confidence would have been greater than the costs incurred by providing aspiring leaders with sufficient latitude to test their ostensible skills and abilities. However, as modern business environments are essentially dominance hierarchies, in which high-ranking individuals can unilaterally influence organizational decision-making, leadership overconfidence is today less effectively observed and regulated from the bottom up.

If overconfident individuals are indeed more likely to be selected for positions of leadership, it is worth considering what other biases may be expected to co-occur with an elevated perception of one's abilities. ELT suggests that leaders may be selected on the basis of the very qualities that ultimately threaten their capacity for effective leadership. These qualities include a number of traits that might emerge from overconfidence, such as lack of self-awareness, inflated self- evaluations, defensiveness in the face of error, and failure to learn from experience. Such qualities might all be functional in maintaining one's positive public image and increasing the chances of promotion to a leadership role, but they may also make leaders more prone to a number of decision-making biases including hindsight biases, illusions of control, confirmation biases, anchoring and adjustment biases, and escalating commitment. Leaders may be particularly prone to these biases as they likely stem from the same self- enhancement tendencies that promote overconfidence and in turn increase one's chances for leadership selection.

Consider how overconfidence is likely to affect anchoring and adjustment. Following an initial estimate, adjustment can occur in response to new data as it comes to hand, but such adjustments are typically insufficient, with final decisions being "anchored" to initial values. When people are overconfident in their initial estimates they may be more subject to anchoring biases. Leadership overconfidence might also intensify the dangers of escalating commitment, another adaptive decision-making bias. Once a significant amount of time and money is committed to a particular project, the likelihood of changing course usually decreases. When people receive feedback that a planned project is failing they often allocate more money and resources to the project than if they receive positive feedback. Overconfident leaders may be especially vulnerable to this bias as they may overestimate the chances of success despite the contrary evidence.

These are various examples of evolved decision-making biases that may impede effective leadership in modern organizations. More research is needed to examine the impact of these biases on leader decision making and how to avoid them.

Implications for Research and Practice

Testing the possible relationship between overconfidence, leadership selection, and decision-making biases might be achieved with a three-prong strategy. Firstly, future research should seek to show that individual differences in overconfidence do indeed increase the chances of selection to leadership positions within organizational settings. This could be achieved by assessing the overconfidence of those in more senior management roles and comparing it to the overconfidence of those they lead. Alternatively, future research might capture trait-level overconfidence of individuals as they pass through recruitment centers and use this as a predictor of selection and promotion over time.

Second, experimental work could seek to test the proposed positive relationship between overconfidence and increased errors in judgment and decision making on biases that are related to the elevation of one's personal sense of self (e.g., escalation of commitment). If this relationship were found to disassociate from more general decision-making biases (e.g., base-rate neglect) it would provide evidence of an underlying mechanism that may well drive both the chances of leadership selection and the chances of faulty decision making.

Third, if overconfidence is indeed related to a general need to self-enhance, then meeting that self-enhancement goal should serve to attenuate overconfidence. Leader overconfidence might then be overcome through self- affirmation processes. Self-affirmation involves reminding people of their self-worth, making them less motivated to justify their decisions and defend their position.

Self-affirmation procedures have been found to reduce cognitive biases and improve decision making. Leaders who find themselves at the helm by virtue of their *over*confidence are inevitably going to encounter situations in which they are overstretched. Improving their self-worth temporarily through a self-affirmation manipulation might prevent them to sticking with a course of action that might damage the organization.

Thus, evolved cognitive biases such as overconfidence and anchoring effects might impede leadership in modern organizations. Further research is needed into the effects of these biases on leader decision making and how they can be avoided or suppressed.

Psychological Adaptations for Dominance

A third barrier to effective leadership, according to ELT, stems from the competition inherent to the process of evolution via natural selection. An individual's reproductive success is always relative: How well does an individual with a particular trait do compared to other individuals with alternative traits? Because natural selection operates on variation between individuals, one person's gain in reproductive success is often another person's loss. An implication is that humans have evolved psychological mechanisms designed to dominate and exploit others, ascend social hierarchies, and prevent rivals from achieving dominance.

ELT suggests that leadership encapsulates two different forms of hierarchies. The first is the traditional dominance hierarchy that results from competition for scarce resources, where the strongest and most determined individual in the group, usually a male, prevails and controls group resources and directs group activities. Dominance is part of our primate heritage. Our closest genetic relatives all live in groups characterized by dominance and power hierarchies. It is not surprising that modern humans retain the vestiges of these dominance hierarchies.

Yet, humans have taken a somewhat different evolutionary trajectory from other primates by going out to live on the savannah in which the best strategy to survive was to cooperate with each other in large groups. To be able to live and function in highly cooperative groups requires mechanisms and procedures for coordinating social activities, sharing resources, keeping groups together, and leveraging the benefits of participatory decision-making. This phase of evolution caused attenuation of the traditional dominance hierarchy, replacing it with a decision-making hierarchy benefiting the entire group rather than a few powerful individuals.

Dominance was thus replaced by leader- ship, whereby individuals voluntarily coordinated their actions and goals with people they believed could help them achieve group goals. In return, individual leaders competed with each other to attract followers but this com- petition was based more on prestige and respect than on dominance and coercion. This move away from dominance to prestige-based leadership was a pivotal step in human evolution, accounting for the emergence of egalitarian hunter-gatherer societies with Big Men leaders. The anthropologist Mervyn Meggitt describes a decision-making process in the Mae Enga, a tribe in Papua New Guinea.

The major Big Man then solicits responses from the audience. Ideally everyone present has a voice and being among his own clansmen can speak with complete freedom. The task of the Big Man at this stage is to ensure that all have a chance to offer their opinions and facts in full and to make no attempt to cut off any but obviously irrelevant speeches.

Nonetheless, dominance is still part of our ancient primate heritage and there is plenty of evidence from traditional and modern societies that leaders will coerce followers if they believe they can get away with it. To get your way as a leader it is much easier to dominate than to convince people to follow you. This makes the leader– follower relationship fundamentally ambivalent, for two different reasons. First, many people with leadership aspirations do not become leaders. Accession to leadership is itself a Darwinian process; through a series of events influenced by circumstances and luck one person prevails. The losers join the ranks of the followers and can scheme against the leader to gain power in the future. Second, when they get into power leaders can bully their own group for personal gain.

There are various mechanisms that enable leaders to increase or consolidate their power that are deeply rooted in our evolutionary history. Unfortunately, these mechanisms some- times undermine effective leadership in organizations. First, individuals can achieve power through corruption, bribery, or nepotism. For instance, when leaders distribute resources between themselves and followers they tend to keep more for themselves. It makes good sense from an evolutionary perspective to benefit either one- self or individuals to which a person is closely (genetically) aligned—this is referred to as kin selection—and nepotism is a common strategy in both humans and chimpanzees. Some political leaders in history turned their rule into a hereditary position to directly benefit their offspring. This evolutionary strategy is also seen in family businesses that recruit their prospective leaders from a very small pool of candidates, usually sons or sons- in-laws, making them more prone to leadership failure.

Second, leaders can consolidate their power base through providing public goods generously to followers. In leadership competitions, individuals may be inclined to engage in conspicuous wasteful behaviors to impress rivals and potential followers, for example, by promising tax deductions for the rich or giving out food vouchers. This process is called competitive altruism and it is a common ritual in traditional societies where Big Men compete for status for example though organizing large feasts. Similarly, some business leaders generously hand out bonuses and organize conspicuous company events to please their employees. However, it is a short-term strategy to curry favors and it may ultimately undermine the efficiency of an organization.

Third, leaders can strengthen their position through winning an intergroup competition. Legendary warlords like Alexander the Great, Genghis Khan, and Napoleon were military geniuses who increased their power base through invading their neighbor's territories. Dictators fed on wars and other external threats that justified their existence—swift military action requires a central command-and-control structure. Half of the 20th-century rulers engaged in battles at some point in their reign. Experimental social psychological research suggests that when a democratic leader feels his power position is being threatened, they are more likely to start a conflict with another group than when their position is secure. The same might apply to business leaders. When they feel their power position is unstable, they might be more prone to start a price war to deflect attention but this tactic might have dire consequences for the organization.

Fourth, leaders can dominate groups by controlling the flow of information within an organization. Throughout history, leaders have tried to control the free press, fearing criticism and unrest. Leaders can shut down the media completely or they can turn it into a propaganda machine for their regime. The former Italian Prime Minister Berlusconi owned nearly half of Italy's media, including national television channels, radio stations, newspapers, and magazines. These outlets carefully managed Berlusconi's public image and shielded him from criticism. The problem, of course, is that when leaders are protected from criticism they might make the wrong decisions and sub- ordinates who cannot express their criticism get alienated from the organization.

Finally, leaders might decide to get rid of rivals in order to consolidate power. The African dictator Idi Amin who came to power after a military coup in Uganda decided to exterminate his political rivals and many of the people who supported them. He is estimated to have killed 300,000 people during his 8-year reign. His victims included cabinet ministers, judicial figures, bankers, intellectuals, and a former prime minister. Although this is an extreme example, getting rid of highly talented people in an organization because they are perceived as a threat may be attractive to leaders to strengthen their power base but it does little to serve the interest of the organization.

There are additional costs to dominance for organizations in terms of what power differences do psychologically. In ancestral environments, leaders were kept in check largely because there were only minimal status and wealth differences between leaders and followers. Yet in modern businesses average salaries for CEOs are over 100 times the average worker's salary. Social psychological experiments show that giving someone power increases power abuse. Power also threatens leader–follower relations by decreasing the ability to empathize with subordinates and increasing the use of stereotypes in the appraisal of subordinates . Finally, inequality in resources undermines the cohesion and the solidarity of teams and organizations. Thus, highly asymmetric pay-offs between leaders and followers in many modern organizations may stimulate a kind of leadership that followers naturally resist and that may impede organizational welfare.

The propensity of leaders to use exploitative strategies might be augmented by the selection process of leaders and managers in organizations. When the privileges associated with leadership positions are substantial and there is intense competition for a scarce number of positions, this might select for the wrong kinds of leaders. Power might be particularly appealing for individuals with selfish personalities because they can use this position to promote their evolutionary interests. The dark triad leaders are an example—leaders who score high on narcissism, Machiavellianism, and psychopathy. This triumvirate makes them self-centered, status-obsessive, emotion- ally cold, and aggressive. Unfortunately, part of their talent lies in image management. Out- ward they appear normal and even charming, yet they have difficulty empathizing with others. According to psychologists Babiak and Hare such personality types are overrepresented in top leadership positions in business.

Finally, the competitive selection process of leaders in large corporations might select for individuals, usually males, with high levels of baseline testosterone. According to research, high testosterone individuals thrive in high power positions. Yet as leaders these individuals have difficulties empathizing with others, which undermines their effectiveness. Furthermore, when high testosterone individuals feel their position is being undermined, they counter with aggression.

These examples suggest that human adaptations to dominate may stand in the way of effective leadership. Our evolved tendencies to dominate, which we inherited from primate ancestors, might make us prone to corruption, power abuse, aggression, and conflict when we find ourselves in leadership positions.

Trait Theory of Leadership

The trait theory of leadership focuses on identifying different personality traits and characteristics that are linked to successful leadership across a variety of situations. This line of research emerged as one of the earliest types of investigations into the nature of effective leadership and is tied to the "great man" theory of leadership first proposed by Thomas Carlyle in the mid-1800s.

Rationale

According to Carlyle, history is shaped by extraordinary leaders. This ability to lead is something that people are simply born with, Carlyle believed, and not something that could be developed. Carlyle's ideas inspired early research on leadership, which almost entirely focused on inheritable traits.

Carlyle's theory of leadership was based on the rationale that:

1. Certain traits produce certain patterns of behavior.
2. Patterns are consistent across different situations.
3. People are "born" with leadership traits.

Even today, books, and articles tout the various characteristics necessary to become a great leader, suggesting that leadership is somehow predestined in some (or is at least more likely) while unlikely, if not impossible, in others.

Since the publication of Carlyle's thesis, others psychologists have examined argued the trait-based theory of leadership.

From the 1940s to the 1970s, psychologist Ralph Melvin Stogdill suggested that leadership is the result of the interaction between the individual and the social situation and not merely the result of a predefined set of traits.

Soon after in the 1980s, James M. Kouzes and Barry Z. Posner posited that credibility was a key indicator of leadership skills, characterized by such traits as being honest, forward-looking, inspiring, and competent.

Leadership Traits

While the list of leadership traits can vary by whoever is drawing up the list, a recent study from Spain outlined behavioral traits that separated lower-level supervisors from higher-level supervisors. According to the researchers, the traits most commonly associated with great leadership include:

1. Intelligence and action-oriented judgment: Great leaders and smart and make choices that move the group forward.
2. Eagerness to accept responsibility: Strong leaders take on responsibility and don't pass the blame on to others. They stand by their success and take ownership of their mistakes.

3. Task competence: A great leader is skilled and capable. Members of the group are able to look to the leader for an example of how things should be done.

4. Understanding their followers and their needs: Effective leaders pay attention to group members and genuinely care about helping them succeed. They want each person in the group to succeed and play a role in moving the entire group forward.

5. People skills: Excellent interpersonal skills are essential for leading effectively. Great leaders know how to interact well with other leaders as well as with team members.

6. A need for achievement: Strong leaders have a need to succeed and help the group achieve their goals. They genuinely care about the success of the group and are committed to helping the group reach these milestones.

7. Capacity to motivate people: A great leader knows how to inspire others and motivate them to do their best.

8. Courage and resolution: The best leaders are brave and committed to the goals of the group. They do not hide from challenges.

9. Perseverance: Strong leaders stick with it, even when things get difficult or the group faces significant obstacles.

10. Trustworthiness: Group members need to be able to depend upon and trust the person leading them.

11. Decisiveness: A great leader is capable of making a decision and is confident in his or her choices.

12. Self-Confidence: Many of the best leaders are extremely self-assured. Because they are confident in themselves, followers often begin to share this self-belief.

13. Assertiveness: A great leader is able to be direct and assertive without coming off as overly pushy or aggressive.

14. Adaptability and flexibility: Effective leaders don't get stuck in a rut. They are able to think outside of the box and adapt quickly to changing situations.

15. Emotional stability: In addition to being dependable overall, strong leaders are able to control their emotions and avoid overreactions.

16. Creativity: Perhaps most importantly, great leaders not only possess their own creativity, but they are also able to foster creativity among members of the group.

Controversy

Early studies on leadership focused on the differences between leaders and followers with the assumption that people in leadership positions would display more leadership traits than those in subordinate positions.

What researchers found, however, was that there were relatively few traits that could be used to distinguish between leaders and followers. For example, leaders tended to be higher in traits such as extroversion, self-confidence, and height, but these differences tended to be small.

There are obvious flaws in the trait-based theory. While proponents suggest that certain traits are characteristic of strong leaders, those who possess the traits don't always become leaders.

Some have suggested that this may due to situational variables in which leadership skills only emerge when an opportunity for leadership arises (such as in war, during a political crisis, or in the absence of leadership).

Meanwhile, others have taken a contingency approach to leadership in which certain traits can be more effective in some situations and less so in others. Opinions vary on what those traits are and to what degree they can predict success, if at all.

Leadership in the Internet Age

More controversial yet is the contention that some people don't have the traits to become leaders. Such a belief inherently overlooks social and economic inequities that limit, if not entirely erase, a person's potential to lead.

It also overlooks the changing economy and how leadership is defined when connections are today made both online and offline.

As outlets for leadership continue to change (such as with social media and e-commerce), the traits needed to succeed are different simply because there are fewer intermediaries. Within this realm, the ability to influence is arguably more important than the ability to lead.

Great Man of Leadership Theory

Great Man Theory or Great Man of Leadership Theory, was established on 19th century by Thomas Carlyle, Scottish Philosopher, Historian, Satirical Writer and Essayist. He was one among the significant social commentators of this time and has presented many lectures during his lifetime. Great Man Theory was born from the impact of great heroes and men, who were kings or personalities with wisdom and charisma, evolved in the 19th century when great men were considered as role models to the society. History of the world lies on the biographies of great men. The goal of humanity lies in its highest positions. Herbert Spencer in 1896 critics the great man theory as they are mere products of social environment and a society should make men before a man remakes it. Great men in histories are remembered forever as history recalls through generations. This theory is praised and criticized at the same time.

Moreover, men and environment should shape each other reciprocally, however, the significance of great men are imaginary. Every individual influence his own society or other with his positive or negative ideas or actions could be recognized in history. Great men theory of leadership states that ambitions and clear visions of the effective leaders, politicians, executives, professionalists, sports personalities who often seem to possess an impression, stands apart from the crowd are created as great men. The great men are not made but they are born and great men can arise when there is a need as even today great men are born.

Great Men

Great men are the one with unique personalities and understand the need of the society and in a patriarchic society men are considered as leaders and that's why it is called great man theory and authoritative posts were held by men and passed on to their male generations, later great women leaders were remembered and it was called as great person theory. Women personalities of the world Cleopatra, Jane Auston, Margaret Fuller, Florence Nightingale, Marie Curie, Helen Keller, Annie Besant, Mother Teresa, Queen Elizabeth II, Indira Gandhi, Malala Yousafzai, etc are the noted distinct great women.

Men with inbuilt leadership trait, intelligence, power, charm, authority, persuasiveness, support, high degree of intuition and judgement, special endowment, oddness, courage, with good characteristics stands throughout the history, yet the great men idea was considered as myth as they would emerge magically at the time of need like Jesus, Churchill, Buddha, Muhammad, etc.

Example:

Lincoln was considered as one of the most pivotal icons in the history of US, moreover, the decisions he took at the time of his presidency had a chance of affecting the future socioeconomic welfare of the country. He was the leader in time for the citizens of America. Correspondingly, Trump connects with great man theory where his characters and personalities affect the course of history in either good way or bad. The choices these great men made matters. Researchers and scientists discuss that great men are inborn as the leadership qualities are carried in genes through generations like Charles de Gaulle, Mahatma Gandhi, Abraham Lincoln, Mao Tsetung, Kemal Ataturk, etc. and they were great personalities of their time.

This theory disagrees that leaders are made through education and exposure and individuals cannot be trained to become leaders as great men are born and posses divine blessings. Yet great men are rejected by modern theorists, scientists and researchers as it has no scientific and empirical evidence as born leaders are imaginary and the great men can be created by education, exposure and empowerment. Moreover, the modern world does not rule out the genetic as it has seen great musicians, singers, players by generations yet it rejects the godly power and inborn. Despite all these arguments, the great man theory was believed up to mid 20th century until the behavioural sciences emerged.

Transformational Leadership Theories

Transformational leadership theories believe that people are motivated by the task that must be performed. The more structured an organization is, the greater the success. People give their all to the organization which can be their primary need and they will place their individual interests second. There is an emphasis on cooperation and collective action and stress is included in the long-range goals of an organization. Individuals exist within the context of the community, rather than competing with each other. Accordingly, tasks are designed to be challenging and desirous. The whole system adjusts to place the community above individual egos.

It is odd to regard influential individuals such as Adolf Hitler and Attila the Hun as transformational leaders, but one must be aware that these categories of leadership theories overlap. The analytical caveat is that one must not describe the category so broadly as to include everyone. When engaging in a discussion about the focus on the primary qualities of leadership, there should be heuristic categories, but remember that there must be boundary conditions, even though they may be subjective.

How long has cooperation been in existence? Perhaps this can be best exampled in families that are identified as functional, sibling rivalries and spousal quarreling aside. When relating this to larger organizations, one can identify an extended family and as a result, cooperatives. In all cases, everyone has a common objective, with everyone benefitting from its achievement. Everyone realizes that any rivalty or an attempt by a person(s) to dominate the organization will obliterate any possibility of a collective effort. Every individual is significant and it is to the organization's benefit and success to allow each person to develop to the maximum of her or his potential. The Greeks realized this when in promoting virtue advised that one should be doing whatever s/he is "cut out" to do. At least some forms of a transformational leadership situation can be compared to a well-oiled machine functioning perfectly or a healthy organism, where all the components collaborate as intended.

Comparing organizations or social systems to organisms is not a recent concept, as shown by John Jacques Rousseau's observations in "Social Contract".

We suppose men to have reached the point at which the obstacles in the way of their preservation in the state of nature show their power of resistance to be greater than the resources at the disposal of each individual for his maintenance in that state. That primitive condition can then subsist no longer; and the human race would perish unless it changed its manner of existence.

But, as men cannot engender new forces, but only unite and direct existing ones, they have no other means of preserving themselves than the formation, by aggregation, of a sum of forces great enough to overcome the resistance. These they have to bring into play by means of a single motive power, and cause to act in concert.

In the 1930s, Oswald Spengler purported that societies were organic and had life-cycles. On a darker side, leaders such as Benito Mussolini argued that the individual's will must be submersed in deference to the will of the State. Of course, Mussolini was not the only one espousing this view. Modern history, especially that of the 20th Century, is littered with the Stalin's and Hitler's, each rationalizing their autocracy by an appeal to the superiority of the state, where individuals benefit more from collectivity than from individualism.

Of course, any thinking underpinning a system can be excessive and transformational leadership theories aren't an exception to the rule. Whereas it can be argued that more can be accomplished through a collective action and this is justification for totalitarian states and one can also argue that any individual development, necessary for social competence, is reason to have a participatory society, such as a cooperative. Aristotle argued in his Politics that a society is strengthened with diversity in ideas and capabilities and as a result, democracy was a better form of authority. Game theory, as exemplified in the Prisoner's Dilemma, supports the view that cooperation produces more results than competition and that the strength of that cooperation is enhanced when people of diverse backgrounds and capabilities are encouraged to participate in achieving the common goals and to make decisions collectively. The simple truth is that if everyone is involved in decision-making, they will be more committed to working to achieve making the ideal goal a reality.

A test of the efficacy of transformational leadership theories could be how a group of island survivors fare. It is clear that if there is no cooperation, the chances of survival are greatly diminished. On the other hand, if the necessary tasks are of an urgent nature, there may be a need for a commanding person. William Golding's Lord of the Flies is an excellent scenario from which to draw lessons such as this. Transformational leadership theories could have brought harmony to this situation that ultimately turned out with the characters fighting each other to the point that some lost their lives because of the turmoil.

The leader strives to exhibit the qualities of a good role model - must be paradigm of good character. S/he is the personification of the ideals of the system, its ethos and motivations driving the organization. The manner in which s/he leads is imbued with desirable human qualities, such as intelligence, compassion, noble ethics and exemplary courage. The leader is a counsel to the rest, lending his/her support to enhance the well-being of each essential member of the organization.

Critique

Transformational leadership theories are placed under stress with enormity and urgency of tasks, wartime being an extreme case. A leader cannot wait for decisions based on consensus but needs to act, often immediately. If there are conflicts within the group, it is more difficult to reach a census on what needs to be accomplished. There may be persons who feel themselves to be more capable of achieving an apparent goal and are actually impatient in waiting for others to "catch up" or "get it". For others, there may be peer pressure to conform and organizational members may simply retire, offering no comment; they do not want to be thought of as being quarrelsome and contentious and risking opprobrium from the group.

It is possible that personality sects may emerge from an organization in which there is cooperation and the leader is admired. Numerous examples exist ranging from Fidel Castro to Ronald Reagan, where excessive devotion to a person compromised critical conclusions as to the quality of leadership. In an effort to build consensus, unfortunately mediocrity may result.

A transformational approach may not be as efficient as a more centralized and directive form of leadership. An extreme case of transformational leadership would be anarchy and if the members of an organization have assertive personalities and intelligence, it may take considerable time to arrive at decisions and perform the required tasks. In extreme cases, indecision may lead to the organization's ruin, especially if there are a number of individuals that are more predisposed to being followers rather than decision-makers.

Future of Theory

Since the 1950s, there has been a consistent increase of certain individuals wanting to gain power for themselves. Monarchies collapsed in the 19th Century, it was the end of colonialism. The common thread was empowerment and as a result, the beginning of recognition of individual worth. On a local level, people began to distrust authority, especially in the latter quarter of the 20th Century with former President Richard Nixon's impeachment and following with numerous government officials convicted of illegal activities and thus receiving prison terms. The Viet-Nam War, then classified only as a police action, brought people into the streets in protest in addition to a growing movement to spread power to the people. Numerous cooperatives of all types - food, land, and housing - were started. This was followed by a period of narcissism, self-help programs and pop psychology. Now, with world political economies under stress, people once again are questioning authority not only in the United States, but worldwide as well. As a result, transformational leadership theories will become even more relevant, although it may not be recognized as such. Modern communications, especially the ever-increasing of the popularity and availability of the Internet have empowered people with knowledge and opportunities abound for self-development that have never before been seen. Thus, it is incumbent upon leaders to realize and acknowledge that populations are highly capable of thinking for themselves.

Pro's

- Transformational leadership theories emphasizes the task and organizational integrity and this helps focus one's attention to more appropriately defining a task.
- The transformational theories emphasizes cooperation, ethics and community in addition to the higher human values.
- Long-range goals are emphasized which leads to increasing the survivability of a system.
- It has been showed in studies, such as in gaming theory, that cooperation, as opposed to competition, is more successful in achieving goals.
- Transformational leadership theories are adaptive and can be tailored to support the fulfillment of the most pressing of needs in people.
- There is greater stability of a leader's position, as there is greater support by those who are being led.
- Transformational leadership theories can bring harmony to a situation that could otherwise be exacerbated by a quarrelsome organization.
- If one has an educated population, transformational leadership theories are more likely to work.

Con's

- Even if everyone is motivated to do a task it does not assure a successful completion of that task. Over-enthusiasm for the leader may cloud the group's judgment as to whether the objectives of an organization are realistic.

- There can be over-dependence upon the leader.
- Members of the organization may resent that their ability to act as individuals has been restricted.
- People have different personalities, and some may be more ambitious than others may, with the latter feeling as if they are being pushed beyond their capacities.
- Some individuals may work better as individuals as opposed to collaborating in a team environment.
- There may be cases when it is difficult to assess whether there is cooperation or mere conformity. People may want simply to "go along to get along".
- There is the danger of the presence of personality cults, where a leader is so revered that s/he is only the personality that drives activity.
- The enormity of a task and a fractious or highly competitive environment may compromise the ability of a leader, applying the concepts of transformational leadership theories, to gain consensus.

Tannenbaum and Schmidt Continuum

The Tannenbaum and Schmidt Continuum is a simple model of leadership theory which shows the relationship between the level of freedom that a manager chooses to give to a team, and the level of authority used by the manager.

Delegation: Tannenbaum and Schmidt Continuum

Delegation and Team Development

The Tannenbaum and Schmidt Continuum is a simple model of leadership theory which shows the relationship between the level of freedom that a manager chooses to give to a team, and the level of authority used by the manager. As the team's freedom is increased, so the manager's authority decreases. This is a positive way for both teams and managers to develop. As a manager, one of your responsibilities is to develop your team. You should delegate and ask a team to make its own decisions to varying degrees according to their abilities. There is a rising scale of levels of delegated freedom that you can use when working with your team.

Over time, a manager should aim to take the team from one end to the other, up the scale, at which point you should also aim to have developed one or a number of potential successors from within your team to take over from you. This process can take a year or two, or even longer, so be patient, explain what you're doing, and be aware constantly of how your team is responding and developing.

When examining and applying the Tannenbaum and Schmidt principles, it's extremely important to remember: irrespective of the amount of responsibility and freedom delegated by a manager to a team, the manager retains accountability for any catastrophic problems that result. Delegating freedom and decision-making responsibility to a team absolutely does not absolve the manager of accountability. That's why delegating, whether to teams or individuals, requires a very grown-up manager. If everything goes well, the team must get the credit; if it all goes horribly wrong, the manager must take the blame. This is entirely fair, because the manager is ultimately responsible for judging the seriousness of any given situation - including the risks entailed - and the level of freedom that can safely be granted to the team to deal with it. This is not actually part of the Tannenbaum and Schmidt Continuum, but it's vital to apply this philosophy or the model will definitely be weakened, or at worse completely back-fire.

Here are the Tannenbaum and Schmidt Continuum levels of delegated freedom, with some added explanation that should make it easier to understand and apply:

1. The Manager decides and announces the decision.

The manager reviews options in light of aims, issues, priorities, timescale, etc., then decides the action and informs the team of the decision. The manager will probably have considered how the team will react, but the team plays no active part in making the decision. The team may well perceive that the manager has not considered the team's welfare at all. This is seen by the team as a purely task-based decision, which is generally a characteristic of X-Theory management style.

2. The manager decides and then 'sells' the decision to the group.

The manager makes the decision as in 1 above, and then explains reasons for the decision to the team, particularly the positive benefits that the team will enjoy from the decision. In so doing the manager is seen by the team to recognise the team's importance, and to have some concern for the team.

3. The manager presents the decision with background ideas and invites questions.

The manager presents the decision along with some of the background which led to the decision. The team is invited to ask questions and discuss with the manager the rationale behind the decision, which enables the team to understand and accept or agree with the decision more easily than in 1 and 2 above. This more participative and involving approach enables the team to appreciate the issues and reasons for the decision, and the implications of all the options. This will have a more motivational approach than 1 or 2 because of the higher level of team involvement and discussion.

4. The manager suggests a provisional decision and invites discussion about it.

The manager discusses and reviews the provisional decision with the team on the basis that the manager will take on board the views and then finally decide. This enables the team to have some real influence over the shape of the manager's final decision. This also acknowledges that the team has something to contribute to the decision-making process, which is more involving and therefore motivating than the previous level.

5. The manager presents the situation or problem, gets suggestions, then decides.

The manager presents the situation, and maybe some options, to the team. The team is encouraged and expected to offer ideas and additional options, and discuss implications of each possible course of action. The manager then decides which option to take. This level is one of high and specific involvement for the team, and is appropriate particularly when the team has more detailed knowledge or experience of the issues than the manager. Being high-involvement and high-influence for the team this level provides more motivation and freedom than any previous level.

6. The manager explains the situation, defines the parameters and asks the team to decide.

At this level the manager has effectively delegated responsibility for the decision to the team, albeit within the manager's stated limits. The manager may or may not choose to be a part of the team which decides. While this level appears to gives a huge responsibility to the team, the manager can control the risk and outcomes to an extent, according to the constraints that he stipulates. This level is more motivational than any previous, and requires a mature team for any serious situation or problem. (Remember that the team must get the credit for all the positive outcomes from the decision, while the manager remains accountable for any resulting problems or disasters. This isn't strictly included in the original Tannenbaum and Schmidt definitions, so it needs pointing out because it's such an important aspect of delegating and motivating, and leadership.)

7. The manager allows the team to identify the problem, develop the options, and decide on the action, within the manager's received limits.

This is obviously an extreme level of freedom, whereby the team is effectively doing what the manager did in level 1. The team is given responsibility for identifying and analysing the situation or problem; the process for resolving it; developing and assessing options; evaluating implications, and then deciding on and implementing a course of action. The manager also states in advance that he/she will support the decision and help the team implement it. The manager may or may not be part of the team, and if so then he/she has no more authority than anyone else in the team. The only constraints and parameters for the team are the ones that the manager had imposed on him from above. (Again, the manager retains accountability for any resulting disasters, while the team must get the credit for all successes.) This level is potentially the most motivational of all, but also potentially the most disastrous. Not surprisingly the team must be mature and competent, and capable of acting at what is a genuinely strategic decision-making level.

Leadership Models

Leadership models may be defined as guides that suggest specific leadership behaviors to use in a specific environment or situation. In addition, they often use a graphic representation to show the required leadership behaviour.

Three models are discussed:

- Managerial Grid - Focuses on a leader's concern for task and concern for people to predict leadership outcomes.
- Four Framework Approach - Uses four common concepts to guide leadership behavior in specific situations.
- Situational Leadership - Guides a leader on the type of coaching required to develop a worker in a specific situation.

Four Framework Approach

In the *Four Framework Approach,* Bolman and Deal suggest that leaders display leadership behaviors in one of four types of frameworks: Structural, Human Resource, Political, or Symbolic:

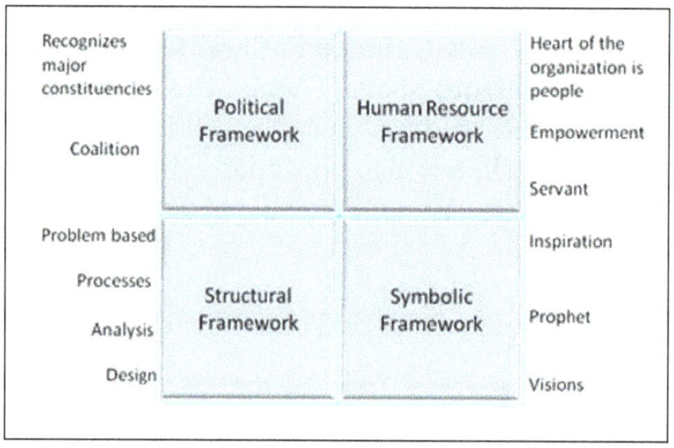

This model suggests that leaders operate in one of these four categories and there are times when one approach is more appropriate and times when it would not be. That is, any style can be effective or ineffective, depending upon the situation. Relying on only one of these approaches would be inadequate, thus we should strive to be conscious of all four approaches, and not just rely on one or two.

For example, during a major organization change, a Structural leadership style may be more effective than a Symbolic leadership style; during a period when strong growth is needed, the Symbolic approach may be more appropriate. We also need to understand ourselves as each of us tends to have a preferred approach. We need to be conscious of these at all times and be aware of the limitations of just favoring one approach.

The four leadership behaviors are:

- Structural Framework - Structural Leaders focus on structure, strategy, environment, implementation, experimentation, and adaptation. In an effective leadership situation, the leader is a social architect whose leadership style is analysis and design. While in an ineffective leadership situation, the leader is a petty tyrant whose leadership style is petty details.
- Human Resource Framework - Human Resource Leaders believe in people and communicate that belief; they are visible and accessible; they empower, increase participation, support, share information, and move decision making down into the organization. In an effective leadership situation, the leader is a catalyst and servant whose leadership style is support, advocating, and empowerment. While in an ineffective leadership situation, the leader is a pushover, whose leadership style is abdication and fraud.
- Political Framework - Political leaders clarify what they want and what they can get; assess the distribution of power and interests, build linkages to other stakeholders, use persuasion first, but will use negotiation and coercion if necessary. In an effective leadership situation, the leader is an advocate, whose leadership style is coalition and team building. While in an ineffective leadership situation, the leader is a hustler, whose leadership style is manipulation.
- Symbolic Framework - Symbolic leaders view organizations as a stage or theater to play certain roles and give impressions, use symbols to capture attention, frame experience by providing plausible interpretations of experiences, and discover and communicate a vision. In an effective leadership situation, the leader is a prophet, whose leadership style is inspiration. While in an ineffective leadership situation, the leader is a fanatic or fool, whose leadership style is smoke and mirrors.

Situational Leadership

The situational leadership theory, developed by Paul Hersey and Ken Blanchard, is based upon two continuums — the required level of *supervision* and *arousal* required to coach workers in specific situations so that they develop into great performers:

- Supervision (directing) - The employee's skill and knowledge level determines the level of supervision. On one end of the continuum is over-supervision, while the other end is under-supervision. The goal is to hit the sweet-spot. Under-supervision leads to miscommunication, lack of coordination, and the perception by subordinates that the leader does not care. Over-supervision stifles initiative, breeds resentment, and lowers morale. The goal is to provide the correct amount of supervision that is determined by the employee's skill and knowledge level.

- Arousal (supporting) - The employee's skill and knowledge level determines the amount of arousal or emotional support required. This emotional support raises or lowers the task holder's arousal level (the inner-drive within our self-system). A certain level of arousal motivates us toward change (learning). However, too much or too little will over or under stimulate our behavior. In highly cognitive tasks a low arousal is required as over-simulation may occur (and vice-versa).

Ken Blanchard later refined the model and changed the term *Situational Leadership Theory* to simply *Situational Leadership*. In his model, leadership is the act of providing the correct amount of supervision (Directing Behavior) and arousal (Supportive Behavior), which in turn, produces the best learning and developmental environment as shown in the model below:

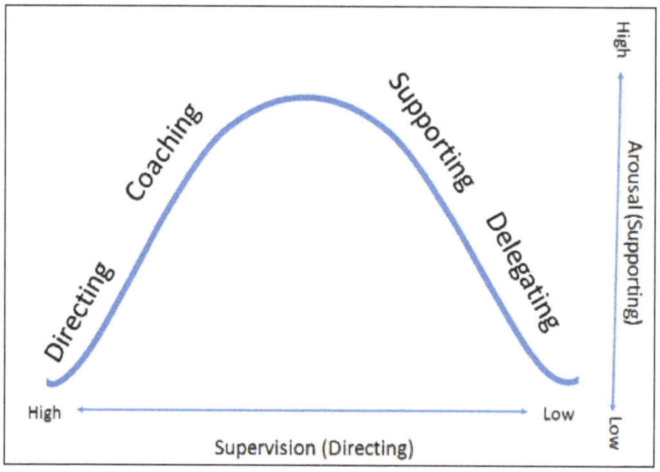

Situational Leadership is basically is a four-step model, however, depending upon the situation, you can jump into any step as required (depending on how well an employee can perform and is motivated to perform):

- Directing - Provide a lot of direction (learner does not know how to perform) and a small amount of support.
- Coaching - Decrease direction (so that learner can learn by trial and error) and increase support (needs emotional support due to some failure).
- Supporting - Decrease direction even more (so that learner can become self-supporting) and decrease support.
- Delegating - Provide direction and support on an as-needed basis.

Blake and Mouton's Managerial Grid

Blake and Mouton of the University of Texas developed a two-dimensional concept of leadership style called 'Managerial Grid'—built on the work of the Ohio State and Michigan Studies—to explain leadership behaviour.

They pointed out that leadership style is a blend wherein task-oriented and relation-oriented behaviour are mixed in different degrees.

The two-dimensional model and five different types of leadership styles are shown in Figure below In the grid, the X-axis represents the 'concern for production' while the Y-axis represents the 'concern for people'. Concern for production means the managerial attitudes about the volume of output, procedures and efficiency of work, etc.

And, concern for people refers to the degree of personal commitment, responsibility based on trust and satisfying inter-personal relations, self-esteem of the workers, etc. A manager is concerned with both the task and the people as he has to get things done through people.

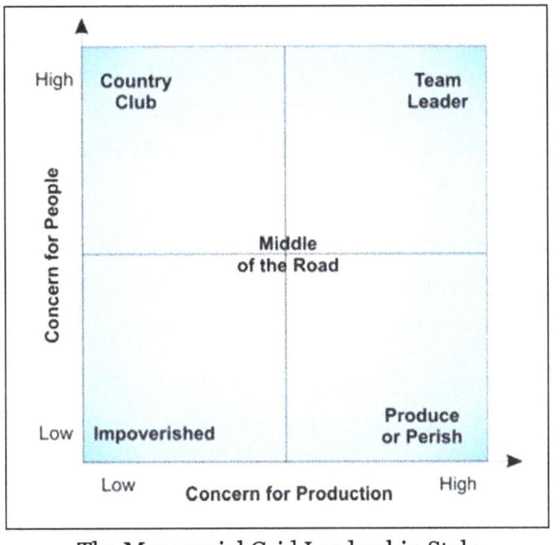

The Managerial Grid Leadership Style

The managerial grid identifies five combinations of these two factors. The five leadership styles are explained below:

Impoverished Management Style

In this style, the manager shows less concern for both production and people. It implies the manager's less interest in the position. In this situation minimum effort is needed for getting the work done and sustaining organisation membership. The leader acts as an observer, avoiding controversy and confrontation.

Country Club Management Style

Under this style the manager is highly concerned with' the people. He tries to establish close personal relationship. Adequate attention to the needs of people leads to a comfortable organisation environment and work culture. The leader has maximum concern for people and minimum concern for production.

Middle of the Road Management Style

In this case, the manager gives emphasis on both production and relationship with the people. Proper organisation performance is possible through balancing the necessity of getting work done through maintaining morale of the people at a satisfactory level. The leader balances tasks with concern for people through compromise.

Task Management Style

In this situation, the manager is mainly concerned with production and has little concern for people. He gives emphasis on getting the tasks done to increase production. The task is well-planned and the authority is well-defined. This is the task-oriented or autocratic style of leadership. The leader leads the people with instructions and discipline.

Team Management Style

In this case, the manager has maximum concern for both production and people. This is the team leadership style in which the leader consults with his team and harmonies organisational goals. Work performed by committed people and inter-dependence through common organisational goals leads to the relationships of trust and respect. This style is considered to be the best leadership style.

Managerial grid approach helps the managers to identify their own leadership styles. It is a useful framework for assessing the styles of leadership. It has been used successfully in improving the attitudes and behaviour of people throughout an organisation.

This approach is very popular among the managers. But it is highly controversial among the theorists who consider it to be only a tool, not a theory of leadership—because it lacks empirical evidence. According to their opinion, it is an attitudinal and conceptual description of leadership. It does not point out the reason for failure of a manager in one part of the grid or the other.

Three Levels of Leadership Model

The Three Levels of Leadership Model is for practicing leaders who want to grow and be better at what they do. It applies to any leader in a group or organization, whether you are an Inc 500 Company CEO or a weekend sports coach.

The Three Levels of Leadership Model, also known as the 3 P's Model of Leadership, is a tool for developing the skills to lead yourself and your role in leading others.

The Three Levels Leadership Model is a tool that helps you to improve your know-how, presence, and skill and helps you understand what to do as a leader.

The model provides some of the tools you need to develop yourself as an effective leader.

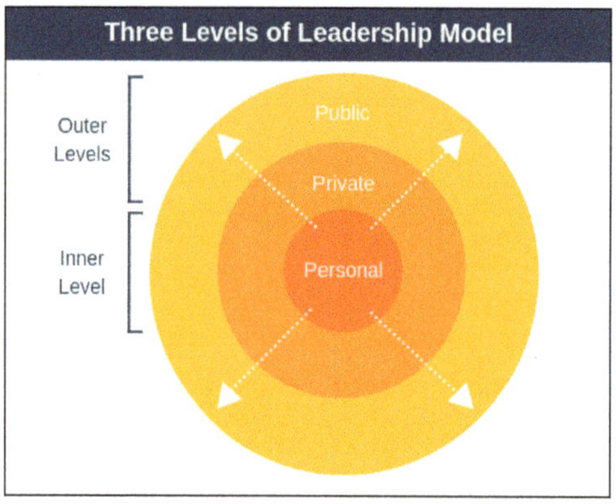

The Three Levels of Leadership model has three levels: Public, Private, and Personal Leadership. The outer two circles represent the Public and Private Leadership Levels. They focus on the range of behavioral elements you need to influence a single person (Private Leadership) or two or more people (Public Leadership).

The central circle represents the Personal Leadership. This level concerns your presence. It also includes your know-how, your skills, your beliefs, your emotions, and your habits. Personal Leadership drives the effectiveness of Private and Public leadership roles.

According to the model, you need to work on all three levels in parallel to be an effective leader.

For example, imagine you have been asked to lead a team to establish a new warehouse. You've never been involved in a construction project before. Consequently, if you don't develop the personal know-how, there will be an upper limit to your ability in performing as a leader on the project.

Public Leadership

Public Leadership is about leading a team and driving collective action, so you get results. By paying attention to your Personal Leadership skills, you can grow your Public Leadership abilities.

The Four Dimensions of Leadership

As the leader, the Public and Private Leadership Levels are what you work on to attend to the four dimensions of leadership.

Leadership is a process where you address these four dimensions:

1. Maintaining a shared motivating purpose,
2. Driving action towards progress & results,
3. Upholding group unity,
4. Paying attention to individuals.

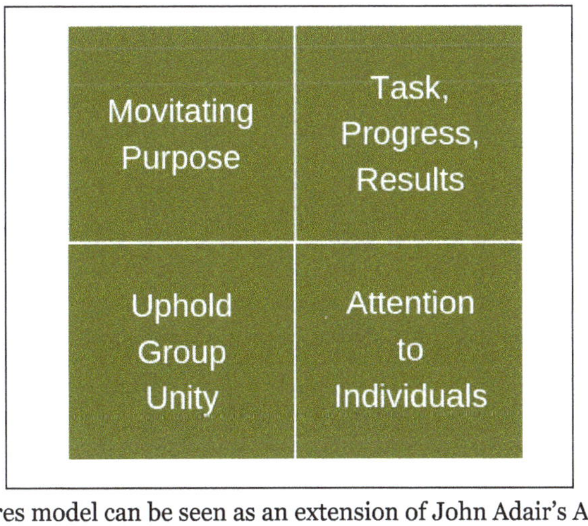

The four squares model can be seen as an extension of John Adair's Action Centred Leadership and the three circles concept.

Private Leadership

Your team or group is made up of individuals. They are all people who have unique traits, behaviors, skills, and emotions.

The skills for a one-on-one chat are unique and are very different from the skills for leading a group.

Imagine one team member is underperforming. You've got to have one of 'those' chats. In your mind, you've already judged your colleague. At times it can be disarming for you too. You confront your colleague only to find out they are dealing with a difficult personal situation, and this is affecting their ability to perform.

The situation requires specific interpersonal communication.

Personal Leadership

Let's say you were watching football last night, and your team lost. You think it would be easy to put it at the back of your mind, but losing irritates and, you are in a less than stellar mood. During a meeting, you find that you are losing control and biting back at a colleague.

When you practice Personal Leadership, you have an increased awareness of how you are using your private and public leadership skills and so perform your role better. With self-reflection, you can identify your areas of weakness, and work on those over time.

There are three key elements to focus your attention on when developing yourself.

- Know-how & skill.
- Attitude towards others.
- Self-mastery.

Self-mastery helps you develop your leadership presence and abilities. By learning to adjust to a range of different leadership situations, you can build trusting relationships.

Leadership Presence

Leadership presence is one of the main features of the Three Levels Model of Leadership, so what exactly is it?

Leadership Presence is the state of being present with a person, whereby you are showing up as a complete version of yourself.

You engage with one particular colleague and have a conversation about your 360-degree feedback assessment. You are giving your colleague your undivided attention, speaking honestly and respectfully and not ducking any issues from the feedback. You are uninhibited and allow your personality to flow, without getting caught by any worries and anxieties about the situation.

Your colleagues can feel your authenticity, and you have a radiating effect on them. When practicing leadership presence, you are in the moment, feeling confident and leading well.

Three Levels of Leadership Example

As a real leader, you to have to adjust to outside influences. Using your Personal Leadership skills, you can build self-awareness and the skills to adapt your behavior to certain situations.

For example, you have recently completed a 360-degree assessment with each of your team members. You discover from the feedback that you tend to put off making decisions with one particular stakeholder. The team suggests you are not listening adequately during stakeholder meetings.

You decide to attend a course and improve your listening skills. By choosing this action, you are applying the Personal Level of the model. You are developing new skills that will benefit you.

You can then apply your new skills in the Private and Public levels and improve communication with the team and the stakeholder. The group sees improvement in your decision making and as a result, is performing better.

Your journey towards self-mastery requires you to embark on a lifelong journey of Personal Growth. By holding this as central to developing your leadership skills, you can become a more impactful leader.

Advantages and Disadvantages

There are several advantages and disadvantages to the Three Levels of Leadership model.

Advantages

- The Model combines the strengths (and addresses weaknesses) of other leadership theories.
- A practical approach to effective leadership development centered around servant leadership and being your authentic self.
- Centers the leader's effectiveness on developing yourself by addressing limiting beliefs, emotions, and unconscious habits and self-mastery.

Disadvantages

- The journey of self-development can be challenging for some people.
- It is difficult to see your weaknesses without the reflection of others.
- There are no supporting programs for leadership development using the model, so implementing the model needs to be self-directed.
- As a relatively new model, the Three Levels of Leadership model needs to be reviewed in the field to understand it's actual effectiveness.

Hersey-Blanchard Model

The Hersey-Blanchard Model suggests that there is no single leadership style that is better than another. Instead of focusing on workplace factors, the model suggests leaders adjust their styles to the followers and their abilities.

Under the model, successful leadership is both task-relevant and relationship-relevant. It is an adaptive, flexible style, whereby leaders are encouraged to consider their followers—individuals or a team—then consider the factors that affect the work environment before choosing how they will lead. This ensures they will meet their goals.

Because the Hersey-Blanchard model depends on a leader's decision-making skills, it uses an individualistic rather than a group approach.

The Hersey-Blanchard Model is also referred to as the Situational Leadership Model or Theory.

The Hersey-Blanchard Model, or situational leadership, was developed by author Paul Hersey, and leadership expert Ken Blanchard, author of "The One Minute Manager." The model is not a static leadership style. Instead, it is flexible, wherein the manager adapts management style to various factors in the workplace including his or her relationship with other employees.

That means managers who live by the model must choose the leadership style as it relates to the maturity of followers. For example, if follower maturity is high, the model suggests the leader provide minimal guidance. By contrast, if follower maturity is low, the manager may need to provide explicit directions and supervise work closely in order to ensure the group has clarity on their goals and how they are expected to achieve them.

The maturity level of followers is divided into three categories: high, moderate, and low. High maturity includes highly capable and confident individuals who are experienced and work well on their own. Moderate maturity is generally divided into two groups—the first are employees who are capable, but lack enough confidence to take on the responsibility to do so, and the second has the confidence but is not willing to do the task at hand. Low maturity employees are not skilled enough to do the task but are very enthusiastic.

Special Considerations

Hersey-Blanchard Model and Leadership Styles

Hersey and Blanchard came up with four different types of leadership styles based on the task and relationships leaders come in contact with in the workplace. According to the model, the following are styles of leadership managers can use:

- Delegating style: A low-task, low-relationship style wherein the leader allows the group to take responsibility for task decisions. This is best used with high maturity followers.
- Participating style: A low-task, high-relationship style that emphasizes shared ideas and decisions. Managers using the participating style tend to use it with moderate followers who are not only experienced but with those who aren't as confident to do the tasks assigned.

- Selling style: Refers to a high-task, high-relationship style, in which the leader attempts to sell his ideas to the group by explaining task directions in a persuasive manner. This, too, is used with moderate followers. Unlike the previous style, these followers have the ability but are unwilling to do the job.
- Telling style: Refers a high-task, low-relationship style wherein the leader gives explicit directions and supervises work closely. This style is geared toward low maturity followers.

Applying the Model and Its Limitations

This leadership method lets executives, managers, and other positions of authority take charge of their followers based on the acumen, understanding, and context of the group. By taking into consideration how the strengths, weaknesses, and awareness of the followers can affect their performance and the outcomes of the project, leaders can apply an appropriate structure and degree of control to achieve the desired result.

There are limitations to the model that may be beyond the leader's control. The position and authority of the leader may be restricted by the operational chain-of-command or hierarchy for an organization, which could force them to adopt rigid styles rather than adapt to follower maturity. Furthermore, time constraints, a narrow field of options, and limits on available assets can also force managers to act based on the circumstances they face, eliminating the possibility of enacting strategies built around follower maturity.

Advantages and Disadvantages of the Hersey-Blanchard Model

Although this leadership model may be sound in theory, it may not necessarily be applicable in every situation. so it comes with advantages and disadvantages.

Some of the advantages of using an adaptive leadership style are that leaders can change their style at their own discretion at any time. Secondly, employees may find a leader who adapts to shifting changes in the workforce as a desirable trait. It is also a simple and easy-to-apply leadership style, meaning a manager can quickly evaluate a situation and make decisions as he or she sees fit.

On the downside, situational leadership may put too much responsibility on the manager, whose decisions may be flawed. The model may not also be applicable to different cultures. The model may also prioritize relationships and tasks, as opposed to a company's long-term goals.

References

- Leadership-philosophy-guide: cleverism.com, Retrieved 3 April, 2019
- Authentic-leadership: techtarget.com, Retrieved 2 January, 2019
- Servant-leadership: investopedia.com, Retrieved 26 May, 2019
- Leadership-and-the-contingency-theory: cleverism.com, Retrieved 14 July, 2019
- Fiedler's-contingency-theory: leadership-central.com, Retrieved 9 March, 2019
- Situational-theories-of-leadership, principlesmanagement: lumenlearning.com, Retrieved 12 May, 2019
- Vroom-yetton-jago-decision-model: free-management-ebooks.com, Retrieved 22 April, 2019

- Lead-path-goal, leader: nwlink.com, Retrieved 18 February, 2019
- What-is-the-trait-theory-of-leadership: verywellmind.com, Retrieved 7 August, 2019
- Great-man-theory: communicationtheory.org, Retrieved 17 July, 2019
- Transformational-leadership-theories: leadership-central.com, Retrieved 27 June, 2019
- Leadmodels, leader: nwlink.com, Retrieved 25 January, 2019
- Blake-and-moutons-managerial-grid, leadership: yourarticlelibrary.com, Retrieved 2 August, 2019
- Three-levels-of-leadership-model: expertprogrammanagement.com, Retrieved 12 March, 2019
- Hersey-and-blanchard-model: investopedia.com, Retrieved 4 June, 2019

4

Leadership Qualities, Traits and Ethics

Some of the qualities which are important in a leader are motivation, vision, thoroughness, continuous improvement and creativity. Compassion is another value which is highly regarded in a leader. This chapter discusses in detail these qualities, traits and ethics which are desired in a leader.

Leadership Qualities

we can define leadership based on common elements that we can all agree on. Here are 10 ways to define the art of leading:

Vision

Leading means having a vision and sharing it with others. Only when you get to inspire others, it is possible to share a common goal towards which to direct the efforts and dedication of the entire team. What is your vision?

Motivation

A leader knows how to motivate better than anyone else; it is one of their main functions as people managers. Through motivation, a leader channels their coworkers energy and professional potential in order to achieve objectives.

Serving

The leader is at the service of the team, and not the other way around. Group members must have and feel the support of their leader, the tools needed to do their jobs properly must be available to them, they must have recognition for their efforts and know that there is a person paying attention in order to correct bad habits. That is all part of a leadership which serves the team, and not the opposite.

Empathy

One of the basic qualities of any leader seeking success is precisely emotional intelligence, that ability – often innate – that makes leaders put themselves in the place of others, understand their concerns and solve problems. Leaders know the secrets of their businesses and therefore can empathize with customers and members of their teams: that empathy gets to inspire and establish links that will ultimately lead to success.

Creativity

The definition of leadership also has to do with creativity. Good leaders are able to create an environment that will encourage all the members of their team to develop their skills and imagination, so that they can contribute to the common project and vision of the company. If you want to lead successfully, respect the creativity of others and learn from the people around you; their ideas will surely prove to be positive for you.

Thoroughness

A good leader sets the bar high for their people, because they want to reach the goals and bring the best ou of their teams. Only a demanding leader will achieve great results. In addition to this thoroughness, the leader must know how to listen, in order to know the needs of the people, and then provide the necessary time and resources for them to do their job properly, and therefore meet what is demanded of them.

Managing

The leader must be at the forefront to lead and guide their team throughout the whole process until the goal is reached. But besides being that "torchbearer", leaders also know when to step back and make their team take the initiative. In this way, the team gets the chance to develop, both personally and professionally. Pure management focuses on the tasks, real leadership focuses on the people.

Team Building

True leadership is about working in a team to reach a common goal. People management is one of the most difficult tasks faced by leaders. Thanks to the positive attitude, essential in good leaders, and the trust in their workmates, people get better results. Team-aware leaders take responsibility when something is wrong, and reward the group after a job well done.

Taking Risks

The leader is the one responsible for taking the risks that others are not willing to take. They are confident enough to make a decision, and if they make a mistake, the leader must have the courage to rectify, assume their guilt and take the right path, without blaming it on the team. Good leaders know how to get ahead of their time, they see opportunities where others can't and know how to spread the enthusiasm for their vision to try to make it real.

Improving

True leadership seeks continuous improvement. Leaders have the ability to turn the people in their teams into stars, people who have improved and developed their skills through the influence of their leader.

In short, the definition of leadership has nothing to do with the hierarchy or anyone's position within the company; it has nothing to do with imposing views but its about listening to those who know. Leadership is the attitude assumed by those looking for something different, who are committed to achieving a goal and whose conviction they manage to transmit to others through enthusiasm and optimism in order to reach a common goal.

Self-Motivation for Leaders

Self-motivation for the leaders is of paramount of importance because as leaders they should be self-motivated first before motivating their team members. Self-motivated leaders contribute to the realization of the organizational vision by providing strategic direction and motivation to the teams.

Importance of Self-Motivation for the Leaders

1. Effect of Self-Motivation on Personal and Team Productivity: Lack of self-motivation, not only hampers the personal productivity but it equally affects the productivity of all the team members. A zealous and passionate leader will create an environment of excitement and motivate the team members for delivering their best.
2. Level of Confidence: Leaders derive pleasure in the completion of complex and challenging long-term pending projects with success, which will eventually act as a natural confidence booster for the leader.
3. Self-Motivation helps in Reducing Stress: In the absence of self-motivation, leaders may experience an accentuated level of stress which may lead to adverse thinking, self-criticism and criticism of others for not being able to deliver the required deliverables.
4. Living without any regrets: Enhanced self-motivation helps in continuous improvement of a leader and controlling self-regrets. By way of self-evaluation, leaders can assess their strengths and weaknesses; identify the possible areas of opportunities and deal with the challenges at work with fresh zeal and vigour.
5. Career Advancement Opportunities: Career advancement can be considered as the outcome of self-motivation. Self-motivated leaders are in a better position to meet their goals successfully, climb the ladders of success and progress professionally by attaining newer heights.

Apart from the above-described factors, leaders who are highly self-motivated enjoy the following benefits:

1. It helps the leaders in defining clear goals and also in finding out ways for attaining those goals more consistently.
2. Self-motivated leaders motivate others to adopt their style of leadership and in dealing with the day to day responsibilities.
3. Leaders who are self-motivated evolve and improve continuously, as they attain new heights of motivation after every achievement.

Improvement of the Self-Motivation Level of a Leaders

1. Physical Fitness: Leaders, who mainly follow a disciplined and a strict health regime for staying fit physically and mentally, are expected to have an enhanced level of self-motivation.

2. Networking: A leader's self-motivation level will improve if they are surrounded by a motivated company or a group of people. By attending seminars, conferences or various workshops, leaders can become self-motivated and recharged.
3. Getting back to the Basics: Leaders who have a high sense of self-motivation are focused in their approach and follow a disciplined routine. They stick to certain good habits which they follow religiously and without fail. Whether, it's a habit of reading motivational books or an inspiring content, following a disciplined lifestyle or any other right habit, they perform them on a regular basis.
4. Remaining Focused: Self-motivated leaders are sure about their strategies and how they plan to achieve their goals. They can visualize the big picture along with the challenges ahead.
5. Be Accountable: By developing a high sense of accountability, leaders become self-motivated to complete the assignments within the stipulated deadlines and resources.
6. Have Fun: Self-motivated leaders derive pleasure and look for ways to have fun and enjoy working.

Various Impediments that affect the Self-Motivation of Leaders

1. Bad Habits: For meeting the desired outcomes, leaders should be able to assess those factors which hold them from reaching their desired goals and be able to work towards getting rid of such habits by replacing them with positive or productive habits.
2. Lack of Proper Resources: In the absence of availability of proper or optimal resources, leaders fail to meet the desired goals. They may have issues related to the shortage of funds, lack of training or availability of the required skilled personnel, technological limitations or management upsurges.
3. Effective leaders should not stop at that: instead, they should explore or find out ways to acquire them by indulging in brainstorming discussions, setting clear priorities and preferences, obtaining the needed resources one at a time instead of everything by breaking down the goals into small achievable options. It will help them to achieve cost advantages and in overcoming the stress which they undergo due to the pressures of pending assignment and non-achievement of the desired results.
4. Lack of Desire: Leaders should try to indulge in those activities which they enjoy performing, instead of sticking to those practices which sucks their time and energy, but then they derive no pleasure from doing it.
5. External Pressures or Circumstances: External pressures or circumstances thwart the self-motivation level of the leaders which could be because of the failure in meeting the expectations of others and failure in getting the desired support or cooperation from others for achieving the desired goals.

Thus we can conclude that self-motivation for a leader is an essential pre-requisite and those who have a high sense of self-motivation are in a better position to achieve the strategic outcomes and propel organizational growth and productivity. Self-motivated leaders stimulate a sense of passion or excitement amongst the team members to achieve challenging goals, improve the existing systems and processes by championing excellent change initiatives with the support of others and manage resources optimally. They play a crucial role in driving organizational excellence by setting up examples before the team, monitoring progress periodically and plugging in the loopholes with proactive remedies or solutions.

Many factors thwart the self-motivation of leaders which may range from personal factors like bad habits to environmental factors or circumstantial factors. Leaders lose the required motivation due to the lack of availability of the needed resources such as technology, skills, finances or human resources. Efficient and highly motivated leaders are charged up to perform better and overcome all the challenges by exploring ways or alternatives to meet the desired results, defining and implementing powerful strategies and by establishing the processes in place.

Techniques for Developing Self-Motivation

Various self-motivation techniques are practiced by leaders for ensuring achievement of the pre-defined objectives. Self-motivated leaders evolve and improve continuously, learn from their mistakes and are flexible enough in working upon their areas of development.

Let's find out below, some of the crucial benefits which leaders can derive by practicing self-motivation techniques at work:

- Leaders who can efficiently exercise self-motivation at their workplaces can establish clear goals and work towards the realization of those goals consistently.
- Others are motivated as well to follow your behavior or the leadership approaches while dealing with their day to day responsibilities.
- It fosters a sense of responsibility and promotes further self-development or improvement of the leader by way of continuous learning and being inspired by the achievements at work.

Techniques of Self-Motivation

- Listening and Leading: By way of active listening and exemplification of experiences, leaders strengthen the bond of respect between the leader and the follower; can attain outcomes and resolve the most complex issues with enhanced confidence.

Benefits of Listening and Leading

- Exemplification of self-motivation by establishing goals and in developing a robust plan of action for achieving them.
- Leading and listening help in focusing the motivational energy in a more positive direction as it facilitates clarity in communication of goals, strategies and what is expected out of the team members.
- By way of active listening, newer methods or approaches for dealing with the tasks can be derived. Continuous improvement at work can be achieved by identifying innovative solutions to various issues which is an outcome of a collaborative team environment and creative problem solving involving active listening skills.

Challenging & Empowering Oneself and Education: Following are the benefits of using education and empowerment as a technique of self-motivation:

- Leaders who are self-empowered develop the required competence for taking up the extra responsibilities and delivering professional synergies at work.
- Leaders can grow and work on their weaknesses by way of self-education and self-coaching. Education helps in keeping the motivation levels very high for contributing exceptionally in the professional as well as personal front.
- Self-empowerment helps a leader to address the challenges efficiently and successfully. With success in challenging endeavors, leaders with a high sense of self-empowerment are motivated for accepting more challenges.

Rewarding and Recognizing Individual Achievements:

- Leaders should reward themselves for their small or significant accomplishments; this will motivate improving continuously and achieving superior milestones at work. They must acknowledge their achievements and commend themselves for their excellent work as this will enhance their overall performance and productivity at work.
- Leaders reward themselves by giving up time for others or by acting as mentors for others and guiding them on various organizational as well as personal matters by sharing their experiences.
- By thinking of people who inspired others to achieve and following their footsteps, leaders can motivate themselves.

Leadership Traits

Leadership traits refer to personal qualities that define effective leaders. Leadership refers to the ability of an individual or an organization to guide individuals, teams, or organizations toward the fulfillment of goals and objectives. It plays an important function in management, as it helps maximize efficiency and achieve strategic and organizational goals. Leaders help motivate others, provide guidance, build morale, improve the work environment, and initiate action.

List of Effective Leadership Traits

A common misconception is that individuals are just naturally gifted with leadership skills. The truth is that leadership traits, like other skills, can be acquired with time and practice. Below are seven traits of an effective leader:

Effective Communicators

Leaders are excellent communicators, able to clearly and concisely explain problems and solutions. Leaders know when to talk and when to listen. In addition, leaders are able to communicate on different levels: one-on-one, via phone, email, etc.

Accountable and Responsible

Leaders hold themselves accountable and take responsibility for any mistakes. Leaders support and encourage individuality while abiding by organizational structure, rules, and policies that need to be followed.

Confident

Virtually all good leaders share the leadership trait of confidence. They are able to make tough decisions and lead with authority. By being confident, leaders are able to reassure and inspire others, establish open communications, and encourage teamwork.

People-oriented

Leaders are typically people-oriented and team players. They're able to foster a team culture, involve others in decision-making, and show concern for each team member. By being people-oriented, leaders are able to energize and motivate others. By making each individual feel important and vital to the team's success, they secure the best efforts from each member of the team.

Emotionally Stable

Leaders exercise good control and regulation over their own behavior and are able to tolerate frustration and stress. Leaders are able to cope with changes in an environment without having an intense emotional reaction.

Traits of a Bad Leader

Listed below are the traits that bad leaders commonly exhibit:

- Too bossy,
- Fearful of change,
- Unwilling or unable to communicate effectively,
- Dismissive of ideas other than their own,

- Lacking empathy,
- Inconsistent,
- Prone to blame others rather than accept responsibility themselves,

  Indecisive.

Forward Thinking

One of the key traits that differentiate good leaders from other people in the organization is a forward-thinking mindset. The best leaders naturally draw people to be followers. In order to follow, people first need to see that they will be going somewhere and that the path is headed in a positive direction.

Forward thinkers focus on the future and pursue a vision. This doesn't mean that they are oblivious to the present, but it does mean that they will not be stuck in the present. To the forward thinker, the present is a stepping stone to the future.

Forward thinkers shape the future by making things happen. A leader who is a forward thinker displays the following behaviors:

- They have an open mind: They see possibilities rather than difficulties. They see opportunities rather than problems. The forward thinker is a broad thinker. They are receptive to ideas and input from wherever it might come. They are both watching for and seeking new ideas from various sources.
- They are not trapped by conventional thinking or stuck in the past: The forward thinker questions current practices, frequently asking "why" and "why not". A forward thinker isn't trapped by the "not invented here" syndrome and never falls for the answer of "that's not the way we do things here".
- They welcome change and accept risk: Forward thinkers go against the natural tendency to maintain status quo. Most people strive to be comfortable. Where others fear change, the forward thinker values change. They are willing to move forward on a path even without knowing all of the answers. They recognize risks and accept possible setbacks as learning experiences.

- They invest in the future: With a focus on the needs of tomorrow, forward thinkers work on self-development. They coach and provide growth experiences for the people around them, knowing that they are building capabilities to be accessed down the road as well as contributing to the career successes of their people.
- They see the bigger picture: Forward thinkers know that details are important, but they see everything in the context of where they are going and what the future holds. They see the complete puzzle of the future, piece by piece.
- They build a vision and stick to it: Forward thinkers gather input and build a shared vision, then they relentlessly drive toward that vision. They over-communicate the vision to keep the team on course.
- They accept responsibility: Because their very nature is to break away from the crowd, forward thinkers have a greater sense of responsibility. They are willing to bear the weight of their decisions and accept the consequences.
- They value teamwork and collaboration: Forward thinkers are focused on the big picture, making them well aware that achievement of the vision is not an individual activity. They rely on their team and therefore share the victories and successes with them.
- They have perseverance: Moving away from the known and into the unknown, the forward thinker has the will to face naysayers and prejudice. They are able to get back on their feet when they get knocked down. Always ready to revise and regroup, they continue to move forward.

Forward thinkers produce energy and excitement in the team that they lead because all of them share in the vision and recognize that they are accomplishing something of significance. The forward thinker's team is inevitably engaged.

Honesty

A leader can motivate followers and inspire them to rise above in life. If they want to achieve respect and trust from the followers, they need to be honest and must value integrity. Much of it, leadership that is, depends on the techniques involved in motivating followers and arranging required sources to accomplish a goal.

Honesty is also referred by positivity and integrity. The ability to develop trust in followers and legitimacy is based on honesty.

Effective leaders always follow these principles. They draft and lead the way, they produce a vision of upcoming missions, inspire people, help others and encourage their team members. They set a strong example with their honesty to inspire followers and other people. People always demand honest leaders like Martin Luther King or Sir Abraham Lincoln.

When you become a leader, before starting the leadership program, assume that people think of you as a dishonest human. In order to show them that you are an honest individual, you will have to prove yourself. People will never take you as an honest person just because you have never been caught lying. Admitting your mistakes in front of people gives them a strong, positive vibe about your honesty.

Opportunities to display honesty do not just occur on a daily basis. By being honest to your own self, your organization and outside, you will increase your sphere of influence. People will trust you implicitly, and will look up to you as a person who is worth following. You will further inspire them to follow the path of honesty.

Honesty is claimed to be one of the crucial elements of great leadership. Great leaders follow the five rule goal that are:

Model the Path

According to this rule, the leader should explain values and goals honestly to his followers/employees. A leader should set a good example for others and inspire them for being honest.

Inspire a Joint Vision and Aim

An honest leader envisages a better future for his organization and followers and enlists them to his people so they can be involved in the decision-making process, which motivates them.

Challenge the framework and Current Process

An honest leader searches for various new opportunities for his followers and organization. The leader would never fear from taking the risks in newer experiments.

Inspire other to take the reign in their hands and Act

Leaders collaborate with people's need and mobilize their teams. Great leaders never retreat from empowering their team members.

Encourage People's Efforts and Appreciate them

An honest leader never claims all the success on his own account, a leader recognizes, appreciates and rewards the contributions along with celebrating the value and success.

Need of Transparency

Four reasons why that transparency and culture of trust is necessary:

Better Relationships

Employees don't just quit their jobs, they quit their bosses. In fact, a revealed that 37 percent of the 3,008 employees surveyed were likely to leave their jobs due to a poor opinion about their boss's performance.

When it comes to building solid workplace relationships, trust takes center stage. Take Unbounce, for example. It took transparency to another level with its "Inside Unbounce" blog, a staff-authored, un-curated window in the organization. Not only does this demonstrate transparency to potential job seekers, customers, etc., it also keeps employees involved and up to date on company happenings, successes and feedback.

Better Alignment

Employee alignment, for transparency's sake, means taking a look at the big picture and seeking to understand everyone's role within it. This is easily done when employers practice transparency in the workplace. Transparent leadership results in employees who understand the company vision and how their efforts help achieve company-wide goals.

Better Solutions

When leaders are transparent, problems are solved faster. By being open and honest about company problems, employees can help find solutions. And two heads (or however many heads make up the company) are better than one.

Social sharing app Buffer makes company performance public with progress reports on customer support, blog performance, business performance and more. Not only does doing so increase accountability, it also highlights issues and encourages employees to find solutions.

Better Engagement

A culture that values transparency in the workplace breeds engaged employees. In fact, Harvard Business Review's 2013 employee engagement survey revealed that 70 percent of those surveyed say they're most engaged when senior leadership continually updates and communicates company strategy.

When it comes to engaging employees, it's best to be open about company matters. LinkedIn CEO Jeff Weiner fosters an organization built on transparency. He even takes the time to hold bi-weekly meetings, during which he updates employees on company matters and listens to their suggestions.

Intelligent Leadership

Intelligent Leadership is a comprehensive leadership concept. It is designed for exceptional people who want to break through the (largely self-imposed) limits that prevent them from reaching their full potential. It is effective, strategic, operationally sound, and is practiced by energetic, passionate people. Intelligent Leadership doesn't just happen, but is the product of intentional choices and practices that have the ability to unlock opportunities beyond what might be apparent at first.

Intelligent Leadership involves cultivating the heart, mind, and soul in order to bring exceptional leadership skills to an organization. In John Mattone's book *Intelligent Leadership*, he describes a process based on empirical research that uses a leader's inner-core strengths and outer-core competencies.

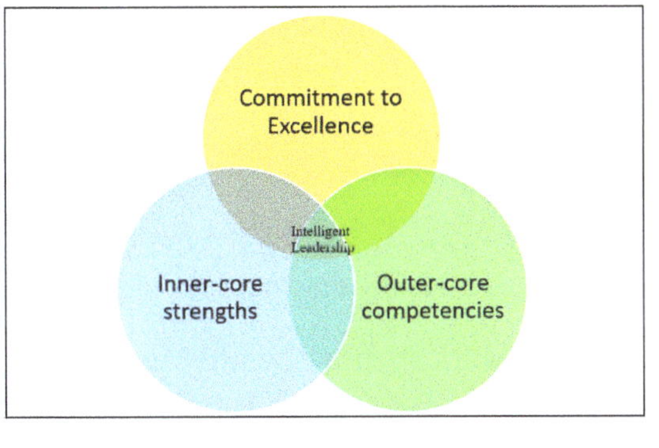

Intelligent leadership rests in the sweet spot of commitment to excellence, inner-core strengths, and outer-core competencies.

Inner-core strengths include traits like character, positive emotions, positive beliefs, self-concept, and values. Outer-core leadership competencies are made up of a person's capabilities, commitment, and connectedness. When inner and outer core are aligned, and when a leader recognizes what they:

- Can do,
- Will do, and
- Must do.

They have the building blocks for Intelligent Leadership success. With the guidance of the intelligent leader's ever-improving competence, teams come to form powerful, engaging organizational cultures where people make their own free choice to commit to giving their best effort and continually seeking to improve. The intelligent leader – the outstanding leader – must possess a clear vision of the capabilities, commitment, and alignment of inner-core values and outer-core competencies required to lead effectively. The definition of leadership success isn't really unique to each organization, though each *leader* is unique. There exist some fundamental, universal target behaviors and characteristics of Intelligent Leadership, and John Mattone has explored them in great depth.

Ways it Differs from Traditional Leadership

Traditional leadership as we usually think of it is goal-oriented. It has to be. Why bother having a leader if there are no goals to be accomplished? Intelligent Leadership is, in addition, vision-oriented: what is our situation right now, what is our best possible outcome, and how can we put our resources and strengths toward achieving that? Leaders must be skilled at guiding operations toward goals, and there are countless ways to do this, good and bad. Setting down objectives and ensuring proper resources are available are positive, effective ways of guiding a team toward goals. Micromanaging, or at the other extreme, trying to lead by fiat ("Make it happen, however you have to do it."), are ineffective ways of doing moving toward goals.

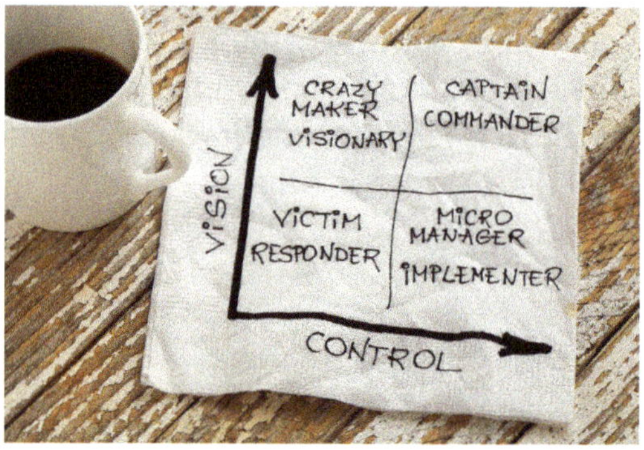

Micromanagement is remarkably counterproductive in a leader.

A leader cannot be focused on the past, but must be able to look realistically at the present situation, with its good qualities and its bad ones. With Intelligent Leadership, a leader not only has a focus on the here and now, but also puts practices into place to ensure the good work outlives their tenure. This involves recognizing and cultivating emerging leadership. Leaders cannot lead effectively unless they know themselves. We all know that trying to be someone you fundamentally are not eventually derails. Therefore, leaders must know, "This is how I am." Intelligent leaders, in addition to knowing "This is how I am," know their own character and values, as well as how they are manifested outwardly in their work.

In summary, the main difference between leadership and Intelligent Leadership is that the latter takes it to a more expansive level. John Mattone didn't just come up with these concepts from scratch, but developed them as the result of extensive global experience over the span of more than three decades. He has also conducted extensive research on talent management and executive development, consulting with hundreds of organizations, and has leadership coaching experience with over 200 executives.

Need for Intelligent Leadership

Any organization that wants continuing success needs Intelligent Leadership. Theoretically, an organization might not require Intelligent Leadership if it were temporary, devoted to a single goal, and ready to disband once that's over, but even that would be short-sighted. Intelligent Leadership isn't only devoted to getting excellent results right now, or this business quarter, but indefinitely thereafter. Implementing Intelligent Leadership requires first finding leaders and future leaders with the potential for greatness, and helping them develop their unique leadership gifts and talents while understanding their own weaknesses so they can address them. And it continues with keeping an eye out for emerging leaders of tomorrow, because succession planning is essential to any organization that wants long-term prosperity.

The world in general, and the business world in particular, will only become more complex, more demanding, and more accountable in the Information Age. A business that doesn't care whether it exists in ten or 15 years may not need to worry much about leadership, but some would argue that guiding an organization to a singular accomplishment isn't really leadership at all. In short, the realities of today's world require Intelligent Leadership.

Ways Leadership Coaches Help

Leadership coaching helps leaders further fine-tune strengths, while bridging skills and performance gaps.

Coaches, in general, can have outsized influence on people's lives. John Mattone regularly asks executives to tell him about the great leaders in their lives, and often that person is a former coach. Great leaders often have role models as inspiration, but when it comes to the people who actually made a difference in their lives, a parent, teacher, or coach is often credited. Leadership coaches can make an immense difference to the person who is soon to assume a leadership role. When someone must perform as a leader before having been adequately trained and coached, the learning curve is steeper, and the risks are higher.

Perhaps it is ironic, then that when he coaches executives, John Mattone explains that taking the more difficult path is the right decision. Saying no to decisions that don't align with what is true and ethical can be difficult. But the difficulty is short-term. Over the long term, making those difficult decisions lead to better-operating results without the stain of ethical or moral lapses and other long-term consequences.

Targeted coaching that aims for real prescriptions for strengthening both a leader's inner and outer core characteristics helps today's and tomorrow's leaders recognize and seize the amazing opportunities they will encounter. At the same time, coaching helps them avoid and mitigate risks that are increasingly common in a fast-paced, high-stakes business world. It is the leaders who are willing to understand what's in their hearts and minds, and who are honest and objective about their inner- and outer-core characteristics that have the greatest chance of not just being good leaders, but of being legendary ones.

Benefits of Intelligent Leadership

Even the best leader is imperfect, and no one should think of Intelligent Leadership as being entirely without flaws, but the benefits of Intelligent Leadership can be disproportionately good compared to the effort that goes into it. One of the main benefits of Intelligent Leadership is that everyone works within the security of knowing their leader has consistency of character. The leader is not going to change the rules, lie, or otherwise throw people under the proverbial bus to make things easier in the short run.

Another critically important benefit of Intelligent Leadership is that it saves time. Intelligent Leadership is deliberate and clear in communication. Team members don't get mixed signals or conflicting instructions, so time isn't wasted clearing up confusion or going back and redoing things that were done incorrectly. Everyone moves forward, without having to backtrack, and that fuels momentum to accomplish big goals.

Clear, deliberate communication saves time and empowers team members.

Intelligent leaders set an example for others, and at the same time they make sure others know how valued they are. Everyone, whatever their function in an organization, needs to feel appreciated in order to bother giving their best, and Intelligent Leadership understands and practices this. At the same time, intelligent leaders continually thirst for wisdom. They know they never will have "arrived," because the world will continue to change, like it or not. The benefits of Intelligent Leadership are evident in the moment, and they're evident over time. *Today*, team members know what is expected of them and know they are appreciated. *Tomorrow*, they will be able to look back on something amazing and have the satisfaction of knowing they were a valued part of it.

Some Real-Life Examples of Intelligent Leadership

Examples of outstanding leadership take different paths and arrive at different destinations, but they all combine passion, humanity, hard work, and accountability. One example is Theo Epstein, President of Baseball Operations for the Chicago Cubs. Not much united Americans in the fall of 2016, but even the most casual baseball fans couldn't help but be moved by Game 7 of the World Series that made the Cubs into champions. Epstein has demonstrated the importance of understanding the human qualities of players that turn a group of athletes into a true team: one that is greater than the sum of its parts.

Jeff Bezos would make most people's lists of leadership superstars, having revolutionized retail with Amazon.com, and having revolutionized the business of IT with Amazon Web Services. Amazon has even won Academy Awards, leading some to wonder if there's anything this company *can't* do. Chief executive officer of Lloyd's of London Inga Beale has had tremendous impact on business in the City of London. She has focused on modernizing Lloyd's of London by embracing technology, and assists London Mayor Sadiq Khan in an advisory role. She has been granted the title of dame by the Order of the British Empire, and has been outspokenly committed to increasing workplace diversity.

Intelligent leadership allows long-established organizations to continue to develop and thrive.

Zimbabwean Strive Masiyiwa is not only successful in business, but is a devout philanthropist, having founded with his wife the Higher Life Foundation that provides scholarships and food to destitute orphans in his country. He has also used his considerable influence to pursue sustainable investment and leadership in environmental policy to help preserve the African continent's natural resources. Intelligent Leadership isn't about fitting into a mold, but about shaping one's own destiny with tools like hard work, integrity, compassion, and the ability to listen.

Whether or not a person reaches the status of world-renowned leader, their character (or lack thereof) has an enormous impact on how they are remembered, regarded, and talked about. The conscious choices we make wherever we stand on the corporate ladder add up to strong or weak character. It's often not easy to make the right choices, and everyone is sure to make mistakes sometimes. But Intelligent Leadership puts a person in a contest not with others, but with themselves, and a habit of continually striving for improvement, authenticity, and just plain doing what is right, even if it's hard, is what eventually turns a good leader into a great one.

Leadership Competencies

Leadership behaviors as well as skills which contribute to superior performance are known as the leadership competencies. The organisations can assist in the identification and development of the leaders of the next generation by the adoption of an approach to leadership that is competency based. Researchers from around the world have identified certain essential competencies for leadership. Apart from these, the future strategies and trends of the business also needs to drive the development of leadership competencies that are new. Even though some of the leadership competencies are vital for every organisation, a firm needs to define the attributes of leadership which are distinctive to a particular firm for the creation of competitive advantage.

The top level leaders, aspiring managers and mangers are all concerned with the development of the competencies that are required to help them in becoming more effective leaders. Over 100 years of research on leadership have identified and outlined the successful abilities and skills which are associated with the effectiveness of leadership.

Better leadership is promoted by focusing on skill development and leadership competencies. However, the skills that are required for a certain position might change as it is dependent on the specific level of leadership in that organization. The use of the competency approach will help the organisations in determining the specific competencies that are required for different positions at different levels in a particular organisation. Certain vital leadership competencies have been identified by the "Centre for Creative Leadership" and these are consistent throughout the organisations. According to them, the overall structure is divided into competencies that are needed for leading the organization, leading other people in the organization and for leading the self.

When the HR professionals select and develop leaders, they need to give consideration to the competencies that are possessed by the individual and then compare them with the competencies that are required for further development to be able to achieve success in the role of leadership.

Thus, by looking at the current capabilities of the person and comparing them to the skills and competencies that are essential for the position of leadership, the organisations will be able to make decisions in the hiring, development and promotion of leaders in a better way. Some of the top leadership competencies and the way in which they can be developed are given below.

Leadership Competencies and how to Develop them

Social Intelligence (SI)

SI is among the best predictors as far as effective leadership is concerned. However, the research on it is poor and it is also not very well-understood. Social intelligence is very wide but it can be viewed best with respect to the understanding of social situations as well as dynamics and the ability to be able to operate in an efficient way in a number of social situations. As per the research conducted social intelligence, which is described as the sensitivity to social situations, "constellation of social performance" and skills of role playing are very crucial for effective leadership.

Development of Social Intelligence

You need to expose yourself to different types of people, different kinds of social situations along with the work for the development of social perceptiveness and also the ability of engaging other people in a conversation.

Interpersonal Skills

Interpersonal skills might be viewed as a "subset of social intelligence". However, they form an aspect of social effectiveness that is more relationship-oriented. The soft skills of leadership that is often spoken about are represented in the best way by the interpersonal skills.

Development of Interpersonal Skills

For the development of interpersonal skills, first of all you need to become an active listener, then you need to work on speaking and conversational skills. You can even join networking groups and toastmasters for this purpose and also work on the personal relationships that you share with your relatives, friends or with the significant other. Such types of skills generalise to relationships in the workplace.

Emotional Intelligence/Skills (EI)

Emotional intelligence is a complement to social intelligence and is the ability of the individual to be able to communicate at a level that is emotional, be able to have an understanding of emotional situations and emotions and also stay in tune with emotions that are our own. These are related especially to the leadership "charisma".

Development of Emotional Intelligence

For developing emotional intelligence you need to practice reading the nonverbal cues of others especially the cues that are related to emotions. You can need to learn to have a control over your emotions as well as your emotional outbursts. You need to practice the way to express your feelings and become an "actor" who is emotionally very effective and learn the way to express your emotions in an appropriate way.

Prudence

It is among the cardinal virtues of Aristotle. It is a synonym of wisdom and is the ability of being able to understand the perspectives of others by being open and considering the viewpoint of the others.

Development of Prudence

For the purpose of developing prudence, you need to listen to others. You have to work towards being more broad minded and also more open minded. You have to learn to ask for the views and opinions of others and take them into consideration when choosing a particular course of action.

Courage

Fortitude or courage is another cardinal virtue. This includes the courage of taking calculated risks along with the courage of standing up for what you believe in and doing the things that are right.

Development of Courage

Some degree of effort is required for this. However, its roots lie in the development as well as the holding of personal values that are strong. In case you value someone or something very truly, you will possess the courage of standing up by your principles as well as by your people.

Conflict Management

This is an interpersonal skill of a "higher order" which helps assisting your colleagues for either avoiding or resolving the conflicts of interpersonal nature. When the members of an organisation are in conflict with each other, the leaders are generally called upon for the purpose of adjudicating. However, the ability to either avoid or to resolve the situations of conflict that are your own are also involved in this.

Development of Conflict Management Skills

Courses as well as workshops are available for the purpose of assisting you in understanding and learning the strategies of conflict management. A vital aspect of conflict management is to help the parties involved in the conflict to compromise (wherein each party should be having the flexibility of giving up something) or to collaborate (a win-win outcome).

Decision Making

The ability of making good decisions or to lead a process of good decision making is among the core competencies of the leaders. The ways of making decisions can be better or worse but the good leader knows when the decision has to be made, when the peers and subordinates have to be consulted and brought into the process of decision making and when the time is right for taking a step back and allow others to make decisions.

Development of Decision Making Skills

The best way of honing the skills of decision making is experience along with the study of the situations where the decisions have gone wrong or have gone right. It has been seen that people learn more often from the mistakes that they have committed rather from the success that they have achieved.

Political Skills

It is a fact that all the organisations or groups at their core are full of politics. In order to move ahead people attempt to gain allies, break rules and push forward their personal agendas. A leader who is effective is also a good player politically and has knowledge regarding the rules that need to be followed for playing the game and is also able to manage political behaviour in order to prevent it from resulting in the dysfunction of the group or the organisation.

Development of Political Competencies

In the same way as several of the other leadership competencies that are highly developed, the political skills are acquired by means of learning as a result of experience and also the learning that is related to social dynamics and about people.

Influence Skills

Leadership, at its core is all about influencing the behaviour of other people. Therefore, a great leader is someone who is a master of social influence and has the ability to wield power in a fair and effective way. You can become all the more influential in the role of leadership if you have the ability to call on your interpersonal or soft skills.

Development of Influence Skills

Reasoned as well as well-thought out arguments can be made if you have been trained in debating. Viewing the things from the perspective of the other person may assist you in understanding what are the things expected by them from a negotiation and this will let you focus on a situation that I win-win.

Area Competence/Expertise

Most of the people would put in at the first position in the list, however, in today's age, the significance of knowledge in every aspect of the job is less important than what it used to be earlier. In creative firms or high-tech industries, the team members might be possessing knowledge that is more relevant and also more expertise in comparison to the leaders. Still, it is vital that the expertise in particular situations, industries or organisations where they are in leadership roles are developed by the leaders.

Development of Area Competencies

Development is a process which is lifelong, similar to all the other competencies. Leaders who are effective gain their competence and expertise and attempt to gain as much knowledge as they can regarding their organization, product and also the members of their team. You need to study the organization and also study the competitors of the organization.

Apart from the above mentioned competencies the leaders should also possess the competencies of agility, speed, passion and focus in order to be successful. Such skills however cannot be taught and if an organization requires as well as supports these competencies as a basis of its success, they have to be instilled by means of an imbedded system of leadership development. Success of such a program is dependent on five crucial factors which include –

- Support that is provided by the Executive Leadership.
- Work assignments that are challenging.
- The right people.
- Supportive environment of work.
- Instead of a course of skills, there should be a Leadership Development System.

The factor that is the most critical is the unwavering support that can be provided by the Executive Leadership of the organisation. If the development of the fifth element is championed by the top leadership of the organization, the leaders produced by the system will make sure that the work environment is supportive which helps to provide work assignments that are challenging for the right people. This will also facilitate the process of building the leadership teams that are strong throughout the organization. Research has also revealed that the teams that which are produced via an embedded system in an organization hold the key to the sustained success of the business in the long term.

Contrary to the belief that popularly exists, no white knight is there. This means that the "right" Chief Executive will not be able to solve all the organizational problems. Therefore, in reality, the requirements of leadership of a winning organization which is able to stand the test of time go far beyond the organization's Chief Executive. It extends to the leadership team along with the procedures, structures and systems that are put in place by them. Over a period of time, it is the organizational systems as well as the broad leadership of an organization that are crucial particularly in the periods that involve high levels of expectations and stress.

Inspiration in Leadership

It is a world in which one employee can threaten a century-old brand's reputation with one social media post, and a management team will be challenged to articulate its viewpoint on the issues of the day, often the next crisis hasn't even been imagined. Organizations will be required to rethink fundamentals, especially their relationship to society and to the natural world.

This constantly shifting landscape represents peril and opportunity in equal measure, creating a new set of questions for executives. Among them: Is your approach to governance fit for an ever-flattening world? Is your organization's culture suited for unprecedented levels of transparency? Is middle management in your organization capable of leading through a minefield of issues each with its own uncertainties?

In a world in which the power to elevate or undermine organizations increasingly rests in the individual employees' hands, the primary goal for leadership development is simple: Enable workers to make wise decisions on their own. These decisions should be independent of the constraints of traditional control functions and dictates of command-and-control management. Put another way, teaching workers to do the next right thing, rather than the next thing right, is the surest way to ensure that organizations win in our reshaped world.

The global study is based on comprehensive data collected from more than 16,000 employees of for-profit, not-for-profit and governmental organizations in 17 countries. With insights into organizational and individual behavior and how they impact performance, "The HOW Report" offers a road map for 21st century leaders. And while the implications for all leaders vary, there are three takeaways from the research that stand out for anyone thinking about organizational health:

1. Inspired employees are the key to outperformance. Global management teams understandably obsess about employee engagement. But ultimately, leadership in a world of infinite choices — where so much power to build value sits with individual employees — is about inspiration.

Inspired employees demonstrate three key characteristics: They are authentically dedicated — proud of their organization for how it acts in the world and therefore self-driven; deeply accountable — seizing authority, meeting obligations; and fully responsible — leaning in, stretching themselves and helping others. Inspired employees are also extraordinarily productive. "The HOW Report" characterizes inspiration as 27 percent more predictive of performance than engagement.

The reason for this disparity is the difference in the relationships between engaged and inspired employees and their organizations. Engagement is contingent and transactional, only as strong as the organization's short-term performance and the employee's career trajectory. Eventually, that transaction — externally driven by rewards, perks and other incentives — will expire. Inspiration — fueled internally by deeply held beliefs and the connection between those beliefs and work — is enduring and profound. Engaged employees usually don't think like owners; inspired employees not only embrace a state of interdependence with their companies, they are passionate about pushing their organizations in new directions based on deeply held beliefs around what must be done for it to achieve its purpose.

2. Most leaders struggle to inspire (Inspirational leaders demonstrate four critical abilities): scaling values, such as instilling a deep commitment to a standard to which people at all levels hold themselves accountable; pursuing significance, such as enlisting all employees in a commitment to a shared, purpose-inspired mission; heightening consciousness, such as building healthy and sustainable interdependency among employees, partners, stakeholders, customers and society; and fostering freedom, such as creating space by carefully promoting freedom from traditional constraints like hierarchy, and filling that space with carefully nurtured freedom to express oneself, experiment and exercise leadership.

Unfortunately, many leaders struggle to inspire. This is to be expected; most of today's corporate managers developed management practices and habits designed for the closed systems of the 20th century workplace. They lack the playbook to inspire today's workforce — especially one that is increasingly populated by millennials who are more insistent on the need to experience meaning and values at work.

This problem is especially evident at scale. The larger the organization in "The HOW Report" data set, the less likely senior management was to exhibit inspirational leadership qualities. Such findings demonstrate that we need to break the mold for how we select and develop leaders, helping them understand how to put purpose and values at the core of how they manage.

3.The best leaders focus on character and freedom. According to data from The HOW Report, when managers focus on shaping character across an organization, 96 percent of their workforces rate them as effective leaders, compared to 52 percent in organizations that lack this focus. Such organizations are also more than three times as likely to deliver high performance (82 percent vs. 25 percent), according to their employees.

Certainly, building character at an organizational and individual level is no small task. It demands leaders create time and space for themselves and employees to pause and reconnect with the values most important to them, then architect strategies and operating models that provide compelling answers to how daily work and organizational mission connect with employee purpose, and cultivate greater empathy and consciousness toward the other actors they engage with every day. Then they need to not only knock down traditional operational constraints like hierarchy, outdate policies and poorly crafted incentive structures, they need to create freedom for employees to bring their full selves to work, including all their passions, beliefs and ideas.

Data from "The How Report" shows that high-character organizations outperform their low-character peers in long-term orientation, resilience and good decision-making. This is because a focus on character creates license for employees to take bold risks, pursue big challenges, and become full partners in reshaping stale organizational environments. High-character organizations invariably tend to be high-trust organizations, creating virtuous circles where colleagues admit mistakes, ask tough questions, challenge conventional thinking and share information. They also innovate, which is the key to long-term growth.

Indeed, businesses, organizations and governments around the world are constantly launching innovation programs, but innovation remains the most elusive of achievements because of a lack of trust. Companies that lack organizational trust — when fear crowds out imagination — are the least likely places to foster the kind of risk-taking and experimentation that leads to new ideas and initiative. High trust, on the other hand, encourages risk-taking, which fosters innovation, which is the key driver of performance. And our research shows that employees who work in high trust environments are 32 times more likely to take risks that might benefit the company, 11 times more likely to see higher levels of innovation relative to their competition, and six times more likely to achieve higher levels of performance compared with others in their industry.

Effective leadership in our reshaped world is about how business gets done, not how much business gets done. Adapting to this new reality will demand a significant shift in outlook and behavior from senior managers. Only when they emphasize character and foster freedom — through a complete overhaul of organizational frameworks, systems and processes — can leaders truly inspire employees to win in today's markets.

Leadership Vision

Leaders have vision. They share a dream and direction that other people want to share and follow. The leadership vision goes beyond your written organizational mission statement and your vision statement. The vision of leadership permeates the workplace and is manifested in the actions, beliefs, values, and goals of your organization's leaders. This vision attracts and affects every employee who is engaged in living this set of actions, beliefs, values, and goals. They want to share your vision.

Executing leadership vision may be among the toughest core competencies for leaders to develop. To successfully execute your leadership vision, you must be able to define the vision, strategy, and tactical plan for your organization, and then effectively communicate it to your team in a way that engages and focuses them around a common goal. The three secrets to successfully executing your leadership vision are defining and communicating your vision, strategic vision, and planning and prioritizing for long-term goals.

Define and Communicate Vision

What happens when you lead a team with no vision? Everyone ends up working, and often working quite hard, but important goals are never achieved. A vision brings the team together under a common goal so that your team is not simply working, but is working together to create something that moves you closer to realizing your leadership vision.

Leadership vision is a vivid, aspirational picture of the future of your organization. It is long-term and measurable. Your vision answers the question: Where are we going? You need to be crystal clear in your definition of what that destination looks like, even if you do not yet know exactly how you are going to get there. This definition gives you and your team the ability to know exactly where you are located within the vision at any given time and whether you are getting closer to or further away from that destination. That destination must be exciting, not just to you and the people on your leadership team who may have helped you craft it, but also to the people who are charged with fulfilling it. It is not enough to simply define a vision, you also must create buy-in from your team and your stakeholders to execute it.

Space X is an aerospace organization with the vision to enable human life on Mars. There are many obstacles in the team's path to achieving that vision. Advances in human understanding and technology to sustain life on the trip to the red planet have not yet been accomplished. That does not deter individuals on the Space X team from trying because, as they put it on their website, they were "founded under the belief that a future where humanity is out exploring the stars is fundamentally more exciting than one where we are not." Inspiring? Absolutely.

Buy-in starts with how clear and exciting your leadership vision is, but it's only sustained through the way you communicate it, celebrate it, and live it every day. People need to understand your leadership vision, be reminded of it, and see how you role model your vision to remain personally invested in it. But, perhaps most importantly, they need to understand the context and its overall intention. They need to understand the Why. Why are we going there?

Strategic Thinking

When a financial news magazine asked executives what makes the world's most respected companies truly great, the top factors they name are having strong management and a sound business strategy. Although great strategic thinking may be among the rarest of executive skills, it is certainly one of the most important.

Your strategy defines how you will achieve your leadership vision based on a number of internal and external factors. Vision is the search for meaning. Strategy is the route that we take to get there. It is simply the search for advantage, and it also ensures you are planning for potential issues in your market. Both of these things factor heavily into our strategic thinking because the strategy can never be done in the absence of destination, and the destination cannot be reached without a clear route.

Strategic thinking can be developed by constructing "memories of the future." When you think back to one of your fondest past memories what comes to your mind? You may vividly see people with whom you share the memory; see your surroundings; and sense the sights, sounds, and smells that were around you at that time. Do you recall how you felt during this memory?

That is exactly the clarity you need to create your memory of the future. What is it that you see, hear, experience, and feel? Make your leadership vision as clear as though it has happened to you already, and then you can start constructing the route—the strategy—that will take you there. This route should be a 2- to 3-year trip, and you must be able to measure your progress.

Being a great strategic thinker does not mean being able to do it all alone. In fact, it is the opposite. You must always find ways to bring in different views and perspectives about your business to inform your thinking. Your direct reports and external advisers can help you identify that your ideas and assumptions are free from confirmation bias, or that you are willing to walk away from the herd in your industry.

Plans and Prioritizes

An aspiring young manager in a small U.S.-based medical supply organization found out the hard way how vision and strategy without a plan leads to burnout and frustration. He went to work for the organization largely because he felt connected to the energy of the CEO who was innovative, energetic, and full of great ideas. The young man felt compelled to work under him as a role model and a mentor. He was initially ecstatic to land the job, and the first year seemed to offer him the chance to participate in exciting growth. The manager loved getting to know the industry and working with his colleagues. He believed in the CEO's leadership vision and the mission of the organization and truly felt as though he was going to make an impact.

But, as the first year turned to the second, the manager began to feel the wear of misused time and unfocused energy. The CEO continually came up with great new ideas—ideas that never left the conference room. Due to a lack of structure, focus, and follow-through, the CEO would simply float the idea without assigning responsibility or structure to anyone. As a result of misdirected goals, this young man and the rest of the team became overextended and frustrated. They moved numbly from one idea of the week to the next, never truly completing a project or celebrating a win.

Your team needs structure and a plan to execute your leadership vision. They need to achieve closure and key wins related to their work, which they are pouring their energy and expertise into accomplishing, on a daily basis.

Your leadership vision is what drives the actions of your team, and although internal and external factors may force you to adjust your strategy and plans, the mission should remain unchanged. Define a clear, compelling leadership vision that you and your team can enthusiastically support. Then communicate it and continuously demonstrate your own commitment to your vision. Think strategically about the factors that drive your organization or team and develop a strategic plan that is realistically optimistic, unbiased, and influenced by multiple perspectives. The achievement of your strategy will be determined by how well you implement and monitor your annual plans and key initiatives.

Core Competency: Executes Vision

Considers a broad range of internal and external factors when creating strategies and implementing plans. Translates business vision and strategy into plans and sequenced priorities to best deliver results and leverage resources.

Executes Leadership Vision Competency Skills

- Define and Communicate Vision: Communicates a compelling picture of the future that connects and motivates others to action.
- Strategic Thinking: Sees the big picture of future possibility and creates strategic connections leading to competitive advantage.
- Plans and Prioritizes: Formulates objectives and priorities, implements and monitors plans in alignment with the long-term strategy of the organization.

Executes Leadership Vision Toolkit

To get your team thinking about vision and communicating a compelling picture of the future, facilitate the following exercise:

1. Assign small groups (no more than six members to each group) and have each group select a facilitator.
2. Task each group to develop an aspirational headline and visual cover story about your organization ten years in the future.
3. Allow for a few minutes of individual thinking time, and then the group facilitator selects a person to start the story.
4. The story continues to build as it moves around the group and each member adds specifics to the story.

Role of Optimism in Leadership

Optimists make strong leaders since they are open to innovation, demonstrate big picture thinking, inspire employees, and deal with adversity with a positive attitude. Intel co-founder Robert Noyce once said that optimism is "an essential ingredient of innovation. How else can the individual welcome change over security, adventure over staying in safe places?".

Trilby Johnson wrote, "Money follows joy. Joy does not follow money." In the Hospitality industry, employees are taught the tenants of customer service and achieving or exceeding guest satisfaction. That is not easily done without a positive attitude and a smile. When you think of the industry's most inspiring stories around guest service, you think of stories like the one Horst Schultze, founder of Ritz Carlton told about one of the night bellmen in his current company, The Capella Hotel Group, who accompanied a guest with appendicitis to the hospital and stayed with him all night. Yes, that takes a caring soul and an empathetic leader, but when you think about those who stand out, they are almost always joyful, warm and optimistic.

Optimism of your Potential Leader

Joy is a state of mind. "Being joyful requires feeling connected to other people in life, with nature, by appreciating the arts, and it requires an acceptance of life, as it is, in the present. Some believe that joy is a conscious commitment to be happy, to have a sense of contentment for the moment, despite life's challenges." states Cheryl McDonald, PsyD.

It is a long-held belief that people prefer leaders who have a happy, joyful, and optimistic attitude. It requires so much less energy than being around someone who is negative or pessimistic. When we look at some of the best leaders, people like John Fitzgerald Kennedy, Mahatma Ghandi, and Martin Luther King come to mind, and business leaders like Jamie Dimon, Elon Musk, and Jeff Bezos also rise to the top of most lists.

This extends to leaders like Chris Nassetta at the helm of Hilton. He loves to say "yes!" Those who are closest to him know this is just who he is. He genuinely enjoys being in front of guests, employees, and his close-knit team.

In November 2016, Arne Sorenson wrote about the passing of his 89 year old mother whose "optimistic spirit" shaped who he is today. He tells of the story of her life challenges growing up in the Great Depression and the optimism that many in her generation had. She overcame a lot and raised one of the most thoughtful and successful leaders in today's day. Now at the top of the largest hotel company in the world, the pressure is intense for people like Arne to marry optimism with realism and to face life with gratitude and joy. Or is it? Is it hard to choose to be joyful?

When looking for potential leaders, either internally or externally, organizations would benefit from using assessment tools to look for positive traits such as optimism, resilience and empathy. Using assessment tools provides robust data to guide selection and succession decisions and helps ensure that candidates are a good cultural fit.

Traits of a Charismatic Leadership

These charismatic leaders have a quality which is hard to pin down, but which attracts followers and inspires people to action. Transformational leaders are often highly charismatic because they are capable of initiating and maintaining a significant level of change in the organization.

The following are some of the most prominent characteristics of charismatic leadership.

Communication

Charismatic leaders have extraordinary skills in communication. This helps to motivate employees through tough times and also help them stay grounded when things are good. The leaders are equally comfortable communicating one-to-one or in a group setting.

Maturity

Though they have a very powerful personality, a charismatic leader also has maturity and character. They don't believe in empty showmanship, but they draw on their wisdom and knowledge which they have accumulated over the years of life and business experiences. They behave in a mature and responsible manner on all occasions.

Humility

Charismatic leaders also have a sense of humility. They place a lot of value on each employee, and have the ability to truly listen to their concerns. The charismatic leader is able to convince the employee of the value that they bring to the organization, and show them how their contributions impact the strategic interests of the company. They inspire great loyalty from their employees.

Compassion

Successful charismatic leaders are also compassionate. Charisma alone may not be enough, because there's a very real possibility that it can disintegrate into mere hero worship. Compassion, integrity, honesty, and fortitude are also qualities that successful charismatic leaders exhibit.

Substance

Charisma can exist without substance, but only for a very short time. Flashy and glitzy behavior may capture the attention of people, but eventually they will want something substantial beneath the facade. A charismatic leader must not only talk the talk, but also walk the walk. Charm gets him the face time, and substance closes the deal.

Confidence

It goes without saying that charismatic leaders are truly confident. They are the glass half full kind of people, and are comfortable with who they are. They understand themselves well and do not try to be anyone else. Charismatic leaders are secure and confident enough to be comfortable in their own skin.

Positive body Language

One of the first things that you'd notice about a charismatic leader is their warm, open, and positive body language. They make eye contact with were that they are talking to, smile, and introduce themselves to strangers with the genuine joy of making a new contact. They have an endearing swagger, and they are authentic.

Listening Skills

Charismatic leaders are extremely good listeners. When they listen to you, they don't fidget or look distracted. A charismatic leader pays attention to what is being said, and listens with interest. They are engaged in the conversation and act with empathy.

Self-monitoring

One of the attributes of charismatic leaders is that they often tend to watch themselves. They are aware of their powerful personality, and the fact that their followers are watching them constantly. For this reason, they consider it important to portray a good image of themselves to their followers. This can be achieved only with self-monitoring.

Self-improvement

A charismatic leader understands that he has certain qualities that make him different from others, and that these are the qualities that get him attention and make him charismatic. So he also knows how important it is to continually improve himself.

Traits of an Ethical Leader

Ethical leaders always know how to do the right thing. It may be difficult to define exactly what "right" is, but a leader who is ethical is not afraid to do what they truly believe to be right – even if it is unpopular, unprofitable, or inconvenient.

Here are 10 ethical leadership characteristics:

Justice

An ethical leader is always fair and just. They have no favorites, and treat everyone equally. Under an ethical leader, no employee has any reason to fear biased treatment on the basis of gender, ethnicity, nationality, or any other factor.

Respect others

One of the most important traits of ethical leadership is the respect that is given to followers. An ethical leader shows respect all members of the team by listening to them attentively, valuing their contributions, being compassionate, and being generous while considering opposing viewpoints.

Honesty

It goes without saying that anyone who is ethical will also be honest and loyal. Honesty is particularly important to be an effective ethical leader, because followers trust honest and dependable leaders. Ethical leaders convey facts transparently, no matter how unpopular they may be.

Humane

Being humane is one of the most revealing traits of a leader who is ethical and moral. Ethical leaders place importance in being kind, and act in a manner that is always beneficial to the team.

Focus on Teambuilding

Ethical leaders foster a sense of community and team spirit within the organization. When an ethical leader strives to achieve goals, it is not just personal goals that they're concerned about. They make genuine efforts to achieve goals that benefit the entire organization – not just themselves.

Value Driven Decision-making

In ethical leadership, all decisions are first checked to ensure that they are in accordance with the overall organizational values. Only those decisions that meet this criterion are implemented.

Encourages Initiative

Under an ethical leader, employees thrive and flourish. Employees are rewarded for coming up with innovative ideas, and are encouraged to do what it takes to improve the way things are done. Employees are praised for taking the first step rather than waiting for somebody else to do it for them.

Leadership by Example

Ethical leadership is not just about talking the talk, this type of leader also walks the walk. The high expectations that an ethical leader has of employees are also applicable on the individual level. Leaders expect others to do the right thing by leading from example.

Values Awareness

An ethical leader will regularly discuss the high values and expectations that they place on themselves, other employees, and the organization. By regularly communicating and discussing values, they ensure that there is consistent understanding across the organization.

No tolerance for Ethical violations

An ethical leader expects employees to do the right thing at all times, not just when it is convenient for them. Don't expect a leader of such high values to overlook or tolerate ethical violations

Leadership Values and Workplace Ethics

Leaders know what they value. They also recognize the importance of ethical behavior. The best leaders exhibit both their core values and their ethics in their leadership style and actions. Your leadership ethics and values should be visible because you live them in your actions every single day.

A lack of trust is a problem in many workplaces. If leaders never identified their values in these workplaces, the mistrust is understandable. People don't know what they can expect. If leaders have identified and shared their values, living the values daily-visibly will create trust. To say one sentiment and to do another will damage trust possibly forever.

To walk your talk as a leader is the most significant way in which you demonstrate why employees can trust you and that you are an ethical and principled leader.

Dr. Duane C. Tway calls trust a construct because it is constructed of these three components: "the capacity for trusting, the perception of competence, and the perception of intentions."

Workplace ethics take the same route. If the organization's leadership has a code of conduct and ethical expectations, they become an organization joke if the leaders fail to live up to their published code. Leaders that exhibit ethical behavior powerfully influence the actions of others.

To really make a difference in your organization, you need to do all three. There are few statements supporting this view:

> "Within the organizations, in which we have had the opportunity to serve, the core values were communicated by actions mostly—in the ways in which business is conducted on a day-to-day basis, and not so much in words directly spoken or written.

"I am a strong advocate of demonstrated values more than written or spoken—actions speak louder. But, I also believe that written values that reinforce and support specific actions, and specific actions that reinforce and support written values, make a powerful combination. Their power far exceeds the power of one or the other by itself. If it is written down and demonstrated in action, we can really hold our feet to the fire when we need to."

Choose your Leadership Values

The following are examples of values. You might use these values as the starting point for discussing values within your organization:

Ambition, competency, individuality, equality, integrity, service, responsibility, accuracy, respect, dedication, diversity, improvement, enjoyment/fun, loyalty, credibility, honesty, transparency, innovativeness, teamwork, excellence, accountability, empowerment, quality, efficiency, dignity, collaboration, stewardship, empathy, accomplishment, courage, wisdom, independence, security, challenge, influence, learning, compassion, friendliness, discipline/order, generosity, persistence, optimism, dependability, flexibility, reliability, responsibility, customer service.

As a leader, choose the values and the ethics that are most important to you, the values and ethics that you believe in and that define your character. Then live them visibly every day at work. Living your values is one of the most powerful tools available to you to help you lead and influence others. Don't waste your best opportunity to deeply engage the minds and hearts of your workers and customers.

Consciously Choose your Organization Values

Organizations that are effective, customer-centric, and employee-oriented, develop a clear, concise and shared meaning of values/beliefs, priorities, and direction within their organization.

They want every employee to understand the values, contribute to the values, and live the values. Once defined, the values should impact every aspect of your organization.

You must support and nurture this impact or identifying the values will have been a waste of your time. People will feel fooled and misled unless they see the impact of the exercise within your organization every day.

Leaders must lead in every aspect of selecting and living organization values.

Examples of Workplace Values

These samples of workplace values were developed by several organizations with facilitation by their leaders.

A Human Resources Development office chose these values as a reflection of how they want the organization to perceive them.

- Integrity,
- Belonging/Caring,
- Helping/Contributing,
- Inner Harmony, Peace of Mind,
- Personal Growth, Learning, and Self-Actualization,

- Achievement/Accomplishment,
- Financial Stability,
- Fun.

A University Student Health Center staff developed the acronym "I CARE" as a tool for remembering and expressing values. In the final document, each word is defined by a series of value statements which describe how the value is expressed in their workplace.

- Integrity.
- Compassion.
- Accountability.
- Respect.
- Excellence.

Characteristics of a Successful Leadership Style

Much is written about what makes successful leaders. This series will focus on the characteristics, traits and actions that many leaders believe are key.

- Choose to lead.
- Be the person others choose to follow.
- Provide vision for the future.
- Provide inspiration.
- Make other people feel important and appreciated.
- Live your values. Behave ethically.
- Leaders set the pace through your expectations and example.
- Establish an environment of continuous improvement.
- Provide opportunities for people to grow, both personally and professionally.
- Care and act with compassion.

Compassion in Leadership

It has been researched that many leaders refrain from showing compassion at their work place. There are multiple reasons due to which they do so, discussing some of these below:

- Showing compassion would mean agreement with the subordinates: Many people think that being compassionate would mean that they are agreeing with whatever have been done by subordinates, which is not true. One can always be compassionate and simultaneously not defend the performance of the subordinate. An effective leader can always make statements like "I think u have landed in a real hard situation because of yourself, still I feel for you. Good luck."
- Being compassionate means you cannot hold people accountable:This is wrong thinking. You can be compassionate and simultaneously you can hold others accountable for not meeting the high expectations set on them. An effective leader should ambiguously sketch the expectations from the followers in terms of their behaviour, conclusions and effect. Recurring assessments should be done. It should be ensured that the followers understand the expectations set on them.
- Being compassionate means falling into the trap of caterpillars: Being compassionate doesn't mean that you are responsible for other person's feelings. Sometimes you need to just listen effectively, put across your concern for the persons, and possibly assist them in discovering solutions for non work issues. Being compassionate means you are not only supporting your organization and your followers but you are also helping yourself.

Sometimes leaders show compassion only towards appropriate and zero error people, which is not correct. Compassion should be shown to all people who work with you, are ready to act efficiently and who look towards you for support when they land in trouble. Even if they are stuck in some bad situation, an effective leader should try to respond and show compassion to them.

- Being compassionate can encourage healthy relationships as well as can ensure a more empathetic work environment: Compassionate leaders always put others needs before their own. They create a tuning with others thoughts and feelings. But the problem is during the process of stress releasing, leaders themselves go into stress as unavoidable result of leading. But effective leaders know how to handle the stress created at workplace. Fact is that compassion should be firstly created and found within, only then it can be shown to others.

Thus, effective leaders should be compassionate. They should ensure clear and transparent communication with the employees and clients. They should set an example for others. They should ensure expression of their emotions both precisely and candidly.

An effective and compassionate leader should keep in mind the effect of his words and statements on others. He/she should deal with their emotions very efficiently and optimistically. He/she should leave rigidity and try to be flexible. This is because being compassionate leads to positivity in the organization. It also encourages healthy relationships. It boost up the energy levels of people within the organization aswell as ensures flexibility. It offsets the adverse reactions of favouritism and bias.

To conclude, compassionate leaders are effective leaders. A leader possessing compassion trait will always be optimistic. He would be sensible enough, i. e., he would be conscious about his own feelings, about impact of his words on the followers and he would be focussed on others needs and feelings. He would be very much responsive and would show empathy to others. Compassionate leaders are in fair situation of dealing with crisis, encourage followers to better actions and are effective and efficient communicators.

References

- What-is-leadership-ways-to-define: game-learn.com, Retrieved 3 May, 2019
- Self-motivation-for-leaders: managementstudyguide.com, Retrieved 12 April, 2019
- Leadership-traits-list, soft-skills: corporatefinanceinstitute.com, Retrieved 18 February, 2019
- Forward-thinking-key-traits-of-leadership: ohmanufacturing.org, Retrieved 7 June, 2019
- Honesty-is-the-core-of-leadership: thehrdigest.com, Retrieved 6 March, 2019
- Intelligent-leadership: johnmattone.com, Retrieved 28 January, 2019
- How-to-develop-leadership-competencies: educba.com, Retrieved 30 July, 2019
- Importance-inspirational-leadership-reshaped-world: chieflearningofficer.com, Retrieved 13 January, 2019
- Secrets-to-leadership-vision-success: crestcomleadership.com, Retrieved 2 March, 2019
- The-role-of-optimism-in-leadership: onpointconsultingllc.com, Retrieved 22 August, 2019
- Charismatic-leadership-characteristics: yscouts.com, Retrieved 10 May, 2019
- Ethical-leadership-characteristics: yscouts.com, Retrieved 21 February, 2019
- Leadership-values-and-workplace-ethics: thebalancecareers.com, Retrieved 24 April, 2019
- Importance-of-compassion-in-leadership: managementstudyguide.com, Retrieved 14 June, 2019

5

Leadership Practices and Challenges

There are various practices and challenges which are associated with the role of a leader. Primary among these is the ability of team building. The leader also plays an integral role in strengthening the bonds between team members. The chapter closely examines these key concepts of leadership practices and challenges to provide an extensive understanding of the subject.

Team Building

Working on a successful team is an important learning experience for future leaders. It demonstrates that not everything can be done by one person, and shows them what it takes to create a team. A leader who's been part of a good team will be able to build good teams because she knows what they look and feel like.

One of the most important tasks of leadership, in fact, is being able to put together a good team and to support its members in doing their best.

Team

Everyone knows what a team is: a group of people working together toward a common goal, right? Well, yes and no. A team is a group with a common goal, but lots of groups have a common goal. And a team works together, but lots of groups work together. The members of the United States Congress work together toward a common goal (making the laws that are best for the country), but each member has her own private interests and beliefs her own agenda. The Congress is no more a team than is a soccer "team" of six-year-olds, each of whom plays as if he's the only person on the field.

A team is a group of people with a commitment to one another, to the team, to a high level of achievement, to a common goal, and to a common vision. They understand that team success depends on the work of every member.

A good team functions as a single organism. Not only do members work together toward a common goal, but they complement and support one another so that their work seems effortless. Compare that soccer team of six-year-olds and their individual agendas with the Brazilian national team in its heyday. Everyone seemed to know not only what all his teammates were doing, but what they were going to do. Passes always hit their mark, as if there were some sort of mysterious force among team members that directed their kicks. Obviously, their "magic" was the result of endless practice, but it was also the result of a shared passion for accomplishment and a shared vision of just that effortless, automatic play that made all other teams look clumsy.

So a team has a shared interest in accomplishment and a shared vision, both of which are different from a shared goal. The need for accomplishment provides a driving force. The vision provides not only a goal, but directions and a compass for reaching it. It keeps everyone moving in the same direction, at the same speed, working together to create as little friction and as efficient a journey as possible.

One of the ways that teams reduce friction is through their members' commitment to working as a team. They're willing to give up most of their need for individual recognition for success in reaching the goal. It's the accomplishments of the team as a whole that become important, and members of good teams hold themselves and one another accountable.

When it's working well, a team is more like a single individual doing a lot of things at once than it is a conglomeration of single individuals, each doing their own thing. The whole becomes greater than the sum of its parts: the team can accomplish more as a team than all its individual members could achieve if each were working alone.

Team Building

So how do you create that kind of team, a group of individuals that functions as a single unit, even if each has a different task? There are really two ways to look at team building. The first is putting together a team from scratch for a specific purpose. That purpose may be for the short term (e.g., running a fundraising campaign with a limited scope) or much more momentous and lengthy (starting and staffing a long-term initiative meant to change the community permanently).

Members of teams need three kinds of skills: technical or functional (i.e., the expertise in the field that they and the team are working in); problem-solving; and interpersonal. The ideal would be to find individuals who embody all these skills, but the reality is you'll probably have to choose some people specifically for each of these strengths. All are obviously important. Effectively accomplishing the tasks of the team requires technical and functional skills; approaching those tasks in a reasonable way calls for a high level of problem-solving skills; and keeping the work of the team from being derailed by internal conflict, jealousy, or other similar issues demands a great deal of sensitivity and interpersonal skill.

In addition to looking for skills, you have to find the right people for the right jobs on the team, and assemble a group that fits together well. Judging how people will fit in with one another is a matter, to some extent, of following hunches, listening to what your instincts tell you about personalities and the ways people present themselves, the kinds of words they use, their body language, etc. These are often as important as their backgrounds and training for determining whether they would be good additions to a particular team.

In some ways, assembling a team from scratch is easier than the second type of team building, which requires turning that group you've just hired or an already-existing group into a real team that works well together. In the case of an already-existing group, you have few choices about who's going to be a member. There may be long-standing antagonism or conflict between some of the people involved, or some may be difficult personalities to deal with. If people weren't chosen to fit together in the first place, they may or may not fit together well now.

Building a team in this second sense takes strong leadership and a vision that the team can buy into. In addition to trying to help team members learn to work together as a unit, you have to find ways to build commitment to the idea of a team and to the team itself, as well as to meeting the challenge the team has been given. Sometimes, an existing group is already a team, or almost a team. They may already share a vision, and have some idea about how to realize it. If that's not true, however, it can take a lot of time and effort to make it true, and you have to be willing to be patient.

Advantages and Disadvantages of Teams

Putting together a team of skilled people may be the best choice for accomplishing a particular task or it may not. Like most other ways of addressing tasks, teams have advantages and disadvantages. Some of their strong points include:

- A team broadens what individuals can do. Team members gain from the fact that being part of a group makes it possible to do things they couldn't necessarily do alone. A good team supports and enhances the skills and learning of its members, and brings out the best in them. Humans are, after all, social animals, and, as a species, we've worked in teams for a long time. Try killing and butchering a mammoth single-handedly.
- Several heads mean a wider range of ideas. Teams can be more imaginative than individuals, and come at things from a larger number of perspectives.
- Teams can have a greater array of talents and skills than can be found in a single individual. That obviously increases both their effectiveness and the variety of what they can address.
- Team members learn new skills from their colleagues. This increases their own range, and also constantly broadens the team's capabilities.
- Teamwork is more efficient than a number of individuals working solo . The members of a good team know how to assign tasks to the appropriate people, and how to coordinate what they're doing for the maximum effect.
- Teamwork provides relief when someone is having a problem. There is always backup and help available, and the stress is less because you're not the only one doing the job.
- By the same token, the fact that each member knows he's responsible to others works to make him more effective. No one wants to let others down, or to be seen as the weak link. When a team is working well, all its members are aware of their parts in the overall mission, and try to make sure that others' work isn't wasted because of them.
- A team member has more ownership of what she's doing. She's involved in the planning of the team's actions, and she can see how her job fits into the larger purpose of the team and the organization. She doesn't feel like she's working in a vacuum.
- Good teams can build leaders. They give everyone a chance to show what he can do, and to exercise leadership when that's appropriate.
- A shared vision keeps everyone moving forward.

That's a pretty impressive array of strengths, but there are weaknesses as well.

- Team decision-making takes longer than individual decision-making, and can be a great deal more difficult.
- Depending upon the task or problem, team effort can be wasted effort. Some things can be more easily dealt with by individuals.
- The team's success may hang on the work of the weakest or least effective team member.
- Once a team gets rolling in a particular direction, even if it's the wrong direction, it develops momentum. It may be harder for a team than for an individual to get back on a better track.
- Especially at the beginning when members are still getting familiar with one another, the work of teams can bog down in interpersonal issues, resentments, and blame.
- On the other hand, once team members are bonded and committed to one another and the team, they may be reluctant to tell others when their work is unsatisfactory or to point out that the team isn't getting anywhere.
- Individuals on the team may lose motivation because of the lack of individual recognition for the value of their work. The balance between team effort and individual recognition is a delicate one.

Need of Building Teams

Social psychologists have looked at the differences between the ways people perform when there are others around and when there aren't. From these observations have come some general guidelines for when a team is likely to be more effective than an individual. Some of the most important are:

- The people in the team, in general, have the skills to tackle the task at hand.
- The task requires the complementary skills of a number of people.
- The task specifically requires several people (moving a piano, for instance).
- The success of the task is not based on the performance of the weakest team member.
- Team members have experience working in teams.
- The perceived importance of the task is high.
- Group commitment to the task is high.

Not all of these conditions need to be obtained for a team to be a good choice, but some should. The more of them that are present, the more likely that a team will be successful.

By the same token, the negatives of these guidelines (e.g, people in general don't have the skills to handle the task) indicate that a team is not likely to be an effective way to deal with the task at hand. In addition to those negatives, teams are unlikely to be necessary or successful when one expert member alone is capable of handling the task, and when there is an immediate deadline.

Given those guidelines, a team can be used in almost any situation that requires the work of several people. There are, however, some particular times when teams might work especially well.

- Creating a strategic plan for addressing community issues. A participatory approach to planning would involve building a community team to develop a strategic plan.
- Starting up a new organization or initiative. You might form a community team to plan for a new entity.
- Starting a new program or intervention within an organization or initiative. A community team might plan or begin to implement a new intervention.
- Starting a coalition. Once again, a community team might be helpful in getting a new coalition planned and going.
- Planning and carrying out a community assessment. A diverse team to plan, communicate with the community, gather and analyze information, and report on findings would make for an accurate and efficient assessment.
- Evaluating an organization, initiative, or intervention. Evaluation is often best accomplished by a team of evaluators who bring different perspectives to the process.
- Spearheading an advocacy campaign *with a specific goal.* Here, a team to handle communication, outreach to the community, and contact with legislators and other policy makers could make all the difference.
- Running a fundraising event or campaign. Whether you're putting on a tag sale to finance a new printer, or trying to raise $50,000 to support your initiative, a good team can spread the work around, and make success more probable.
- Staffing and running an organization or initiative. Staff members might be organized into teams with each team having responsibility for some area of the work of the entity. Another possibility here, especially in smaller organizations, is that the whole staff functions as a single team, working toward a shared vision.
- Engaging in ongoing advocacy. A team approach might make advocacy more effective, especially if team members represent different elements of the population.
- Performing a particular function within a community program or initiative. Many health and human service organizations form teams to address specific issues or populations. A health clinic might have a physician, a social worker, a nurse -midwife, one or two physician's assistants or nurse practitioners, and some RNs all working together as a team to assess and treat families. Mental health centers often take a team approach, with a case manager and several therapists serving a number of people. Child care providers, teachers (especially in middle schools, where the team approach is standard), street outreach workers, and others often also work in this way.

- Changing the community over the long term. Community organizing and community development are long-term processes. They're often difficult and frustrating, and they rely on the dedication of those engaged in the work. A team approach not only makes more activity possible, it keeps everyone involved aware of what everyone else is doing. This means that the team can be more efficient and not duplicate services, and that it has the ability to change what it's doing as new information comes in. Mutual support can also add to a team's effectiveness and staying power over the long haul.

Aspects of Good Team

Every good team is not the same, but really good ones often have a number of similar characteristics. In their book, Organizing Genius: The Secrets of Creative Collaboration, Warren Bennis and Patricia Ward Biederman looked at six famous groups, including the Manhattan Project team, to understand the factors that foster creative collaboration. Here are their 15 "Take Home Lessons"about "Great Groups. A "Great Group" is Bennis and Biederman's version of Katzenbach and Smith 's "high-performance team":

- Greatness starts with superb people: Those who see things differently, have a knack for finding interesting and important problems, have skill in problem solving, see connections, and are "deep generalists" with broad interests and multiple frames of reference.

- Great Groups and great leaders create each other: The best leaders create and maintain situations in which others can make a difference.

- Every Great Group has a strong leader: Leaders might act as "pragmatic dreamers" with original but attainable visions, as "curators" who recognize and select for excellence in others, as coordinators of volunteer associations around "great projects," or as "conductors" who understand the work and what it takes to produce it.

- Leaders of Great Groups love talent and know where to find it: Talented people smell out places full of promise and energy where the future is being made. Leaders help connect groups to networks of people, ideas, and resources that enhance the group's work. More diverse networks increase the chances that new connections will be made. Participants know that their inclusion in the group is a sign of excellence.

- Great Groups are full of talented people who can work together: Members accept their responsibilities to share information and advance the work. They tolerate personal idiosyncrasies, and try to be good colleagues who advance the common purpose.

- Great Groups think they are on a mission from God: Members believe that they are doing something vital. The work is more a crusade than a job. A powerful vision helps them see losses as sacrifice. Their clear, collective purpose makes everything they do seem meaningful and valuable. Members of older generations tell newer ones what they are doing and why, and how new members can contribute.

- Every Great Group is an island, but an island with a bridge to the mainland: People trying to change the world need to be isolated from it, free from its distractions, yet able to tap into its resources. The work should be intense and fun.

- Great Groups see themselves as winning underdogs. They are feisty. They are Davids slinging fresh ideas at Goliath. They see themselves as wily opponents in the face of bigger competitors.
- Great Groups always have an enemy: They are involved in a "War on Drugs" or a "War on Poverty." This raises the stakes of the competition, helping the group rally and define itself.
- People in Great Groups have blinders on. They have a passion for the task at hand. They are unusually devoted to the work.
- Great Groups are optimistic, not realistic: They are talented people who believe that they will accomplish great things together. The difficulty of the task adds to its joy.
- In Great Groups the right person has the right job. Talented people are allowed to do the work they are best suited to doing.
- The leaders of Great Groups give them what they need and free them from the rest: Leaders help bring in a "worthy challenge," a task that enables people to use their talents fully. They provide the tools needed for the work, and help share information and ideas by convening weekly colloquia in which problems and dilemmas are addressed and new ideas are explored. They help members manage stress, model and support a climate of civility, and protect the group from the broader institution and environment.
- Great Groups ship: They are places of action, not merely think tanks. They do hands-on work that delivers products and services by deadlines.
- Great work is its own reward: They are engaged in solving hard, meaningful problems. The work matters to people to those served and to those doing it.

Elements of Team Building

Building a good team involves a great deal more than simply choosing members. That's only the first step, and you may not even have the chance to do that if you're working with an already-existing group. Developing and communicating a vision, planning the team's mission to match the vision, working out how people will function together, and then fine-tuning it over time are only some of the other elements of team building.

The following are guidelines, and are not meant to be a step-by-step guide to team building. Some elements of the process may get worked out over time in the course of the team's activities. Others may reach critical points and be dealt with then. Each team is unique, and there is no single formula for success or excellence.

Choosing Team Members

Whether you're hiring new staff people especially for a team, or choosing from among the existing staff members of an organization, there are a number of factors to consider.

- Start with the best people you can find. No team is any better than its members, and finding the best people for the jobs at hand is tremendously important. "Best" doesn't always simply mean someone who can do the work better than anyone else, however. Someone may be a terrific practitioner, but difficult to work with, or jealous of others' successes. It may make more sense to choose someone who's only second best (although still very good) at the work, but better at being a member of a team.

- Choose team members so they'll have a good fit. The issue of fit was mentioned earlier, and it can't be overstressed. In order for team members to fit together well, they must connect on a number of levels.
    - Personality: People don't necessarily need to become best friends, but they need at least to respect, and, better yet, to like one another. They're going to be spending a lot of time together: it's far more conducive to the team's success if time spent together is seen as pleasant. In addition, the more people like and respect one another, the more they'll communicate, and the more loyalty they'll feel to the team and its work. Both of these conditions add to the effectiveness of the team. As team members are chosen, therefore, it's essential to consider whether each person is likely to get along well with the others, and what she'll add to or take away from the personality of the team.
    - World view: Especially in health, human service, and community work, it's important that the overall goals of everyone involved be similar. If some team members see participant empowerment as paramount, and others see participants as annoying and obstructive, there will be friction. Not only will team members disagree and perhaps work against one another, but the whole purpose of the team's work will be weakened. It's vital, therefore, that the basic vision of the team's purpose be shared. In choosing team members, people's attitudes and general world views need to play a large role.
    - Work ethic: Team members don't have to be workaholics, but they need to have similar work ethics and similar conceptions of what doing a good job means. If that's the case, then no one will get upset because he's doing more work than others, or because one person isn't pulling his weight.
    - Ability to use disagreement and conflict well: Team members need to be able to disagree positively, and to use their disagreements and differences about the work to come up with better solutions. They have to be willing to voice those disagreements, because disagreement is often a wellspring for good ideas. At the same time, they have to be able to remove such disagreements from the personal, and look at them as problems to be solved with creativity and mutual respect.
- Look for members with a diversity of backgrounds and perspectives. It seems obvious that the more different frames of reference that can be brought to bear on an issue or a community, the better. Teams that are diverse in a number of ways background, training, culture, etc. Bring a range of skills and perspectives to the work they do. Choosing team members with an eye for what they bring to the mix can create a more dynamic and creative group.
- Look for members with a commitment to the concept of working as a team. Teamwork often requires that people put aside their individual interests in order to accomplish the team's goals. Team members need to understand just what it means to work as part of a team. They have to be willing to compromise especially when they know they 're right and

to maintain a team atmosphere of civility and mutual respect. More to the point, they have to check their egos at the door if the team is to work well.

- Look for team members committed the team's guiding vision. The vision may be one that's jointly developed, or it may already exist before the team is formed. In either case, belief in it and a willingness to strive toward its realization are a large part of what will make a team successful in the long run. Anyone you choose needs to have the passion needed to make that kind of commitment, and the sense of the world that will allow commitment to the team's particular vision.
- Find people with a sense of humor. The work of community-based and grass roots organizations and initiatives is always hard, often frustrating, and seldom pays well, if at all. People need a sense of humor and fun attitude to maintain their enthusiasm, and to deal with the disappointments or failures that are an inevitable part of even the most successful efforts. The gallows humor that some people find appalling in health and human service situations is often just as necessary to the smooth functioning of the organization as the competence and devotion of the staff in the work they do.

Once a group of team members is assembled (whether by hiring, by choosing from among the staff of an existing organization, or by taking an existing group) has to be turned into an actual team. The less care taken in assembling the group, the more difficult this task will be. All of what follows applies both to teams chosen carefully for specific purposes and to preexisting groups that must become teams. Some of the points, however, (working out personal issues, or making the team concept clear) are particularly relevant for those groups not as carefully selected.

- Start with the vision. As mentioned several times above, a team needs a vision to be passionate about. This vision can be developed in a number of ways:
    - It may be the vision of a strong and creative leader. A transformative leader has a vision that draws others with it.
    - It may simply be putting flesh on the bones of what the team is already doing. Changing the form of the work of an organization to a team approach, for instance, may not involve a change in vision, but simply a clearer statement of, or a new commitment to, what has already been the organization's goal and purpose.
    - It may be a group vision. One way to start is to get it to develop its guiding vision. For a team where the leadership is collaborative, the vision almost has to come out of a group process. Where there is a designated leader, she can simply join the group in developing the vision, so it will be hers also.
    - It may come out of an organization-wide or community-wide strategic planning process. The vision may speak directly to the needs of the community or of the target population.

Regardless of how the vision is arrived at, the team needs to buy into it if it is going to be successful. That means either the vision has to be consistent with what team members are already committed to, or that they have to be part of its development.

- Build team bonds. At the outset, it's often useful to build cohesiveness through some type of bonding activity appropriate to the nature of the group (e.g., You wouldn't take a team of seniors on a rigorous wilderness experience.) Some possibilities:

- A retreat: A full-day or several-day meeting in a place where team members can get to know one another and develop their commitment to the team and its purpose.
- Specific bonding activities: Activities where success is only possible through teamwork. Where it's physically possible, Outward Bound-type activities like rock climbing, mountain hikes, or cooperative games can serve these ends. Group problem-solving, perhaps centered on the team's task, is another possibility. Laughter is an important element here, as well as the chance to work together.
- Socializing: Preparing and eating meals together, doing some enjoyable activity such as a picnic, making music, going to a play, etc. with or without families, can create ties among team members.
- Creating team traditions: Eating lunch together, a regular lunchtime or after work card game, fake "awards," or a continually passed-on e-mail story that everyone contributes to can help cement the team.

- Make sure that the concept of a team is absolutely clear, and that everyone understands what that means for themselves.
- Involve the team in jointly planning how it will function and what the team and each of its members will do. The more control team members have over their work, the more likely they are to do it well.
- Address personal issues: (This may be an ongoing necessity. It should start at the formation of the team in order to try to resolve issues as early as possible.) Any personal issues that get in the way of the smooth functioning of the team need to be confronted and resolved at the beginning. Some of these can be worked out privately with a single person, while others may need the whole group's attention. Some common issues to address:
    - Conflicts or other issues between or among members of the group: You can't necessarily make people like each other. But you can insist that they face and resolve conflicts, that they be civil, and that they not let their antagonism get in the way of the work of the team.
    - A need for individual recognition: Individuals may put themselves forward constantly (correctly or incorrectly) as the originators of ideas, the solvers of problems, the driving force behind team successes, etc. There are times when this is appropriate, but if it's constant, it can destroy the cohesiveness of the team.
    - An inability to compromise or let go of ideas: Flexibility is a prime characteristic of a good team member. It's important to put ideas on the table, but it's also important to understand when to let go of them, or to incorporate some aspects of them into someone else's conception for the sake of progress.
    - Lack of commitment to the work: In order for a team to function well, every member

has to believe in what he's doing, and do his job as well as he can. If folks aren't committed to the work, that simply won't happen.

Problems arising from these kinds of issues can be the hardest to solve, but if they're left to fester, they can destroy a team.

- Establish team norms: Teams should be in agreement about the ways members treat one another and how issues are resolved. The team standards should be generated by the team as a whole, and hashed out so that everyone sees them as fair and reasonable.
    - Areas that might be covered include:
- Civility: Even in the heat of argument, there should be general agreement that name-calling, personal attacks, threats, and the like are off limits. Discussion can be heated, but shouldn't threaten the glue that holds the team together.
- Conflict resolution: There should be clear avenues for dealing with conflict that minimize the possibility of leaving it unresolved, or of it resulting in permanent splits between or among team members.
- Communication: Team members need easy and direct access to one another, and also need to pass information around quickly and efficiently, so that no one is left out of the loop. Establishing systems to maintain this level of communication is an important piece of team formation.
- Responsibilities: Team members already know their job responsibilities, but they also need to understand their personal responsibilities for maintaining the team. Someone having a problem with another team member's behavior, for instance, should be responsible for bringing it up in the appropriate way, rather than waiting for the other to change, or for someone else to notice and take care of it. Other similar responsibilities might include helping to keep everyone focused on the task, offering help when others are struggling, calling attention to problems in the work or among team members, etc.
- Importance of the team and the mission: It can't be forced, but it adds greatly to team effectiveness if one of the norms is that the collective goal comes first, and if everyone on the team buys into it. If that can be established, the team is almost sure to be successful.
- Hash out the logistics of working as a team: How does a team work best? Your team needs to establish how it can do its best work. Who's going to be responsible for what? (Remember that a good team assigns its members the tasks at which they're most competent.) What kind of meeting, conference, and consultation schedules can you establish to make sure that everyone always knows everything she needs to know? How can you keep team thinking and decision-making dynamic, i.e. able and ready to change a course of action or an idea when needed? All of these and many other questions must be addressed in order for the team to work smoothly and well.

One possible way to approach some of these issues is to confer with other successful teams, either within or outside of your organization. They may be able to help you avoid some of the mistakes that they made, and to guide you to some questions you may not have thought of asking.

- Start the team with a task that is both doable and requires teamwork to accomplish. As in spring training for baseball, this will give people a chance to practice working as a team on something relatively simple. Starting with a success will help cement the team, and give it a positive outlook upon which to base its work.
- On a regular basis, go back over both successes and failures to understand what happened and learn for the future. It's important to look at errors and failures as chances for learning, not occasions for blame.
- Provide both individual and team support: Make sure that everyone has what she needs to do her job. Pay attention to team members' personal needs as well. They'll work better if they don't have other things gnawing at them. If they need flexibility because of the needs of small children or elders, make sure they have it. If it will help the team to have food or amusement, or just space available for breaks, see what you can do about accommodating it. If people need resources such as a library, access to particular Internet sites, etc., try to provide it for them. If someone needs an afternoon off, make sure she takes it. In other words, do everything you can to make people happy, comfortable, and functional. It will pay dividends in quality of work life and quality of work for everyone.
- Give people something extra for working as a team: You can pay people more if you have the money to. More likely, you can offer them more flexibility, more power over their jobs, a better chance at successfully achieving their shared vision, better working conditions and quality of working life. Whatever it is, offer something to let people know you appreciate what they're doing.
- Reward accomplishments like crazy: Reward the whole team for successes, and reward individuals for particularly good work. You may want to institute a system whereby team members recommend their colleagues for recognition. Use praise unsparingly, and criticism only when it's absolutely necessary, and your team will accomplish wonders.

Leadership Tips to Manage Every Type of Team

The biggest concern for a leader is to get a job well done. Success only comes after that. In any company, we will find many different types of people to work with. These are the 10 tips to leading every type of team:

Be a Nonconformist

Great leaders constantly challenge their teams. They don't resign themselves, but demand the very best from their workers. Successful leadership will drive the business to the top, and in order to do that it will first encourage the team to get the best out of them.

Learn from Mistakes

Everybody makes mistakes, and so do leaders. The difference is that a good leader will take a mistake as a master class from which to get the best learning, so as to keep focused on success and good results.

Getting Things Done

Leaders spend much of their time managing teams and coordinating people. That may take away from them time to "execute", i.e. to "make things happen. The key to strong leadership is to find ways to make things happen and not let it all be just words.

Know your Business and your Team

In order to make the right decisions and have a unique style to lead our teams successfully, it is necessary to know the business and the people working with us. The leader must look after receiving reliable and complete information directly from their team.

Be Realistic

Oftentimes, the leading style in organizations is the one that lives exclusively on ideals and is unable to analyze reality objectively. Successful leaders must also be realistic, without fearing the fact of facing difficult or unpleasant situations. A good leader maintains the eagerness and is optimistic, without losing sight of the reality around them.

Set Proper Goals and Priorities

The best leadership style is the one that gets to define goals as clearly and concisely as possible. Similarly, learning to prioritize is essential for successfully managing teams and maximizing available resources. Defining our goals and priorities in a clear way will get things actually done.

Monitor

Good leaders must delegate tasks to their teams and trust them until the full implementation of that which has been commanded. However, successful leadership underlines the importance of monitoring tasks, as well as the goals and objectives of the entire organization.

Reward the "Executors"

Leaders always know who those ultimately responsible for getting things done are. Those team members who produce tangible results should be rewarded for their good work. This form of leadership that "rewards" will spread the spirit of improvement and everyone will fight for their rewards.

Bring out the Potential of your Team

The leadership that makes a difference is the one that cares about developing the skills of their team members. Motivating everyone is a guarantee to a better performance. In addition to the rewards previously mentioned, helping them improve in their area will increase everyone's level of commitment to the company.

Work on your Leadership Everyday

Leaders never lose their inspirational spirit. Working on developing our leadership is a constant task in good leaders: read, take courses, go to congresses, participate in conferences, do research on other leaders. In short, develop your leadership every day so as not to stray from the path to success and happiness.

Role of Leader in Strengthening the Bond

As a leader, your primary job is to motivate and guide your team to reach their goals. However, you won't be able to accomplish this if your team doesn't feel a sense of trust and loyalty to you.

One of the best things you can do to establish that connection with your team members is focus on building strong personal relationships with them. It takes time and ongoing effort, but maintaining those relationships is well worth it to have a committed, collaborative team.

Hold Regular Individual Meetings

Established, regular touch points with a leader builds confidence and relationships. An "open door" policy doesn't cut it. As a leader, you must reach out to your team, not the other way around. Have short meetings with a basic agenda where your team member can share his/her thoughts, concerns and ideas. You can also give constructive feedback for their personal development on an ongoing basis.

Include Everyone in Decision Making

The easiest thing leaders can do on a regular basis to strengthen relationships with their reports is to include them in decision making. Asking "What do you think" or "What are your thoughts" will begin to build trust, engage reports and provide a sense of responsibility. When there is shared decision making, morale is higher. Inclusivity brings trust, engagement, responsibility and motivation.

Ask For Feedback on your Management Style

We're used to managers giving feedback to their reports, but how often do you ask for it? "How we doing as a leader and what can our do better?" can be the most powerful questions you can ask. At first, it will be strange for a report to give the honest answer. But when you can get to the point where you are getting honest answers and using that feedback to grow, relationships build quickly.

Make Time for Small Talk

Employees want their leaders to get to know them as human beings, not just workers. In addition to task-oriented conversations, ask your people what they did over the weekend, not just if it was a good weekend. Inquire about the family or vacation photo on their desk. Listen well. Showing your employees that you care about them as humans and not just "task completers" will go a long way.

Ask, Listen, Respond and Recognize

Too often, leaders get so caught up in the day to day, they forget their reports are people with feelings. People perform at a much higher level when they know they're seen, heard and valued. To communicate this, take time every week to ask your reports what's working and what's not. Listen to their answers. Respond with solutions. And recognize a job well done on a regular basis.

Be Transparent about your Mission and Methodology

Sharing your methodology regularly with your team helps strengthen the communication lines between leader and reports. Showing you care about their development and their goals both personal and professional makes you an invaluable mentor.

Once your team understands your mission and methodology it creates a common language, forming a common bond that both parties can work off of for years to come.

Focus on the S.M.A.L.L. Things

The key to building relationship currency is through authentic connections. Leaders can do this consistently by remembering the S.M.A.L.L. things: Show thanks often; Motivate your team; Acknowledge and award hard work; Lead by example; and Learn from your team as much as you teach. The S.M.A.L.L. model creates a two-way exchange you can build on.

Be Thoughtful

Leaders should know their reports personally as well as professionally. This means doing at least a little something for their birthday, knowing preferences that come up daily (she likes tea, not coffee), genuinely asking about their kids, their spouse or their pets, and noticing when something is off. If someone is overly tired or uncharacteristically upset, inquire if they want to share and listen.

Act on their Feedback

Many leaders have regular weekly or monthly meetings where brainstorming and feedback occurs. Often when the meeting ends, that is where the creative ideas die or are put on the shelves with no further actions taken. An easy way to strengthen relations is to simply value their feedback and to implement their ideas. When employees feel heard, a new sense of employer/employee connectedness happens.

Acknowledge your Employees with a Smile

It sounds so simple, but when we humans are stressed and/or are in deep in thought, our jaw clenches, resulting in a look of annoyance. To add perceived insult to injury, leaders who are driven by urgency and a destination become myopic and may fail to recognize those around them. A simple acknowledgment of reports will alleviate the fear that the leader is "mad" or unapproachable.

Challenges of Leadership

Leadership constantly presents challenges to a leader and their abilities. These challenges are an incitation to rise to another level, to test yourself and improve in the process, and to show that you can accomplish something that may seem difficult or even impossible.

Being a leader is in itself a challenge. The challenges of leadership are really of three kinds: external, coming from people and situations; internal, stemming from within the leader himself; and those arising from the nature of the leadership role.

External Challenges

It's almost impossible to imagine a situation where a leader doesn't have to cope with external challenges. In an organization, such issues as lack of funding and other resources, opposition from forces in the community, and interpersonal problems within the organization often rear their heads. Social, economic, and political forces in the larger world can affect the organization as well. To some extent, the measure of any leader is how well he can deal with the constant succession of crises and minor annoyances that threaten the mission of his group. If he is able to solve problems, take advantage of opportunities, and resolve conflict with an air of calm and a minimum of fuss, most of the external issues are hardly noticeable to anyone else.

If the leader doesn't handle external challenges well, the organization probably won't, either. We've all seen examples of this, in organizations where everyone, from the director to the custodian, has a constantly worried look, and news is passed in whispers. When people feel that leaders are stressed or unsure, they themselves become stressed or unsure as well, and the emphasis of the group moves from its mission to the current worrisome situation. The work of the group suffers.

Internal Challenges

While leadership presents to each of us the opportunity to demonstrate the best of what we are, it also exposes our limitations. In many cases, good leaders have to overcome those limitations in order to transmit and follow their vision. Fear, lack of confidence, insecurity, impatience, intolerance (all can act as barriers to leadership. At the same time, acknowledging and overcoming them can turn a mediocre leader into a great one.

It's often very difficult for people, especially those who see themselves as leaders, to admit that they might have personality traits or personal characteristics that interfere with their ability to reach their goals. Part of good leadership is learning to accept the reality of those traits, and working to change them so they don't get in the way.

Challenges Arising from Leadership Itself

Real leadership makes great demands on people. As a leader, you are responsible for your group's vision and mission, for upholding a standard, often for being the group's representative to the rest of the world and its protector as well. These responsibilities might be shared, but in most organizations, one person takes the largest part of the burden.

In addition to its responsibilities, leadership brings such challenges as motivating people - often without seeming to do so - and keeping them from stagnating when they're doing well. Leaders also have to motivate themselves, and not just to seem, but actually to be, enthusiastic about what they're doing. They have to be aware of serving their group and its members and all that that entails. In other words, they have to be leaders all the time.

Most Obvious Leadership Challanges

One obvious - and correct - answer to this question is "all the time," but in fact some times are more likely than others. Leadership is usually the most difficult when the situation is changing or unstable. When a grass roots group is doing well - gathering allies, getting its message across, attracting funding - no one much notices what the director does; but when something unexpected happens, she's expected to take care of it, often in a very public way.

Some particular times when challenges may arise:

- When something new is about to start: When you're beginning a new intervention, trying something different in a program that's been running for a while, stepping up to another stage in your initiative, or hiring a new leader, no one is quite sure what's going to happen. Systems and relationships can break down, and it's often a matter of leadership as to whether the new situation is successful or not.
- When something is about to end: Often at the end of a school year, a particular project or initiative, a training period - anytime when something is coming to an end and things are, by definition, about to change - times get difficult. That may be because of a big push to get finished, or because it's tough to tell what's coming next, or because a close-knit group is splitting up. Whatever the reason, it often takes leadership skills to make sure that the project ends successfully, and everyone moves on to the next phase, whatever that is.
- When times are tough: If there's not enough funding, or an organization or group is being publicly criticized, for instance, its leader usually has to try to solve the problem in some way: find money, reduce expenses, defuse the attacks. Leaders are tested when times are difficult.
- During transitions: There are many ways in which a group can be in transition. It may go - because of a grant or because of other circumstances - from a loosely organized, grass roots collective to a much more formally structured organization. It might grow quickly even too quickly. It might be losing some key people, or changing leaders. One of the most difficult tasks a leader faces is trying to keep a group stable through a period of change.

The challenges of leadership are ongoing and occur daily. Knowing when the greatest challenges are likely to arise, however, can prepare you to meet them successfully.

Ways to Cope up with Challenges

As we discussed above, there are challenges that come from external sources (other people, situations), from internal sources (within the leader herself), and from the circumstances of leadership. We'll examine each of these categories, and consider some strategies for addressing them.

External Challenges

The world surprises us at every turn, throwing up barriers where the way seems clear, and revealing broad highways where there seemed to be only brick walls. Both kinds of surprises -

sometimes the positive more than the negative - present opportunities for exercising leadership, with all the challenges they entail. Some common situations that call for leaders to use their resources include:

- Public criticism, especially uninformed criticism, of your group or mission.
- Flare-ups of others' interpersonal issues, either within the group or outside it.
- Crises, which could be tied to finances, program, politics, public relations (scandals), legal concerns (lawsuits), even spiritual issues (loss of enthusiasm, low morale).
- Disasters. These are different from crises, in that, in a crisis, something important (usually negative, but not always) seems to be happening, and you're trying to control the situation. In a disaster, the worst has already happened, and you're trying to deal with that in some way.
- Opposition and hostility from powerful forces (business groups, local government, an influential organization, etc.)
- A financial or political windfall. Sometimes an unexpected benefit can be harder to handle than a calamity.
- Collaboration with another group or organization may call upon a leader to define clearly the boundaries within which he can operate, and to balance the needs of his own group with those of the collaborative initiative as a whole.

This is by no means a comprehensive list, and most Tool Box users will be able to think of many other possibilities from their own experience. It's clear, however, that leaders are often tested by external events and people. What are some of the general strategies they can use to cope with these and other external - and therefore often unpredictable and uncontrollable - circumstances?

Cope with External Challenges

Be Proactive

Regardless of the situation, it's important for leaders to do something. Waiting is occasionally the right strategy, but even when it is, it makes a group nervous to see its leader apparently not exercising some control.

Be Creative

Try to think "outside the box," i.e. in unexpected but effective ways. If disaster has struck (you've just lost a major source of funding, perhaps), how can you turn what looks like the end of the world into a new beginning? Can you change the way the organization operates to deal with the loss? Can you use the fact that you're about to lose services to gain community and political support? Is this an opportunity to diversify your funding? Can you expand your horizons and your reach through collaboration? Don't just look at the obvious, but consider a situation from all perspectives, and search for unusual ways to make things work.

Face Conflict Squarely

This doesn't mean come out fighting, but rather identify and acknowledge the conflict, and work to resolve it. This is true both for conflict within your group, and conflict between the group and others outside it. Far too many people, leaders included, act as if conflict doesn't exist, because they find it difficult or frightening to deal with. As a result, it only grows worse, and by the time it erupts, it may be nearly impossible to resolve. If it's faced early, nearly any conflict can be resolved in a way that is beneficial for everyone involved. It's a function of leadership to have the courage to name the conflict and work on it.

Always Look for Common Ground

If there's opposition to what you're doing, it may only be to one specific part of it, or may be based on misunderstanding. There are few groups or individuals who don't have some common interests. If you can find those, you may have a basis for solving problems and making it possible for people to work together.

Retain your Objectivity

If you're mediating a conflict within the organization, don't take sides, even if you think you know one side is right. That will come out if you mediate objectively and well. If you're faced with detractors or opposition, don't automatically assume they're villains. What are their concerns, and why do they disagree with what you're doing? Don't get sucked into a fight unless there's really no alternative. Even rabid opposition can often be overcome through a combination of respect, political pressure, and creative problem solving.

Look for Opportunities to Collaborate

This is important both within and outside your group or organization. Within the group, involve as many people as possible in decisions, and make sure they have control over what they do. The more they own their jobs and the organization, the more enthusiastic they'll be, the more effective the organization will be, and the more effective you'll be as a leader.

Outside the organization, try to forge ties with other organizations and groups. Let them know what you're doing, get and give support, and work with them to the extent you can. Make common cause with other groups that have similar interests. In numbers, there is strength, and you'll be stronger as an alliance of groups than any one of you could be individually.

Internal Challenges

Leaders are human. That's hardly news, but it means that they come with all the same problems and failings as everyone else. One of the greatest challenges of leadership is facing your own personal issues, and making sure they don't prevent you from exercising leadership. Acknowledging the attitudes and tendencies that get in your way, and working to overcome them, is absolutely necessary if you're to become an effective leader. Among the most common personal traits that good leaders have to overcome or keep in check are:

- Insecurity: Many people feel, at least some of the time, that they're not up to the tasks they face. They may even believe that they're fooling people with their air of competence, when they know they're really not very capable at all. Insecurity of that sort keeps them from being proactive, from following their vision, from feeling like leaders. It can be crippling to both a leader and her group or organization.

- Defensiveness: Also born of insecurity, defensiveness shows up most often as an inability to take criticism (other people might catch on to the fact that you're as incompetent as *you* know you are), and continuing hostility to anyone, even an ally, who voices it. Defensiveness often also includes a stubborn resistance to change ideas, plans, or assumptions, even if they've been shown to be ineffective.

- Lack of decisiveness: Sometimes it's hard to make a decision. You never know till later - and sometimes not even then - whether you made the right decision. Maybe if you had a few more facts The reality is that leaders are called on to make decisions all the time, often with very little time to consider them. It is important to have as much information as possible, but at some point, you just have to make the decision and live with it. Some decisions are reversible, and some are not, but in either case, it's important to learn to make a decision when necessary and understand that living with the consequences is part of being a leader.

- Inability to be direct when there's a problem: Many people want so badly to be liked, or are so afraid of hurting others, that they find it difficult to say anything negative. They may be reluctant to tell someone he's not doing his job adequately, for instance, or to address an interpersonal problem. Unfortunately, by letting these things go, they only make them worse, which makes them still harder to address. It's essential to learn when firmness is necessary, and to learn how to exercise it.

- Inability to be objective: Neither looking at situations through rose-colored glasses nor being always on the edge of hysteria is conducive to effective leadership. Just as objectivity is important in dealing with external issues, it's important to monitor your own objectivity in general. There's a difference between being an optimistic individual and being unable to see disaster looming because it's too painful to contemplate. By the same token, seeing the possible negatives in an apparently positive situation is not the same as being paralyzed by the assumption that calamity lurks around every corner. The inability to accurately identify the positive and negative in any situation and react appropriately can create serious problems.

- Impatience - with others and with situations: It may seem, given the importance of decisiveness and firmness, that patience is not a virtue a leader needs. In fact, it is perhaps the most important trait to develop. Situations do not resolve themselves instantly, and anyone who's ever been involved in an organization knows that Rule #1 is that everything takes longer than you think it will. People in unfamiliar situations need a while to orient themselves. Leaders who are impatient may make rash decisions, may alienate staff members or volunteers or allies, and can often make situations worse rather than better. It's hard to be patient, but it's worth the effort.

Again, this list is far from complete, but it includes many of the most common stumbling blocks that leaders throw in front of themselves. Fortunately, there are some strategies that can be used to identify and remove those stumbling blocks, or at least cut them down so you can jump over them more easily.

Coping with Internal Challenges

Listen

Listen to people's responses to your ideas, plans, and opinions. Listen more than you talk. Listen to a broad range of people, not just to those who agree with you. Probe to find out why they think or feel the way they do. Assume that everyone has something important to say. If you hear the same things from a number of different and diverse sources, you should at least consider the possibility that they're accurate. If they're about things you do that you can change, you might give it a try.

Ask for 360-degree Feedback and use it

This is feedback (people's views of you) from everyone around you - staff, volunteers, Board, participants, people from other organizations or groups yours works with - anyone you work with in any way. As with listening, if you hear the same thing from a lot of different sources, it's probably true. Act on it. All the feedback in the world won't do you any good unless you do something with it.

Look at what's Going on Around you

Are you the center of controversy and chaos? Or do calm and good feeling seem to reside wherever you do? The chances are that the answer lies somewhere in between these extremes, but it probably should be closer to the calm and good feeling side. Even if you're involved in a battle with the forces of evil, you can foster calm in yourself and those you work with. At the same time, your group could be on top of the world, and you and your colleagues could still be climbing the walls if that's the kind of atmosphere you create.

Reach out for help in Facing Internal Challenges

Most of us find it difficult to change entirely on our own. A psychotherapist, a good friend, a perceptive colleague, or a trusted clergyman might be able to help you gain perspective on issues that you find hard to face. Many people find meditation or some form of self-discovery helpful in understanding themselves and in getting through change. Don't feel you have to do it all on your own.

Challenges Stemming from the Nature of the Leadership Role

A leadership position brings with it unique demands. Leaders can be looked on as authority figures, as saviors, as fixers of things that are broken, as spiritual guides, as mentors, as models, as inspirers, as teachers in short, they may be seen however others choose to see them. This in itself carries a set of challenges, in addition to those posed by what all leaders indeed have to do in order to keep things going. Some of the issues that leaders have to cope with specifically *because* they're leaders are:

- *Keeping an eye on, and communicating, the vision.* As the guardian of a group's vision, it's up to the leader to remind everyone of what that vision is, to keep it in mind in everything the group or organization does, to protect it from funders or others who would try to change it and to make sure it *does* change, if necessary, with changes in circumstances, the needs of the target population, or the available information. That means not being distracted from the bigger picture by day-to-day issues (even as those issues are addressed and resolved). It also means not substituting another, lesser goal (getting enough funding to start a specific program, for instance) that may be contrary to the true vision of the organization.

- Keeping the everyday under control while you continue to pursue the vision: You can't maintain the vision without making sure that there's paper in the printer, that you understand the legal implications of an action you plan to take, that people know what they're supposed to be doing on a given day, that there's enough cash in the bank to meet payroll, and that there's someone there to answer the phone, to pay the bills, and to look for funding. These aren't necessarily all things a leader has to do herself (although there are certainly organizations where that's what happens), but she's responsible for making sure they get done, and that things run smoothly. No matter how transformative she is, no leader can accomplish much if the infrastructure doesn't work.
- Setting an example: If you want others in the group to show mutual respect, to work hard, to embrace the vision and mission of the organization, to include everyone in their thinking and decisions, you have to start by doing those things yourself, and behaving in the ways you want others to behave. A leader who yells at people, consults no one, and assumes his word is law will intentionally or unintentionally train everyone else in the group to be the same way. A leader who acts collaboratively and inclusively will create an organization that functions similarly.
- Maintaining effectiveness over time: One of the hardest lessons of leadership is that you're never done. No matter how well things go, no matter how successful your group or organization or initiative is - unless it's aimed at accomplishing a very specific, time-limited goal - you have to keep at it forever. Even if you get a bill passed or manage to get money for your cause included in the state budget, you have to work to maintain your gains. If you're running a community intervention, you have to recruit participants, refine your methods, do community outreach, raise funds...indefinitely. Maintaining effectiveness is a matter both of monitoring what you do and working to improve it, and of keeping up enthusiasm for the work within the group. It's part of the leader's role to maintain his own enthusiasm and drive, and to communicate and transfer them to others.
- Avoiding burnout: This is a challenge not only for leaders, because a burned out leader can affect the workings of a whole organization. Leader burnout is a product of being overwhelmed by the workload, the frustrations, the stress, and the time demands of the position, multiplied by the number of years spent in it. It can reach a point where the leader no longer cares about the vision, the work of the group, or anything but when he can go home. By that point, the rest of the group is likely to be struggling, feeling rudderless and uncertain. It's crucial that leaders learn to recognize the signs of burnout and - depending on where they are in their lives and a number of other factors - either find ways to renew their commitment or leave.

- *Finding support.* Cliches often become cliches because they're true. It is lonely at the top, largely because a good leader tries to make things go smoothly enough that others aren't aware of the amount of work she's doing. The leader may have no one to share her concerns with, and may have to find her own satisfaction, because others don't recognize the amount and nature of her contribution. The buck may stop with her, but where then does she unburden herself? As mentioned earlier, leaders are human. They need support and comfort as much as anyone else, and it's important that they find it.

Coping with Challenges Stemming from the Nature of the Leadership Role

So how can you continue to be a leader and also continue to be a functioning human being? There are things you can do to retain both your sanity and your competency.

Create Mechanisms to Revisit your Vision

Hold occasional meetings and at-least-yearly retreats to discuss vision and renew commitment. These will serve both to review the vision to see if it still resonates (and to rework it if necessary), and to renew your and others' purpose and pursuit of it. They'll help to remind you of why you're doing this in the first place, give you an opportunity to work on group solidarity, and - ideally - leave you feeling refreshed and ready to carry on.

Share the Burden

Surround yourself with good people who share your vision. If you can find others who are competent and committed to whom you can delegate some of the tasks of leadership, it will both remove pressure from you, and make your group stronger. One of the greatest mistakes a leader can make is to be threatened by others' abilities. In fact, sharing responsibility with capable people makes all of you more effective, and strengthens your leadership.

Having competent people to depend on also means that you can develop systems and know they'll work. Organizational maintenance becomes much easier, and you have more time to devote to the actual pursuit of your vision.

Find an Individual or Group with whom you can discuss the Realities of Leadership

In many communities, some heads of organizations meet on a regular basis to talk about the difficulties and rewards of their situations with others who truly understand. Some such arrangement can be a valuable hedge against burnout, and can also help you gain insight into how you function as a leader. It can introduce you to alternative ways of doing things, as well as giving you a chance to vent, and to realize you're not alone.

Make sure you have Personal Time

The founder and director of a prominent think tank once went seven years without a day off - including Sundays. That's 2,557 straight days of work. (That includes two leap year days, for those of you doing the math.) Even if that doesn't cause burnout, it's not good for your creativity or your understanding of the world. Everything becomes work or related to work: the world holds no other reality, and leadership becomes all you do.

In order to maintain perspective and to keep yourself fresh, you need to take time away from being a leader, and away from your organization or initiative. It's important to have an activity that gets you away from your daily concerns, and to take days off from time to time. Some people meditate every day, others play music regularly, others participate in sports or fitness activities. Your get-away doesn't have to be an everyday thing, but it should be something you love and look forward to, and it should be frequent and regular. It may be as simple as taking a walk with your kids for an hour every evening - whatever it is that relaxes your mind and feeds your soul. Rather than detracting from your effectiveness, your time off will increase it.

Depending upon how you approach it, leadership can be a hard and lonely road, or an exciting and collaborative trip to a new place. The more, and more useful, strategies you can find to cope with its challenges, the better leader you'll be.

Motivation and Inspiration

Being the leader of a team is a huge responsibility, regardless of whether you're the CEO, department manager, or supervisor.

As a leader, it's your job to inspire and motivate the others on your team to work to the very best of their abilities. Being an effective leader demands a number of qualities and characteristics that encourage those around them to succeed.

Provide a Vision and Purpose

Create an inspiring vision of the future that also gives your team a purpose - something to look forward to, and something to work towards. Make this vision achievable and realistic and work with your team towards achieving this goal. Think of practices or services that could help make both yours and their job easier. Use personal stories and anecdotes to explain your vision and inspire your team members, it will make you more relatable and less of a separate entity.

Set Clear Goals

Set clear goals for completing a project so that your team knows what is expected of them. Ensure that your team agrees with goals and deadlines you have set, and can identify with them on a personal level. This way they can be motivated to work harder and achieve those goals, boosting productivity levels in turn. Making sure that your team are in agreement and happy with goals and deadlines you have set will help them feel more involved in their work.

Lead by Example

One of the most powerful motivational tactics you can use is to lead by example. Working hard, showing professional integrity, and having a can-do attitude are all qualities that will have a positive effect on your team members.

If your team recognises that you value the time and effort they put into their work, and you demonstrate the same actions and values you expect from them, it will inspire them to do the same.

Encourage Teamwork

Encourage members to work together as a team by stressing the importance of and the connection between teamwork and achieving group goals. Note the fact that when people work together, work is much easier and quicker to do. You can further motivate your team by linking performance with team goals.

Encouraging teamwork will help individual team members feel less isolated and separate from the workplace. Employees will feel more engaged and a part of a larger community, inspiring them to work harder and enjoy what they do.

Be Optimistic and Positive

Having a positive attitude and an optimist outlook, even when times are tough, can inspire your team members to adopt the same attitude and outlook and continue to work hard. Remaining positive will show your team that it's not the end of the world if things are going wrong, and keep them focused on the greater picture.

You can also help motivate your team by reacting positively to goal or project completion, and to the skills and abilities that each member brings to the team. Make them feel valued and appreciated, and your team will work harder.

Give Praise and Rewards

This is one of the best ways to inspire and motivate your team to work harder. When you praise one person in front of others, it encourages them to work harder or perform better, simultaneously motivating the others to work hard in order to be praised. When a reward is linked to performance, people will work even harder and be more committed to their task in order to win the reward.

Communicate with the Team

You should be contactable at all times so that your team members can ask you questions about a project, get your opinion, offer ideas, and give feedback. Being available for your team plays a key role in motivating them, as it shows that you value the project and their feedback. Making yourself more available also avoids making your team members feel isolated and separate from management. Ensuring you're always available for your team can boost productivity and improve the quality of your work.

Empower Team Members

When you give team members the power or authority to do something with complete control, this helps to motivate them to complete the work. You can also keep motivating your team members to work hard and bring out the best in them by offering constructive feedback. This will result in an empowered, happier, and more productive team.

Leader and Conflict Management

Conflict resolution is a daily occurrence at work that can either propel or disrupt the momentum for a leader, a team or the entire organization. The workplace can become a toxic environment when leaders allow conflict to fester rather than confront it head-on. Managing conflict can be a tricky thing – especially when you are not familiar with the larger ecosystem in which the particular individual or department creating the conflict operates, and how efforts to resolve conflict will reverberate throughout that ecosystem. The workplace is fueled with so many concurrent agendas that you never know which ones may be affected when you resolve conflict solely to benefit and advance your own.

Leaders must act responsibly to be respected. Leadership is not a popularity contest; it is a serious responsibility that primarily involves developing and guiding the full potential in people, teams and the organization at-large. An important part in the process of developing potential is knowing how to see conflict and when to seize the opportunity within the conflict before healthy tension turns into overly disruptive chaos.

Many leaders would rather avoid tension to create the appearance of harmony. What they don't realize is that by avoiding tension all together they are unknowingly creating silos and internal disruption amongst employees. A leader must be expected to neutralize or minimize conflict, not allow it to grow and run rampant.

Unfortunately, in their attempts to keep the peace at work, leaders often create artificial, untrustworthy environments. This is what happens when you are more concerned about being well-liked, avoiding a negative reputation, or being put into a situation that might reveal your leadership vulnerabilities.

To help you create and sustain workplace momentum, employee engagement, and healthy outcomes, here are four ways to deal with conflict resolution at work.

Right Timing

People often create unnecessary conflict. Leaders who avoid conflict at all cost will find themselves regretting it later. Timing is everything when it comes to managing conflict, and the best time to take action is when there is hard evidence/proof that an employee has a track record of wrongdoing that is negatively impacting the performance of others.

If everyone around you knows it must be dealt with and you are still waiting to act, you are losing the respect of your peers and those you lead. Leadership is about taking action and confronting the issues before it's too late. If you wait too long during times of adversity, those around you will begin to make the decisions that you were hesitant to make – and you lose momentum as a leader. When others see that you are not mature enough as a leader to act, this puts your leadership reputation at risk.

Know your Boundaries

Conflict can become something much more complicated and unmanageable if you don't know the limitations and boundaries of your employees. Everyone deals with conflict differently, so you must know the risks and rewards of conflict resolution within the boundaries of each of your employees.

Help others know when they tend to cross the line through careful observation; identify behavioral tendencies that seem to trigger certain attitudes, provoke mindset shifts, or demonstrate a lack of self-awareness. This can be accomplished with consistent coaching sessions where you can begin to set precedence and reinforce performance expectations for each of your employees. This not only allows you to identity their conflict boundaries but more importantly to establish standards that will help prevent conflict from arising.

Leaders who actively engage in coaching and learning about those on his/her team will find themselves dealing with much less conflict. The new workplace represents a growing diversity in the types of people that we lead; you must get to know who they are if you want to understand how they will influence the ecosystem you are trying to create.

Respect Differences

Rather than impose your influence, hierarchy or rank – respect the unique differences in people and learn to see things from differing points of view so you can better understand how to avoid conflict in the future. Conflict resolution is rarely black and white. In fact, there are more and more grey areas these days as the workplace becomes more generationally and culturally diverse than ever before.

Beyond the understanding of how conflict could have been avoided, respecting differences in people can help you better understand how to manage conflict with people in general (and their boundaries as noted in point two).

Common sense tells us that we are most comfortable dealing with those we trust and naturally gravitate towards. As leaders, we must see that each employee represents a unique opportunity for professional growth and development. Business is all about people intelligence, and until we accept this fact, we will continue to unknowingly create tension with those employees we are not comfortable with – and undervalue their contributions in the process.

Confront the Tension

Leadership is often about doing the things that most other people don't like doing. Conflict resolution is one of those things – but as leaders we must confront the tension head-on. Don't wait, but rather activate your leadership to address the conflict before circumstances force your hand.

Conflict can yield an emotional state of mind that makes it more difficult to manage it. As such, we must confront rather than allow it to fester because we failed to address the adversity when it first became apparent. Adversity is very big when it is all you can see. But it is very small when in the presence of all else that surrounds you.

Perception is not always reality and oftentimes we don't confront the most obvious situation before us because we let other points of view distort what we believe to be true. The most effective leaders have the self-awareness and wisdom to confront and diffuse the tension. Conflict resolution is much like any other form of adversity. You either act or you don't. How many times has your gut told you to take action when dealt with adversity, but instead you waited until those around you took the calculated risks that you were hesitant to take yourself?

Leadership is about anticipating the unexpected. Don't complicate matters. Trust yourself enough to take action.

Conflict resolution is about seeing opportunities that others don't see. When dealing with conflict resolution through a lens of opportunity, conflict can be a healthy enabler of growth for your business –and professional growth for all of the people involved. Effective leaders know that the most authentic relationships with their employees, clients and external partners don't truly begin until they experience some form of tension with them.

Leadership and Conflict Resolution

Leadership involves defining and communicating an organization's long-term vision and mission while conflict resolution typically deals with the situation at hand. By articulating what you want to accomplish, providing support for talented subordinates, overcoming obstacles, exploiting opportunities, demanding excellence, behaving ethically, you set a good example for your organization. An effective leader builds teams that work well together. As a leader, you facilitate the resolution of conflicts that distract the team members, decrease productivity, destroy motivation and lead frustration and anger. You also recognize that some conflict is natural and necessary to produce innovative solutions to problems, encourage meaningful communication between team members and leads to clarification and cooperation. Using the Thomas-Kilmann Conflict Mode Instrument, developed in the 1970s by conflict resolution experts Kenneth W.Thomas and Ralph H. Kilmann, you can identify the best way to handle conflict in your organization.

Competitive

Leaders use their position, expertise or persuasive ability to exercise control over their subordinates. In an emergency situation, when a decision needs to made quickly, you typically use the autocratic leadership style to resolve the problem. On an ongoing basis, however, to prevent conflict from festering in the organization, effective team leaders take the time to gather input from subordinates and refrain from behaving as if decisions represent a win or loss for subordinates.

Collaborative

By using the participative leadership style, you foster an environment of cooperation and collaboration that typically enables employees to function effectively as a team. An effective leader quickly diagnoses issues that hinder team productivity, takes prompt corrective action to resolve disagreements and helps the team members to develop the skills necessary to resolve conflicts on their own, without management intervention.

Compromising

By compromising, both sides in a conflict give up something in order to gain an agreement. Effective leaders encourage team members to accept concessions when necessary to maintain a level of productivity rather than continuing to debate or argue. They help team members overcome interpersonal conflicts and promote acceptance of other cultures and experiences in the workplace.

Accommodating

To meet the needs of the team, a team member may surrender his position. When the stakes are low, accommodating the needs of others can promote harmony and foster a productive work environment. However, long-term conflict can arise if more aggressive individuals take advantage of team members who don't act assertively. Effective leaders monitor their team environment and provide coaching and mentoring to members that enables them to function productively together without operating at the expense of others.

Avoiding

When a conflict involves a controversial or unpopular decision, resist the temptation to ignore or avoid it. By defining the root cause of the problem, encouraging active listening, negotiating a resolution and reminding participants to forgive each other once the conflict is over, you can foster a productive team. However, effective leaders also recognize that delegating conflict resolution to a third party, such a facilitator or mediator, can be effective in a situation where emotions remain high even after lengthy discussion.

References

- Team-building, leadership-ideas, leadership: ku.edu, Retrieved 21 March, 2019
- Leadership-tips-to-manage-team: game-learn.com, Retrieved 19 May, 2019
- Easy-ways-to-strengthen-your-bond-with-your-team-members: forbes.com, Retrieved 11 July, 2019
- Leadership-challenges, leadership-ideas, leadership: ku.edu, Retrieved 31 January, 2019
- Leadership-qualities-to-motivate-and-inspire-your-team: deakinco.com, Retrieved 23 June, 2019
- Ways-leaders-effectively-manage-employee-conflict: forbes.com, Retrieved 4 April, 2019
- Leadership-vs-conflict-resolution: smallbusiness.chron.com, Retrieved 15 February, 2019

6

Gender and Leadership

Gender in leadership has been a topic of study for the past few decades, after women have increasingly began to take on leadership positions in different industries. The topics elaborated in this chapter will help in gaining a better perspective about the role which gender plays in leadership as well as the different approaches which men and women undertake in order to lead their teams.

In many areas of society, men have long dominated leadership positions. This dominance was especially apparent in business, where female members of boards of directors and corporate executives had been scarce. Over the past three decades, however, women have entered more leadership positions throughout industry. The trend has provided an opportunity to examine differences in how men and women perform in the role of leaders.

Virginia Rometty, CEO of IBM As CEO of one of the largest companies in the U.S., Virginia Rometty is in a highly influential and visible leadership role.

Conflicting Studies

Nonetheless, studies demonstrating distinct leadership styles between men and woman do not represent the final word. Other research has found limited evidence for significant differences between the behaviors of male and female leaders. In 2011, Anderson and Hanson found differences in decision-making styles, but none linked directly to differences in leadership effectiveness. They found no distinction in types or degree of motivation or in leadership styles overall. Other studies show similar results, challenging the notion that leaders' sex shapes their performance as a leader. Management guru Rosabeth Moss Kanter studied men and women in a large corporation and found that differences in their behavior resulted not from gender but from organizational factors. In Kanter's study, men and women, given the same degree of power and opportunity, behaved in similar ways.

Leadership and Gender Differences

Business ventures are currently facing all sorts of risks that seem to be endangering their very existence. There are economic, political, cultural, environmental, technological, and social challenges that force stakeholders, investors, employees, and state representatives to carefully analyse and project different strategic scenarios in order to sustain long-term business growth.

When looking at the specialized literature concerning the business environment, the analyses are being conducted from different perspectives. Having said that, they do converge toward a universally shared opinion, which is that leadership decisively influences the day-to-day business activities and their results.

Therefore, it is obvious that there should be a vested interest in finding the correct answers to questions that focus on a leader's activities, their competencies, style behaviour, and personality, as many of the already conducted research offer valuable results, whether they are congruent or complementary. Some of these studies show that without a willingness to lead, without a commitment toward the company's mission and vision, and without integrity, the notion of authentic leadership simply does not exist in a business environment. That is why, when choosing or preparing future leaders, there is a need to:

- Evaluate the people's desire to lead and favour a self-reflection process that will offer them answers to questions such as: what do you feel when others are interested in finding out your opinions? During a project, do you like asking your teammates challenging questions? Do you enjoy helping the members of your team finish their tasks on time and in good conditions? How do you value personal interests versus the team's ones? Can you enable an authentic team spirit when working with other people? Do you feel comfortable when other people take your ideas and put them into practice? Do you enjoy helping others to improve their skills and assuming a coaching/mentoring role? When personal conflicts arise, would you rather sort them out within the team, or do you let them continue? What are your feelings when noticing someone else being successful? Can you have a productive discussion when the others are disagreeing with your opinion? Do you see your team's problems as your own? Do you enjoy generating ideas and sharing them with your group?
- Evaluate the leader's commitment to the company's mission and vision. It is hard to imagine how you can convince others to give their best when attempting something that you, as the leader, don't put a real faith in. Certainly, with careful observation, we can notice the fact that, not by accident, the first company leaders were actually the ones who created the company. The founding leaders had a mission and a vision regarding the purpose of their organization, their customers, and the changes that they will create in their belonging industry. They took risks and made personal sacrifices before their company has become a successful one. They hired the first leaders from within the company, trained and groomed them, taught them what to do and how to behave. These leaders, in turn, carried on the samc process until the human hierarchies were created in order for the company to fulfil its mission and vision.
- Evaluate integrity. That means that a leader's actions should be in line with his/her words, he/she should behave according to his/her team's expectations, to be authentic and

express the expectations he/she has from his/her colleagues and teammates. Although that does not sound very difficult, reality shows that these sorts of promises are not all that easy to keep. In fact, it is quite challenging for people to keep their word and be an example, especially when under a great amount of stress.

We cannot conclude that men's leadership skills are more powerful and more important than women's skills or vice versa, but it is clear that gender differences do exist and people should capitalize on them. We consider the word 'complementary' is better than the word 'different' when talking about leadership styles and that it is possible for leaders to develop a series of skills that are not necessarily traditionally linked to their own gender.

Feminine Leadership vs. Masculine Leadership

If we compare male and female leaders, we can see that it is an ever-evolving situation. There are some female principles and characteristics (such as using their intuition in the decision-making process, being careful, getting a good work-life balance, and social responsibility), as being in tune with the basic cultural hypotheses with regard to the way men and women think and act.

In general, women are better equipped for motivation (they are energetic and enthusiastic), communication (they make sure that their employees are well informed), feedback (they update their team in terms of their performance), and aspirations (they set high goals). Men are better at tradition (building knowledge based on past experience), innovation (they are open to new ideas and are willing to take chances), strategy (seeing the big picture), being calm (they tend to keep their emotions in check), delegating (they assign objectives and responsibilities), cooperation (they are good teammates), and persuasion (they sell ideas and win people over).

Furthermore, women tend to be better evaluated in terms of empathy (showing good people management skills and their needs by establishing a strong connection with their team) and communication (by establishing clear demands from others, expressing their thoughts and ideas clearly, and by keeping a solid communication flow) when compared to men. Also, women are better qualified in terms of people skills (sensitivity toward others, being kind, having good listening skills, and developing efficient relationships with their team and their superiors). Contrary to popular belief, women have great results on the leadership scale, which measures their focus on production (women have a great interest in achieving their goals; they have high expectations both from themselves and their colleagues). Men tend to get good results on scales that evaluate the focus on strategic planning and the overall company vision.

We all know that at the beginning of this century, the professional activity was totally different from the reality nowadays. There was no discussion upon flexibility and innovation as phenomena characterizing the global economic conditions and there were no such fast changes in technology. Cameron calls these transformation changes in the culture of Anglo-American capitalism and associates them with the passage to the norms of traditional interaction (aggressiveness, competitiveness, and individualism) to a new leadership style focused on flexibility, team work, and collaboration in problem solving.

Traditionally, the most appreciated leadership characteristics were masculine in their nature. Yet, in the past years, the researchers have shown that many of these traits (assertiveness, individualism, and task orientation) did not always contribute to the efficacy of leadership. Instead of the leadership theory centred on The Great Man, the transformational leadership has emerged, and its efficiency is supported by more and more researchers. It is interesting that many of the traits of the transformational leadership (such as collaboration and empowerment) are associated traditionally with women, which illustrates that many feminine features contribute to the leadership efficacy. Fortune 500 showed how the companies with many female managers have a much higher average productivity of their own capital in comparison with the companies with few female managers. Despite this information, female leaders still deal with many disadvantages. Often, people tend to attribute their success as leaders to some external rather than internal factors and avoid placing them on leadership positions.

Some authors showed that increasing the number of female leaders has been accompanied by changes of theory and practice in leadership. They also specify that the most modern characterization of an efficient leadership found in the literature and in mass media is heavily based on the characteristics considered to be feminine. At the same time, they state that if the leadership roles belong to more women and/or are perceived feminine attributes, we will continue to see a serious cultural change. It is a real success that many analyses emphasize the fact that employees position female leaders better than male leaders in more traits of the transformational leadership (charisma, ability to motivate the employees, and creativity in problem solving). Moreover, these characteristics of leadership are considered a real support for the efficacy of leadership. Subordinates of some of the female leaders are more willing to make supplementary effort, are more satisfied with their leaders, and are more efficient competitively in comparison with the subordinates of male leaders. It was also observed that women work harder than men in the same position, and this difference is explainable by the strict standards and exigencies manifested toward women.

The feminine leadership style was called social-expressive, with personal attention paid to subordinates and with focus on a good work environment; by contrast, the masculine leadership style was described as an instrumental one, focused on giving directions. Helgesen is one who made researches that led to the identification of the differences between the masculine and feminine leadership styles. The works of Hofstede are also very well known at the international level and actually femininity versus masculinity is considered an important cultural dimension. Human traits that are generally attributed to men are more present in some cultures, whereas the ones generally attributed to women appear in other cultures. For example, in a more masculine culture, like the American one, it is expected that in CVs, people's works are presented in superlative terms, as they feel the need to show their qualities and sometimes even more. For people living in a masculine culture, it is important to win, to have recognition, to be promoted, and to accept challenges. On the contrary, in Holland, we should meet more modesty, as there is a feminine culture. People value relationships and cooperation and generally think that work safety is more important than challenges.

Is feminine leadership a solution for modern organizations? In order to answer this question, we took, as our starting point, the opinions of Kouzes and Posner and conducted a research based on the list of the 10 descriptors included in the Checklist of Admired Leaders: Ambitions, Caring, Competent, Determined, Forward-looking, Honest, Imaginative, Inspiring, Loyal, and Self-controlled. In conducting this research, we have taken the following steps:

Step 1: Preparing the research. During this stage, we formulated the goal of the research, we chose the research method, and we built the instrument we needed to conduct it. Also, we defined the respondent group, while also formulating the research hypotheses.

Step 2: Conducting the research. During this stage, the research was launched and the respondents' opinions were gathered.

Step 3: Interpreting the results, verifying that the objectives were completed, and validating the work hypotheses that were initially formulated.

We have taken into consideration the continued development of new businesses, organizational structures, and operational and managerial processes. Many of today's companies are lean, dynamic, and adaptable, which is essential, especially with employees who have different expectations, motivations, and skills than the ones from previous generations. It seems obvious that a successful leader for these types of companies ought to have a different profile from the traditional one.

In order to collect the data, we have constructed a questionnaire consisting of two parts:

Part 1: Composed of questions referring to personal information: age, gender, field of work, professional status (manager/non-manager) and

Part 2: In which respondents are invited to establish the relationship between, on the one hand, the leadership characteristics as seen by Kouzes and Posner and, on the other hand, the gender of a successful leader (in other words, they were asked to assign each characteristic to a gender: masculine, feminine, or they could consider to be neutral). Then, the respondents were asked to order these characteristics on a scale of 1–10, based on their importance to a successful leader.

After analysing the resulted data, we have noticed that descriptors such as Ambitious, Caring, Honest, Imaginative, and Loyal are mainly associated with a female style of leadership, whereas descriptors like Competent and Forward looking tend to be associated with a male style of leadership. We have also noticed the fact that there is no clear answer when looking at the Determined, Inspiring, and Self-controlled descriptors, which means that these concepts are generally equally attributed to male and female leadership.

This research has also helped us observe how people's perception of a successful leader varies when the respondent is a manager or not, male or female, and when they belong to a certain generation (Baby boomers, X or Y). Indeed, the respondents' opinion influenced their preference for several key female leadership characteristics: non-manager respondents said that they appreciated descriptors such as Honest, Imaginative, and Caring more (35% versus 15%). As far as the generation differences are concerned, they were also clearly visible: for people from Generation Y, characteristics such as Imaginative, Ambitious, Honest, Inspiring, and Determined are more valued, which suggests the fact that, over time, there have been changes in mentality that favour the women's style of leadership.

The research has also given us a lot of signals indicating that successful leadership is no longer solely attributed to men and we anticipate that there will be further important changes in the approach based on the social and cultural evolution of our times. For this reason, we will keep following the articles and studies written on this subject and we will analyse the opinions of as many employees.

In Search of 'The Best' Leadership

In the last year, our research has continued with studying the general gender differences presented by Human Synergistic International in Life Styles Inventory (LSI). First of all, we took into account all the 12 styles, grouped into the three clusters:

- Constructive styles—Achievement, Self-Actualizing, Humanistic-Encouraging and Affiliative.
- Passive/Defensive styles—Approval, Conventional, Dependent and Avoidance.
- Aggressive/Defensive styles—Oppositional, Power, Competitive, and Perfectionistic.

Since constructive styles are the ones that are needed for a real leadership potential, we will try to give some recommendations in order to improve in each of us the styles grouped in this cluster and to diminish the influences of the other styles.

According to our research, women and men have split the 12 styles quite equally. Thus, in terms of constructive styles, women tend to be better at Humanistic-Encouraging and Affiliative, whereas men scored better at Achievement and Self-Actualizing. When being defensive, there are more women with passive styles (Approval, Conventional, Dependent, and Avoidance) and there are more men with aggressive styles (Oppositional, Power, Competitive, and Perfectionistic).

Achievement Style

This is clearly an effective thinking style, which increases the leadership potential through a feeling of direction and the capability to establish and attain realistic objectives, better planning, more respect, and self-accomplishment. There are also more promotion opportunities, higher wages, and less stress.

In order to increase the Achievement style, people could work on the following list:

- Focusing more on themselves, by taking into account their real needs.
- Taking risks (not very high, though).
- Establishing and working on attaining objectives.
- Accepting others' help, when this is the case.

According to our research, it is slightly more often attributed to men (but the difference is not really significant).

Self-actualizing Style

This is the style showing the highest level of personal development and generally manifests through an excellent self-acceptance and acceptance of others as they are. In this case, people are very preoccupied with self-development and release of any negative feeling. They have more energy, believe in their instincts, and are open to new experiences. Self-actualizing leaders can see new opportunities in every situation and are more flexible.

In order to be more self-actualizing-oriented, people should focus on:

- Living in present and thinking less about past and future.
- Reducing the temptation to judge others and trying to always accept them as they are.

- Choosing to do pleasant things whenever it is possible and reorganizing the unpleasant ones in order to become better activities.
- Looking at the problems from multiple facets, in order to see the opportunities.
- Allowing their feelings and thoughts to guide them more in their lives.

While women generally seemed to work more in order to obtain the benefits of a self-actualizing style, our research showed that this style was clearly more attributed to men.

Humanistic-Encouraging Style

This style also refers to a positive unconditioned acceptance of others, but in another way. People having this thinking style are very sensitive to the others' needs, value close relationships, and put most of their energy into the others' development. They appreciate sincerely people's strengths and believe in them. They are optimistic and good at inspiring and motivating the others, which makes them great leaders. They are patient and productive.

In order to improve their Humanistic-Encouraging style, people should work on the following:

- Developing their empathy and learning to listen more.
- Asking for ideas and feedback from the others.
- Being more involved and spending more time with other people.
- Focusing on a few persons, encouraging them, and observing the role of this encouragement into their lives.
- Looking for opportunities to help and train others.
- Showing genuine appreciation for what the others do to you and maybe learning to say 'Thank you' more often.
- Being open about their feelings and thoughts, in order to encourage the others to be open as well.

According to our research, women score generally better for this style compared to men.

Affiliative Style

The last, but not the least constructive style is the affiliative one. It refers to a real need for social interaction and interpersonal contact. People having this thinking style value strong relationships more than anything else, work on developing interpersonal skills, and motivate others with a friendly attitude. They are liked because they focus on teamwork and building trust. By having a collaborative style, they are more productive.

In order to increase their affiliative thinking style, people could do more of the following:

- Looking for opportunities to interact with others and even forcing themselves to initiate talks with persons they do not know very well.

- Attending courses and events in order to meet new people.
- Focusing on being very close with somebody, in order to build a trustful relationship and to communicate effectively.

As expected, the results of our research showed that women are generally more affiliative compared to men.

Approval Style

This refers to a defensive approach, based on the need to be accepted by others. While it is absolutely normal to want to be approved, the tendency to understand this as a need inevitably leads to a series of problems related to low self-esteem, too much attention to the others' opinions, and difficulties in conflictual situations and in negotiations. Affiliative managers are not good leaders because they tend to be undecided, to postpone discussions, to avoid conflicts, and not to act immediately.

In order to reduce the need for approval, people should focus on:

- Being more self-oriented and expressing their own opinions.
- Practicing direct approach of confrontations.
- Reflecting on the need for approval and on its causes.
- Recognizing their strengths and the fact that they are valuable persons for what they are and not because the others like them or approve them.

The results of our research showed that women tend to feel the need for approval stronger than men and they should work more on diminishing it.

Conventional Style

Another defensive and potential dangerous approach is the one of acting only according to norms. It is potentially dangerous because this way people risk losing their uniqueness and individuality. Conventional managers are not good leaders, because they prefer the standard rules and procedures and generally work in a very predictable environment that hinders innovation. The Rules are more important than ideas.

In order to become less conventional, people should work on the following:

- Understanding that being conventional generally means fewer opportunities for development.
- Focusing on their unique skills and strengths.
- Taking moderate risks, when it is the case.
- Trying new ways of doing things, avoiding routine.

According to our research, women tend to be a little more conventional than men.

Dependent Style

Dependent managers cannot lead because they rather tend to follow and to depend on the direction of the others. It is quite rare for them to disagree with them or to take a moderate risk, as they are very sensitive to the others' feelings and reactions and it is very hard to say 'no'.

In order to become more independent, people should do the following:

- Learning something new in order to become more achievement-oriented.
- Establishing small objectives, as a series of small steps can mean very much.
- Focusing on making decisions independently.
- Trying to take initiatives and move toward the behaviour of a leader.

The results of our research showed that women tend to be more dependent than men and thus they should work more on the above suggestions.

Avoidance Style

People having the avoidance thinking style need protection and keep distance from any potential danger. They are afraid of failure and tend not to take responsibility for their own behaviour. It is hard for them to express their feelings and, in many cases, they focus on their weaknesses rather than on their strengths.

In order to become less avoidance-oriented, people should work on the following:

- Identifying the causes of the avoidance behaviour.
- Focusing not only on their feelings but also on the relationships with the others.
- Developing self-trust.
- Trying to tell the others what they feel and having this, at least for a period, as an objective by itself.

In our research, we found that women tend to have higher avoidance scores than men.

Oppositional Style

This is an aggressive thinking style that shows a tendency to be in disagreement with the others. People having high scores for this style often appear to be distant and seem to look for the others' mistakes. They have a negative attitude and their humour is sarcastic. This approach is a result of their belief that their ideas are better than the others' ideas. While the oppositional style is not a constructive one, the score should not be very low either, because in that case the others would perceive them as naïve and maybe too flexible persons.

In order to decrease their oppositional style, people should focus on:

- Understanding that people would admire them more if not being so oppositional.

- Not rejecting ideas only because they are not theirs.
- Praising the others more often and avoiding the temptation to criticize.

As expected, the results of our research have shown an increased oppositional style in men when compared to women.

Power Style

The power thinking style measures our tendency to associate our self-recognition with the degree in which we can dominate and control the others. People having this style are motivated by the need for prestige, status, and influence.

In order to decrease their preference toward power, people should focus on the following:

- Trying a more friendly approach and looking at the others' reactions,
- Trusting the others and delegating more,
- Learning to be a mentor for the others,
- Being aware that the need for power actually means a fear,
- Obtaining feedback about their behaviour from neutral sources.

According to our research, as expected, men manifest the need for power considerably more than women do.

Competitive Style

This style reflects the need for always comparing with others and obtaining self-recognition through competition. While this is traditionally associated with the idea of success, it was proven that people should rather focus on performance, excellence, on the process by itself, and not on the result of winning in order to really become successful. Actually, people scoring high at competitive style are very aggressive and have a big fear of failure. Competitive managers are preoccupied with the way they are perceived by the others and focus more on being the winners than on performance.

In order to lead more successfully, people should decrease their competitive orientation, and they could do this by working on:

- Focusing on results, on self-achievement, and not on comparisons with others.
- Striving to always improve and obtain excellent results.
- Cooperating more with others for various projects.
- Accepting the fact that no one can be the best at everything.

The results of our research have revealed higher competitive scores for men than for women.

Perfectionistic Style

As the name of this thinking style suggests, it refers to the degree in which we feel the need to be perceived as 'perfect'. Of course, the need for being perfect comes at quite a high price: it is hard to be relaxed, people seem not to be very close, everything is stressful, and priorities are not really clear. This style generally comes with a low level of self-esteem and an excessive preoccupation for avoiding mistakes. Expectations from self and others are huge, and it is very difficult to cope with emotions and to express them. Perfectionistic managers tend to look too much into details and thus do not see very well the whole. While being perfectionist seems not to be a good thing, too low scores for this style also reveal some issues related to working under the potential and lacking motivation and determination.

In order to become less perfections, people should focus on:

- Understanding that the desire to be perfect is actually harmful and time-consuming and becoming aware of the fact that their work is not the same with their value.
- Improving relationships.
- Lowering expectations in order to obtain more satisfaction.

According to our research and this time unlike our expectations, men seemed to be more perfectionistic than women (with a difference not really significant).

Women in Leadership

Women are gradually making their leadership presence felt in entrepreneurship, administration, education, engineering, health, etc. at regional, national, and global levels. Women are now resolved to break the traditional glass ceiling that barred them from entering leadership positions even if they possessed requisite skills and talent to occupy them.

Women are constantly evolving and reaching new milestones across a wide spectrum of human activities in modern times. The world has witnessed the advent of women leaders such as Hillary Rodham Clinton, Indra Nooyi, Oprah Winfrey, Theresa May, Christine Lagarde, to name a few.

Leadership is not gender-specific. It is a set of leadership qualities inherent or cultivated in person or persons who develop themselves into great leaders with mass following. Leaders can be either men or women.

Although leadership skills are acquired and shown by both men and women, there exists certain differences in the basic traits and qualities possessed by men and women leaders. Men and women mostly show distinctly different styles of leadership.

Characteristics of Women Leadership

In this topic, we have highlighted some of the common characteristic features of women leaders.

Transformational Leadership Style

Women leaders are more transformational than men leaders. They function as a role model for their subordinates. They inspire their team and spend a lot of time coaching their team. They care a lot about their personal development. Women leaders emphasize teamwork and authentic communication as a key to success. For most women leaders, leadership is not meant only for accomplishing organizational goals but for transforming their followers into better people.

Task-Focused

Women leaders are invariably focused on completion of tasks assigned within deadlines. From an operational point, completing day-to-day tasks are necessary to ensure smooth functioning of the company.

Prefer to Work in Collegial Atmosphere

Women leaders generally prefer leading and creating flat organizational structures that enables all to work in a collegial atmosphere interpedently. Flat organizational structure overlooks the experience and knowledge of seasoned employees and the manager. Women leaders usually are critical of hierarchical structure of organization.

Promote Cooperation and Collaboration

To work in collaboration with others is a typical feminine characteristic. Women leaders always promote cooperation and collaboration amongst the team members. In this case, all the members of the team need to be clear of their roles and responsibilities, otherwise, it results in redundant work.

Communication Style

Women leaders tend to be participatory and possess a democratic style of leading people. They seem to abhor 'command and control style' practiced by male leaders. Women often times indirectly communicate their expectations of a given task and allow more space in accomplishing a goal. It sometimes helps the team members use their skills and expertise to complete the task, however, at other times it can be a drawback if the assigned task requires a leader to have direct communication with the members.

Self-Branding

Unlike their male counterparts, women leaders often appear to be modest or silent about their own accomplishments. They are seldom good at branding themselves. However, it is necessary that women leaders learn how to brand themselves by sharing their achievements and skills with others. Unless people know or notice what they are capable of, they cannot recognize the leadership qualities of a women leader.

Women in Leadership – Importance

Any institution, whether it is society or organization, in the present century cannot function effectively without women's equal participation in leadership activities. Women create a perspective that brings to competition and collaboration to organizations and teams.

In today's world, organizations that are led by inclusive leadership teams make effective decisions that deliver better result. In the twenty-first century, the essential qualities required to lead include the ability to collaborate, connect, empathize and communicate. All these qualities are feminine in nature and can help build a more sustainable future.

Many statistics show that companies led by women have better financial results. Leadership by women is vital to increase the pace of societal transformation at home and in the workplace. Women leaders are likely to provide an integrated view of work and family, resulting in an engaged and promising personal and professional future.

Gender parity in leadership is important because true progress cannot happen without a diversity of perspective in leadership roles.

Representation of Women in Different Sectors

Representation of women in different sectors refer to the percentage of women employees working in various sectors. In the past, women were grossly underrepresented in politics, businesses, education, manufacturing, science and technology, etc. However, this situation is changing steadily.

In the US, women are 50.8 percent of the total population. They earn almost 60 percent of undergraduate degrees and 60 percent of all master's degrees. They do fairly well in law, medical degrees, business administration and management. Women account for 47 percent of the US labor force and 49 percent of the college-educated workforce.

Women in the US account for 52 percent of the professional-level and middle-management jobs. However, they lag substantially behind men when it comes to their representation in leadership positions. While 45 percent of the overall S&P (Standard and Poor's) and 37 percent of first or middle level officials and managers in those companies, they are only 25 percent of executive and senior-level official manager.

In the legal field, they are 45 percent of associates but only 20 percent of partners and 17 percent of equity partners. In the medicine sector, women comprise 35.5 percent of all physicians and 26 percent of permanent medical school deans. In case of academia, women are only 30 percent of full professors and 26 percent of college presidents. In politics, women represent only 6.2 percent of the total members of Congress, whereas in the UK 19.4 percent of Members of Parliament are women. They are only 12 percent of governors and only 17 percent of the mayors of the 100 largest American cities. In the UK, 30.8 percent of local councilors are women.

The above-mentioned facts and figures, though indicate a rise in women representation in different sectors, it shows that women representation in decision-making positions is far from being satisfactory. Much remains to be done to increase the number of women at strategic and decision-making positions.

Benefits of Women in Leadership

Women constitute half of the working-age population in the world. Companies led by women seem to have traditionally fared better than their counterparts during times of financial crisis. A study carried out by Pew Research Center on women and leadership suggests that there is little difference between men and women in key leadership traits such as the ability to innovate and intelligence, while many observe that they are even better than men when it comes to being compassionate and organized.

Benefits of women leadership in different sectors are manifold and they are as significant as those from male leadership. Women leadership is found to be good for financial health of an organization. Organizations having females as board members show significantly better financial performance than those having low female representation.

Better financial health of the organization leads to better job opportunities, higher productivity, and more growth and development. Various studies have found that women are equipped with better relationship building skills. They are also found to be good at inspiring and motivating others.

Women Unify Diverse Groups

Women as such symbolize unity and cooperation. They are pivotal to the survival of a family – a basic social organization. This quality of unifying diverse minds in a family is an essential feature of successful leadership. A true leader acts as a unifying force to bind the team or the group of followers together and successfully leads them to achieve the goal. Women possess such quality substantially and this makes them great leaders.

Diversity refers to the existence of different people with different interests, characteristics, and attitudes. A woman leader sees diversity as an advantage to secure a balanced and unique relationship in a group. She continues to lead by unifying diverse interests, attitudes and desires inherent in a group. The idea of diversity also includes respect and acceptance. It means understanding every person is unique and identifying their individual distinctions.

Self-owned qualities like compassion, patience to listen to others, giving due importance to personal development of the followers, democratic approach to solve intrigues and above all womanly consideration of fellow human beings make women a preferred choice for leadership amidst diverse groups. These qualities help the women leaders bind diverse groups together for larger interest and for the realization of the ultimate goals.

Women Improve Interpersonal Relationships

To be a successful professional or a successful leader in this age of science and information technology, communication skills are an absolute necessity. An organization functions smoothly, if there is effective interpersonal, interdepartmental, and external communication system. Within the organization, both upward and downward communication needs to be operating to facilitate effective and timely communication among the employees and departments of the organization.

In matters of building relationships, female leaders are consistently rated higher than their male counterparts. Being skilled at building in-house relationship, women are also quite likely to do well at building outside relationship; for instance, creating new clients or negotiating difficult contracts for the company they lead.

Women fare brilliantly when it comes to communication at personal level. They are quite deft at communicating with others and score higher than men on this front. Ability to communicate with people is a fundamental need to become a successful leader. Women possess this skill naturally.

Women tend to be better listeners than men and this makes them an effective communicator. Good communicators are excellent listeners. Effective communication skills begin with listening. Women are comparatively better at both listening and communicating.

Women Value Accountability

Accountability is also an important leadership quality. Women seldom ignore their accountability on any issue. It is seen that women are more accountable than men. Accountability may not help in motivating others, but is highly inspiring.

A leader who understands the value of accountability never puts the onus of any loss or blunder on the individual members of a team. The leader rather shoulders the responsibility. It motivates the team members to undertake any assignment without any compunction and fear.

Women understand the value of accountability more than the rest. While leading a family, they often come forward to shoulder the accountability for any disruption with an intention to keep the family bonding intact. They contribute largely towards forging unity and cohesion among family members. Such quality of women, when put into practice while leading an organization, a society or a country, works miraculously.

It is often seen that women leaders have increasing number of followers since they start leading people. They never let down their followers and as a matter of fact, people follow them willingly.

Women Embrace Collaboration

Collaboration or being collaborative is defined to be mostly a feminine characteristic. Collaboration is to act willingly together with other members to attain a common pursuit. This makes leaders rise in their career graph because popular support remains with them as long as they are collaborative.

Women leaders have the ability to collaborate with colleagues, clients and employees across teams, functions, and departments because to be collaborative is innate with them. Many studies have agreed that women are more cooperative than men.

A paper from the National Bureau of Economic Research (a non-profit organization based in Massachusetts, the USA) agrees on the fact that women are more attracted to cooperation than men. Men, often overestimate their capabilities, while downplaying those of their colleagues. Women, on the other hand, are a better judge of their abilities and therefore are not averse to suggestions and help from their team members. In short, women make better team players than men.

Women are transformational leaders in general. They understand the individual needs and aspiration of team members and interact with them on a personalized note. This personalized approach of women leaders bind the team members more strongly and they work with dedication towards realizing the goal.

Apart from the above-mentioned benefits, women leaders possess the tendency to look on the positive side of the events or conditions and continue to remain optimistic throughout. Being optimistic, women leaders on many occasions come out with favorable outcome. Optimism leads to development of confidence. At the core of confidence lies faith and trust. Women leaders show more self-confidence and have faith in the followers for good. This helps them win the willing support of the followers which in turn help them achieve success.

Women in Leadership - Enablers

To promote women leadership, countries and organizations need to create a congenial environment so as to facilitate entry of women into mainstream positions. The factors and conditions which ensure smooth journey for a woman to pursue her chosen career and enable her to reach the top are called enablers.

There are a number of enablers that can move women on the right track to achieve their goals. They are, for instance, a supportive family, education, secure social environment, equal employment opportunity, women-friendly house policies of business organizations and public policies.

An enabling socio-cultural, political and business environment is a sine qua non for women occupying leadership positions in the society. What creates an enabling environment for women? Which factors are necessary to enable women to rise to become true leaders? In this chapter, let us discuss some important enablers for effective women leadership.

Supportive Family

Family as the basic social institution has profound influence on individuals. As the seat of the very first integration of individuals into social life, families are the major source of their members' basic personal and social identity, and capacity for love and togetherness.

A supportive family is a great enabler for women leadership. An individual's physical, emotional and psychological development takes shape first in his/her family. An individual is what a family creates him/her.

- As a source of Inspiration – It is the family that inspires an individual to bring out the best in him. Unless the family in which a girl is born provides her the required support, both moral and monetary, she finds it utmost difficult to shape her career as per her will and determination. Many women leaders are nipped in the bud before they come to the forefront. Their family stands on their way to the top.
- As an Effective Enabler – A supportive family helps women members to bring out the best in them. It enables them to hone their talent in the right perspective. When families nurture a positive attitude towards women members and provide them with moral and economic assistance at par with male members, they become an effective enabler for prompting women to leadership positions.
- Family as an Influencing Factor – It is found that most of the successful women leaders in the world are products of their own family. In other words, their families have helped them rise to top positions. Family values and ideals greatly influence the character building of its members, especially a girl or a woman. By providing girls and women the required space, the family enables them to bring their inherent leadership qualities to the foreground.
- As an Empowering Social Institution – A supportive family not only inspires a female member but also empowers her by providing moral, physical, and monetary support. Being empowered, she is spurred to activities to succeed in becoming a leader. Thus, family is the first social institution that empowers women to become what they intend to be.

A supportive family, therefore, provides the basic platform to women to pursue their career goals and establishes themselves as leaders.

Good Education

Education is a great liberator. It liberates women from the shackles of age-old superstitions, traditions, and beliefs that exist in a society. It is rightly said, "If you educate a man you educate an individual, however, if you educate a woman you educate a whole family".

- Education helps women acquire knowledge, understand gender relations, develop a sense of self-worth, a belief in their ability, etc. It enables them to bring out the best in them and make them accepted as a mass leader.
- Education enables women to free themselves from the bondage of ignorance and orthodox beliefs, social evils, gender discrimination, and domestic as well as social violence.
- It creates in them fortitude and self-confidence to fight against every odd on their way to achieve success in life.

- It enlightens them about the larger world and world views. It also acquaints them with women leaders of different countries and their leadership styles. It exposes them to the world and helps them know the conditions of women in different countries and different societies.

Good education brings out the inherent leadership qualities in women and enables them to establish themselves as great leaders.

Secure Social Environment

An enabling social environment is a necessary precondition for growth of sustainable women leadership. For the all-round growth of women and for making them fit for leadership position, a congenial and secure social environment is an utmost necessity. She needs the unconditional support of family, and the society in which she lives in to realize her potentials to the full.

- Communities where women are given due recognition, provided with opportunities and allowed to express themselves, have seen the rise of many women leaders in the passage of time.
- Enable women to become effective leaders – If a favorable secure social environment is provided and women are provided the position to lead, they will prove themselves as effective and successful as or more than that of their male counterparts.
- Encourage and build trust – When a woman feels safe and secure in a given society, she is encouraged to participate in leadership activities in the society. A secure social environment help women build trust in themselves.
- Enhance self-confidence – A secure socio-cultural environment enhances self-confidence in women. It drives away fears and insecurity from them and makes realize their full potential.
- Provide Opportunities – A secure social environment provides multiple opportunities for women to grow and show their leadership qualities. A community, where women are to move, to express themselves and to take part in community building activities, is destined to realize progress and prosperity.

Factors for Building a Secure Social Environment

- Change in the attitude of a male-dominated society towards women.

- Necessary constitutional and legal measures to build a secure social environment.
- Equal consideration of girls and women at par with boys and men in family and society.
- Change in organizational and corporate policies to allow women to reach the top.
- Stringent laws and their effective implementation against women abusers.
- Design an education system suitable for women.
- Inculcate a spirit of co-habitation through peace and order in social members.

There is a need to build a progressive society. Changes need to take place in the attitudes of the majority of the society in which women's progress is hindered. A secure social environment provides ample space to women to grow as leaders. Thus, the society where women realize their full potential and contribute to the task of social building is, indeed, a progressive and democratic society.

Promoting Women Leadership

The need for promoting women leadership is as important as creating an enabling environment for women to hone their leadership qualities. Despite umpteen measures to empower women and see them in leadership positions, the representation of women in such positions across the globe is quite upsetting. Women make up just 4 percent of CEOs in the world's 500 top companies, even a lesser percent of heads of government at national level belongs to women and the least percent of international leadership positions is occupied by women in the world today.

Absence of gender equality in leadership positions not only hampers the due progress in every sphere but also costs the global economy substantially. Hence, there is a need to promote women leadership. Corporate houses or companies need the best of leaders and it will not be fulfilled if the recruitment pool excludes women. Statistics show that women have not yet reached their full potential in leadership positions.

There are several factors that help in promoting women leadership. Following are some of the important measures that can be taken to promote women leadership.

Recruit Women Employees Actively

Recruiting women in various leadership positions by corporate houses and companies on the premises of equal opportunity provisions is the first step to help women rise to important positions. Organizations and sectors hiring people to work for them should issue meaningful equality plans to absorb women members in proportion to men.

Organizations should carry out a thorough analysis of their manpower composition and take immediate measures to maintain gender equality. Employee survey should be used to detect inequalities. Equal opportunity planning should be based on concrete goals and measures as well as the follow-up on their success.

Organizations should look for requisite talents in women to occupy any positions. Gender should not be the sole criteria in selecting or rejecting a person while making appointment to decision-making positions. Emphasis should be laid on the skills and abilities the person possesses and if such skills and abilities are in tune with the requirements of the position.

Organizations should take active interest in treating women applicants at par with the men applicants while selecting persons for higher positions. Women should not be ignored only because they are women.

Provide Training Opportunities

Providing training for women members is a powerful promoter of women leadership. Training for gender equality is a transformative process and it aims to provide knowledge, techniques and tools to develop skills and changes in attitude and behavior.

A recent study on Women Leadership, on more than 3,000 professional women in United States, identified confidence building and leadership training, along with the ability to network with women leaders, as key elements to expanding women's leadership in the years ahead.

Comprehensive training modules for women empowerment and women leadership help build an inclusive business environment and promote gender equality. Training helps women and men to understand the role gender plays and to acquire the knowledge and skills necessary for advancing gender equality in their daily lives.

Formal training such as structured training course and workshops should be regularly organized and informal training through existing employees sharing knowledge and experience should be undertaken periodically to enable women to become fit for higher positions.

Targeted women development programs conducted in women-only environment enables women to increase their ability to navigate their own careers successfully. It also helps them identify and overcome personal and professional challenges and take responsibility for their growth and development.

Training should be included in the annual performance review of the employees and when opportunities arise. It is also important to offer flexibility in the time and location of training (e.g. during work hours) to make it accessible to employees who have family responsibilities. Mentoring program for new employees is also essential to develop the required skills and knowledge for personal and professional growth.

Encourage Women-friendly Culture

There is a need to develop a women-friendly culture in the society and business environment. An inclusive and collaborative culture calls for pro-women changes in the old system of recruitment, training, performance appraisal, promotion, wages, etc. Unless women are treated equally and assessed not on the basis of gender but on the basis of their talents and skills, they cannot make it to leadership positions.

The following measures can help create a women-friendly culture:

Flexible Work Schedules

Organizations should have flexible work programs to suit women employees. Flexibility in work schedule such as providing some days of remote work to employees is quite encouraging. In this case, when an employee needs to stay home to spend time with her children or family or sick parents, the company trusts that they will still get their work done.

Equal Opportunity

Difference in wages between men and women is a challenge specific to women. It is found that women still earn less than men. Discrimination exist in the workplace in various ways. Sexual harassment at workplace is not a thing of the past. Women employees are still falling prey to it. There is a very low representation of women in boardrooms or top paying executive positions.

Organizations should make provisions for ensuring an equal status to women employees at par with their male counterparts. There should be no discrimination on the basis of gender in the organization.

An Effective Career Mapping for Women Employees

Organizations should have an effective career mapping for its employees after they complete their probation period. Development plans, stretch assignments, promotions, and networking opportunities should be equal for men and women who have been rated with similar capabilities. This enables women employees to become aware of opportunities for their development at higher levels and sharpens the visibility to rise to top leadership.

Provisions for Self-care

Organizations employing women should have provisions for self-care. For instance, multinational oil company, Chevron, offers full-fitness and self-care facilities onsite at their global locations. Employees have the opportunity to take care of themselves by working out during the day and getting massages or facials without having to leave their worksite. This enables women to find balance and stay healthy. It encourages women to take up higher responsibilities.

Provisions for Family Support

The most difficult thing for a working woman is to maintain a good balance between her life at home and workplace. Some women being unable to adjust to the stress of both leave to look after their families. In this case, the organization makes suitable provisions to create a stress-free environment for women.

For instance, provisions for offering after school programs beyond day care for children of the women employees such as science camps, math sessions, and other activities in the evening enable women employees with families to retain demanding positions without the worry of leaving their children at home. It reduces the choice women often make between family and work.

Policy Changes to Promote Women Leadership

- High quality and affordable childcare and elder care.
- Paid maternity and paternity leave.
- A right to request part-time work.
- Comprehensive job protection for pregnant workers.
- Higher wages and training for paid caregivers.
- Reforms at elementary and secondary school schedules to meet the needs of digital workplaces.

Ways to Promote Women Business Leaders

- Corporate houses and companies should make high-level decisions to promote women's advancement in the career pipeline and the progress of the situation.
- There should be meaningful equality plans.
- Recruitment processes should promote both genders to seek all kinds of jobs.
- Talent potential among the employees should be recognized and it should be ensured that women are fully considered in the talent management process.
- Men and women should be offered equal training.
- Women should be allowed to experience business operations leadership and line management.
- Provision of proper mentoring for women in their career path.

Gender Equality through Legislations

Gender equality refers to the state of equal access to resources and opportunities irrespective of the gender. It suggests that both men and women are free to develop their personal abilities and make choices without limitations set by stereotypes, rigid gender roles and prejudices. Different behaviors, aspirations, and needs of women and men need to be considered, valued, and favored equally.

Organizations are stronger when its leadership has diverse perspectives and experience to draw from. Leadership positions should not be filled solely on the basis of gender. Every organization should look at the challenges women often face in the workplace and take necessary measures to set the track right for talented and dynamic leaders to rise and inspire new generations.

Need for Legislations for Gender Equality

Gender equality is an inseparable part of human rights and fundamental towards building a just, secure, and democratic society. In order to eliminate barriers to establish gender equality, legislations are being made to provide equal rights and opportunities for women and men in laws and policies and equal access to resources and services within families, communities, governments, and society at large.

Legislations for Gender Equality should aim at:

- Providing equal political and economic rights to women such as the right to vote, right to equal pay for equal work, etc.
- Ensuring equal status to women in business or corporate policies. For instance, women should be given equal consideration in recruitment, training, promotion, and performance appraisal. Organizations must grant a certain period of leave for expecting employees and for those who want to take leave or remain home to care for a sick family member.
- Allowing women to have access to both general and technical education, public and private services.
- Making a secure social environment where women are free from fear or threats to their physical and mental well-being.
- Enabling them to fight against domestic violence in any form and lead a safe family life.
- Making way for whistle blower protection. A whistle blower is defined as an individual who reveals alleged dishonest or illegal activities concerning an employer to the public.

However, legislations cannot serve the purpose of promoting women leadership unless they are properly implemented. In some countries the percentage of women in leadership positions is quite low despite several legislations framed.

Women in Leadership - Barriers

It is established that women leadership has distinct benefits and women leaders are endowed with certain natural qualities such as collaboration, empathy, and considerateness which have become essential ingredients in present leadership trend. However, the subtle gender bias that still persists in the society, community, families, and organizations stand as a strong barrier to women leadership.

Efforts have been made by governments, corporate houses, and social organizations to enable women to give meaning and recognition to their innate leadership qualities and establish themselves as active leaders in the society. It will help build a progressive and developed human society.

However, several barriers still persist that hinder the growth of women into independent leaders. Let us discuss some significant barriers to women leadership in the present time.

The Glass Ceiling

The proverbial "glass ceiling" refers to the existence of intangible and unacknowledged impediments that obstruct the advancement of women and the weaker section of the society in professional or public life.

A host of community-specific practices and views constitute the glass ceiling. Here are some of its characteristics –

- Societies leaning heavily towards the male members of the society.
- Set of socio-cultural and religious practices to deny basic freedom to women.
- Priority to male members in the family and society.
- General but biased perceptions that feminine qualities are inferior to those of masculine.
- Perception that leadership is invariably a male prerogative.

Glass ceiling as a barrier prevents woman from moving up the hierarchies in organizations, governance and other areas. From a vantage point on their career ladder, women can see the top-level positions but are kept from 'reaching the top'.

Glass ceilings as barrier are not based upon a person's inability or lack of expertise and knowledge to carry out assigned tasks. Rather, it relates to women as a community who are knowingly or unknowingly kept from advancing higher because 'they are women'.

Professional Competency

Professional competency refers to possessing abilities and skills by a person to discharge professional duties and responsibilities as efficiently and effectively as possible. The nature and characteristics of such abilities and skills vary from profession to profession.

A number of researches indicate that women and men managers don't differ largely in the competencies they possess. However, stereotypical view of gender role considers women less competent than women. As a result, there exists a gender gap in the assessment of male and female employees. There are instances of less pay for women than that of the men for the same work and equal work hour.

Cultural biases and social arrangement overrate men and underrate women. In order to ascertain the criteria for common competencies for leadership positions, we need to value both the transformational leadership of women and transactional leadership of men. Studies have found that young women are less achieving than young men in technical subjects and areas. Subtle gender bias that persists in organizations and in the society upsets the learning cycle for acquiring new skills and expertise for women after becoming leaders.

Traditional leadership education is not sufficient to help women become successful after assuming leadership positions. Even women rate other women as incompetent. Women are studied to have lower self-confidence, dominance and need for achievement. These findings, though not fully established, create a common assumption that women are less competent than men.

However, recent studies conducted by management institutions and corporate houses reveal that the gender of the leader is less important than the role and responsibilities of the leader's position. There appears to be little difference between women and men leaders in their core competencies such as leading and motivating, mentoring and coaching, managing finances, building teamwork, communicating to employees, conducting appraisals, managing resources, etc.

Gender Disparity

Gender disparity is based on the premises that women and men are unequal and women are less powerful than men. Gender disparity or gender inequality has been a barrier to women leadership since ancient times. It still remains a major barrier to empowerment of women and development of women leadership.

Here, we have highlighted a few major reasons behind the existence of gender disparity:

Discriminating Social Structure

In many societies, especially in Asia, gender discrimination has been accepted as a tradition. Men are given priority in almost every aspect social and cultural life. Women and girls are assigned negligible roles to play in decision-making process affecting family and society.

Patriarchal society, lack of legal awareness in women, considering women's household work as economically insignificant, and male child preference in society aggravate gender disparity in the society.

Low Representation in Leadership Positions

Women have achieved almost parity with men in the number of both employees in the workforce and positions in the middle management level. Women now comprise 57 percent of the total US job market and 52 percent of all management roles and professional occupations, such as physicians and attorneys.

However, the higher one climbs, the wider the gender gap one finds. Women make up only 15 percent board seats, 14 percent of executive officers and paltry 2 percent of CEOs. About 98 percent of Fortune 500 CEO positions are held by men.

Political Apathy

Women are usually not given preference by political parties while choosing candidates for contesting elections. Women are seen as incompetent to fight elections and get elected to legislatures. Women representation in legislatures, judiciary, government and business is not very encouraging even in developed countries despite umpteen measures and a number of institutional interference in the issues of empowering women in the world.

Maintaining Work-Life Balance

Maintaining work-life balance is also a great barrier to women leadership. Women are still attending the bulk of domestic and child care responsibilities at home, even when both spouse are full-time employees. Women in this situation find themselves in dilemma as to how to maintain a perfect balance between home and workplace demands. Maintaining work-life balance is one of the most complex barriers to women leadership.

Women professionals find it quite stressful while trying to balance motherhood and working outside home. The changing nature of work environment especially at the top of the hierarchy that demand round-the-clock work schedule represent an impasse to many women who wish to extend life outside the workplace.

Further, when the women professional climb the ladder of their rising career and as their family grows, their responsibilities multiply. Time spent in the office continues to be seen as a powerful indicator of work commitment that impacts on family life, health, and productivity of men and women at work.

Most employers and businesses have put in place flexible work initiatives so as to attract talented women to the jobs. However, choosing flexibility suggests a lesser engagement with the workforce. Flexibility options are not meeting the needs of senior female talents. Yet, many successful women leaders have both a good family and an enviable career graph. They have not sacrificed either.

Apart from the above barriers to women leadership, there are other society-culture-specific impediments to women's progress into leadership positions. There is need for devising women-friendly policies to inspire women to vie for leadership positions and continue to lead independently.

Permissions

All chapters in this book are published with permission under the Creative Commons Attribution Share Alike License or equivalent. Every chapter published in this book has been scrutinized by our experts. Their significance has been extensively debated. The topics covered herein carry significant information for a comprehensive understanding. They may even be implemented as practical applications or may be referred to as a beginning point for further studies.

We would like to thank the editorial team for lending their expertise to make the book truly unique. They have played a crucial role in the development of this book. Without their invaluable contributions this book wouldn't have been possible. They have made vital efforts to compile up to date information on the varied aspects of this subject to make this book a valuable addition to the collection of many professionals and students.

This book was conceptualized with the vision of imparting up-to-date and integrated information in this field. To ensure the same, a matchless editorial board was set up. Every individual on the board went through rigorous rounds of assessment to prove their worth. After which they invested a large part of their time researching and compiling the most relevant data for our readers.

The editorial board has been involved in producing this book since its inception. They have spent rigorous hours researching and exploring the diverse topics which have resulted in the successful publishing of this book. They have passed on their knowledge of decades through this book. To expedite this challenging task, the publisher supported the team at every step. A small team of assistant editors was also appointed to further simplify the editing procedure and attain best results for the readers.

Apart from the editorial board, the designing team has also invested a significant amount of their time in understanding the subject and creating the most relevant covers. They scrutinized every image to scout for the most suitable representation of the subject and create an appropriate cover for the book.

The publishing team has been an ardent support to the editorial, designing and production team. Their endless efforts to recruit the best for this project, has resulted in the accomplishment of this book. They are a veteran in the field of academics and their pool of knowledge is as vast as their experience in printing. Their expertise and guidance has proved useful at every step. Their uncompromising quality standards have made this book an exceptional effort. Their encouragement from time to time has been an inspiration for everyone.

The publisher and the editorial board hope that this book will prove to be a valuable piece of knowledge for students, practitioners and scholars across the globe.

Index

A

Achievement Style, 215

Affiliative Leader, 43, 98

Affiliative Style, 216

Altruism, 115, 124

Approval Style, 217

Authoritarian Leadership, 15, 50

Autocratic Leadership, 40-41, 50-53, 59, 73, 81, 208

Avoidance Style, 218

B

Big Men Leaders, 115, 120, 123

Bureaucratic Leadership, 53-58

Bureaucratic or ganizations, 118, 120

C

C-suite Leaders, 10

Chain-of-command, 55-57, 145

Charismatic Leadership, 15, 54, 67-69, 104, 110, 120, 173

Coaching Leader, 42, 99

Conceptualization, 90

Conflict Resolution, 6, 114-115, 191, 206-209

Constructive Styles, 215

Contingency Theory, 91, 93-96

D

Delegating Style, 98, 144

Delegation, 93, 133

Democratic Leader, 43, 124

Dependent Style, 218

E

E-commerce, 128

Emotional Intelligence, 4-7, 14, 43, 71, 88, 98, 147, 163

Ethical Leadership, 74-75, 175

Evolutionary Leadership Theory, 80, 114-115, 117, 119

Executive Leadership, 40, 43-44, 166

F

Flow of Information, 27, 124

Four Framework Approach, 136

G

Great Man Theory, 128-129

H

Hands-off Approach, 60-61, 64

Hersey-blanchard Model, 144-145

Humanistic-encouraging Style, 216

I

Intelligent Leadership, 157-162

Interpersonal Skill, 164, 182

J

Job Satisfaction, 35, 61, 70

L

Laissez-faire, 40, 58-67, 78-79

Leadership Competencies, 158, 162-163, 165

Leadership Development, 8-12, 30, 32, 38, 69, 88, 143, 166-167

Leadership Training, 9, 13-14, 30, 229

Leadership Traits, 2, 7, 44, 97, 126-127, 152-153, 223

Leadership Vision, 169-171

Life Styles Inventory, 214

M

Managerial Grid, 41, 136, 138-140

Managerial Leadership, 40, 44-45

O

Opinion Leaders, 47-48

Oppositional Style, 218-219

Organizational Leadership, 6, 9

P

Participative Leadership, 35, 40, 71-74, 209

Passive/defensive Styles, 215

Path-goal Model, 42, 111

Personal Growth, 55, 88, 143, 177

Personal Leadership, 14, 60, 141-143

Power Thinking Style, 219

Private Leadership, 141-142

R

Relationship-oriented Leadership, 70-71

S

Self Management, 5

Self-actualizing Style, 215-216
Self-categorization Theory, 104-105
Self-leadership, 77-79
Self-motivation Level, 149-150
Servant Leadership, 36, 44, 80, 88-91, 143
Situational Leadership, 97-98, 136-138, 144-145
Social Contract, 130
Social Identity Theory, 104-107
Social Intelligence, 163
Strategic Leadership, 15-19, 21-28
Strategic Thinking, 18, 170-171
Symbolic Framework, 137

T

Tannenbaum and Schmidt Continuum, 133-134
Task-oriented Leadership, 69-70
Trait Theory of Leadership, 126
Transactional Leadership, 17, 44-46, 233
Transformational Leadership Theories, 130-133

V

Visionary Leader, 42

W

Workplace Ethics, 176

CPSIA information can be obtained
at www.ICGtesting.com
Printed in the USA
LVHW062012100122
708212LV00002B/193

9 781647 260798